# Are We There Yet?

Hardcover: 979-8-9951957-0-2
Paperback: 979-8-9951957-1-9
Ebook: 979-8-9951957-2-6

Published by: Riverside Press
Enfield, CT
Riversidepressbooks.com

Cover and Typesetting Design by Cornelia Murariu at PixBeeDesign.com
Cover photo L to R: Cheryl (standing), two cousins, Nancy and Andrea on raft

Disclaimer: This memoir is a work of nonfiction based on the author's personal experiences. While the author has taken care to present accurate accounts, certain names and identifying details have been changed to protect the privacy of individuals mentioned.

Library of Congress Control Number: 2026906098

First Edition

# Are We There Yet?

*Four Sisters on a Road Trip
from Connecticut to Maine:
A Nostalgic Journey of
Laughter, Loss, and Resilience*

A MEMOIR

Cheryl Smith Lawson

*A note from the author:*

The chapter titles in this memoir are a compilation of songs from the music of my life; the music of a generation. You may want to read our stories with these songs playing in the background.

Dedicated to my sister, Nancy.

# Contents

# Are We There Yet?

*I slid the closet door open a crack and trembled as I listened for any sound. When I didn't hear anything, I looked out the small opening. It was dark and eerily quiet so we knew that Mom and Dad were asleep. "We can come out now," I whispered to my younger sisters.*

Resiliency is not the first thing that popped into my head when I woke up on the night of my 75th birthday. I heard the sounds of the maple tree as it scratched the window of our little red house in Falmouth, Maine. The cold, gentle wind of a rain storm rocked the branches back and forth. It was the perfect weather for deep sleep—for someone else perhaps, but not for me. When woken abruptly by days I'd rather forget, those gossamer strands of my nightmares made sleep impossible.

As I sat up, I exhaled a breath I hadn't realized I'd been holding in. Unfortunately, my anxiety didn't go along with it as I had hoped. No matter how much I tried not to think of those days, willed myself to conjure up happy memories of times spent with my sisters, my mind wouldn't budge. So, I decided to stop resisting. I slipped out of bed, walked to my computer, and began writing. I haven't stopped since.

This started out as my story—one of four sisters growing up in the 1950s and 1960s. But as I started telling the story of my life, I realized I was actually telling four stories about four lives that happened to intersect, and sometimes collide. Like *Seinfeld*, it was a story about nothing, and yet *everything* that shaped the lives of many women of my generation. At first, I thought I was writing it for myself. Then, I thought I was writing it for my sisters. But as I shared early drafts with friends, their responses were unexpected. Even though we were all Boomers—a term I've always disliked—who grew up in different places, our stories were uncannily alike. I began to think I might be onto something—giving a voice to the universal experiences of women of my generation.

As I shared my manuscript with a wider audience—women of varying ages and even people who don't identify as women—the story still resonated. So maybe I didn't write it just for myself or my sisters, or only the women of my generation. Maybe it was bigger than that. Maybe it was not, and is not, a singular experience to ask, *Are we there yet?* As it turned out, I wrote this for all of us, anyone who ever wanted to know if the path to acceptance has a silver lining when you make it to the end; whether it's simply a road trip or rather a lifetime of healing, of resilience, of learning to forgive.

I came from a family of three biological sisters with whom I shared DNA. But I also met sisters in college, through the Epilepsy Foundation, while traveling, in my teaching career, "upta camp", and by circumstance alone. Many of them, and others as well, became like family. We may not have started out together, our paths may have diverged unexpectedly somewhere down the line, and yet, we look back and find that we've still left a lasting impact on one another's lives. There were the sisters with whom I shared my earliest memories and the sisters I met along the way. Some inspired me, some disappointed me, but all left their mark. I've realized it's more than a random combination of parental DNA that binds us to one another.

Although we lived in Connecticut, New York, and Massachusetts, as we got older, we really wanted to be in Maine, where we had enjoyed childhood summers at Wells Beach. Summers of basking on the sand slathered with Coppertone (I can still smell it!) and teenage romances at the Wells Beach Casino were some of our happiest memories. By the time Labor Day came, we didn't want to leave.

While we stopped asking, *Are we there yet?* in the road trip sense, the question took on an entirely different meaning once my sisters and I arrived in Maine as adults. I had thought that the questions would stop, yet there was one that haunted us for many years: *Will our lives finally be happy here?* While the location had changed, we wondered, would the echoes of memories we'd rather forget still come calling?

We did what we needed to survive in a family that looked perfect from the outside. However, when the front door closed, we lived in fear. We secretly endured confusing adult relationships, alcoholism, and family violence with no one to confide in. Our years together led us from sisterly laughter to inconsolable grief. There were seizures, cancer, betrayals and losses, all of which we could not have imagined in the days of *Howdy Doody*, *American Bandstand*, and the Beatles.

It was a time of rapid change in society as well. Abortion was illegal; we could not get a credit card or a mortgage without a husband to cosign. Women were paid 73 percent less than men to do the same job. Sexual harassment was considered a joke, and people looked down on a mother working outside the home. We came of age during the Civil Rights movement, Timothy Leary, and Vietnam.

Some of us made it through in better shape than others. *Are we there yet?* became a metaphor for the search upon which we each embarked to find self-acceptance, resilience, and forgiveness. We struggled with our differences, both as individuals and as a sisterly unit. We're not quite there yet emotionally, but as strong women, as *sisters*, we're working on it. Some wounds may never heal, but we haven't given up.

These are our stories.

# CHAPTER 1

# "*Dream Along with Me*"

## Perry Como

### Newington, Connecticut, 1952-1953

In 1952, at almost six years old, I proudly walked three blocks all by myself to the Dowd Street bus stop to meet Grampa Smith. William Arthur Smith was born in 1900 in Haverhill, Massachusetts. He left school after eighth grade to become a vaudeville performer. He loved being on the stage—singing, tap dancing, playing the tambourine, and directing shows throughout New England.

While Grampa was a talented performer, Dad was a talented tinkerer, engineer, and builder. My dad, Frederick Joseph Smith, was a gifted student who hoped to go to college to become an engineer after he graduated from Haverhill High School in 1941. The Second World War changed those plans, as it did for many of the men of his generation. He enlisted in the Army Air Force and was stationed in Germany, France, and Luxembourg. He worked with a group of fellow mathematicians to decode the German Enigma machine. He and his men snuck into Normandy before the D-Day invasion to predict the weather, helping General Eisenhower to decide whether to go in on June 5th or 6th.

When Dad returned from WWII, he accepted a job at Remington Rand in Hartford, Connecticut. One day, Dad stopped at Witkower's Book Sellers on Asylum Street and bought a book entitled *Your Dream Home: How to Build It for Less Than $3,500*. Dad and Grampa used house plans from that book to build our first home, a Royal Barry Wills Cape Cod.

Most afternoons, my grandfather Smith took the bus from Hartford to Newington to help Dad on the house, carrying his supper in a brown paper bag. Once his bus arrived, I looked forward to walking back up the hill with him, my little hand in his big weathered one. He greeted me as "Honeybunch" and, as we made our way to Gilbert Road, told me stories about Ireland, with its mystical horses, ancient castles, and wailing banshees.

The sidewalk near the bus stop where I waited for Grampa Smith was shaded by a row of old chestnut trees. While I watched for the bus, I filled my pockets with as many horse chestnuts as I could. They were green and prickly on the outside but, when split open with a rock, each had a shiny brown nut inside. I never ate the nuts; I just liked the feeling of the chestnuts in my pocket. Sometimes the neighborhood boys used them as projectiles to tease us girls as we walked home from school. No throwing for me—I always kept mine. Twirling them around in my pocket like talismans, I thought they would bring me luck. One Thanksgiving Day, years later, my mother tried a new recipe for turkey with chestnut stuffing. I got sick just smelling those chestnuts cooking. No one ate the stuffing that year, not even Mom. It was then that I decided some things are probably better on the outside than the inside.

Dad and Grampa made Mom a little sewing room under the slanted ceiling at the top of the stairs in our Gilbert Road home. Sometimes I liked to sit in the corner watching her work on her old Singer Featherweight. She was a talented seamstress; nothing was too difficult for her. Mom sewed herself elegant 50s-style suits from Vogue patterns: navy blue with white piping, gray with black. She also made curtains for our new house, which had swags and jabots. I didn't know what jabots were back then, but I did think they looked quite fancy. Mom once sewed me a white satin dance costume with big blue polka dots. I excitedly wore it on the big stage of the New Britain Auditorium, where Rosemary Clooney's rousing tune of *Oh, You Beautiful Doll* accompanied the tapping of my little feet in shiny black patent leather tap shoes.

Dad and Grampa spent that winter finishing the upstairs of our little Cape. There were only two bedrooms when we first moved in. The three of us sisters shared one room. Nancy's crib was tucked under the single window at the foot of the double bed Andi and I slept in together. Later, Daddy and Grampa added two bedrooms upstairs for us girls with a Jack and Jill bathroom between them. I had my own room, I suppose because I was the oldest, while Andi and Nancy shared the other.

When our new home was finished, Grampa Smith brought over his new movie camera and filmed the whole house, just as a realtor might do when selling a home today. Having once been in Vaudeville, he loved production and accompanied the movie with signs that he held up for the camera between scenes. My favorite one read: "PLUMMING by ED SMITH."

One night in my new upstairs bedroom, my sleep was interrupted by a major scare. In the dark, I heard a whirring noise coming closer and then circling around my head. I was screaming, thinking something was trying to eat me! Dad ran up the stairs and turned on my bedroom light. He looked around, and said, "Oh, nothing to worry about, Cheryl, it's only a miller." A MILLER! I had no idea what a miller was or whether it was capable of eating me or not. Dad waved the miller out the window and tucked me back into bed. For years afterward, just hearing the word "miller" elicited fear. Eventually, I learned that "miller" was a less common term for a moth. It was only a moth! I was smart enough to know that a moth could never eat me. What was Daddy thinking?

The summer of 1953 brought record heat to the Connecticut River Valley. One morning, I lay on the grass in the shade at the side of the garage trying to keep cool while Daddy and Grampa Smith shingled its roof. I rolled over and there it was: the first four-leaf clover I'd ever found! Grampa Smith, being Irish and full of stories of leprechauns and castles, told me that if I found one, it would bring me good luck. I picked the clover, careful to leave the stem attached, and hollered to my dad and grampa to tell them. After the clover was admired at length by them and every neighborhood kid I could drag into the yard, Dad said that if I'd let him borrow the clover for just a day, he had an idea how I might be able to keep it forever. The next night, when Dad came home from his job at Remington Rand, he handed me my clover. It was encased in a circle of hard, clear resin-like material. Under the clover, also in the resin, was a very small typed slip of paper that said, "CHERYL, July 22, 1953." Dad promised that if I held on to it, it would bring me luck. That clover turned 70 years old this past July. I still have it safely framed in my bedroom. I misplaced the clover for about 20 years when we were packing, moving, and raising children, but I found it again when we unpacked at our current home. During those years, I didn't always have the good luck Daddy promised. I've concluded that maybe a four-leaf clover only works when you know exactly where it is.

Unless we had company, we ate all of our meals as a family at our maple kitchen table. It was pressed up against a wall, papered in a farmland scene, with animals and people, houses and barns, dirt roads and streams, covered bridges and apple trees. My seat was right next to that perfect little world on the wall. I loved to trace my fingers along the dirt roads and across the bridges, over ponds and streams. I counted the sheep, pigs, cows, and horses. I made up stories of the daily adventures of the Wallpaper People and followed them, tracing my fingers along the roads and through the fields. When I close my eyes, I can still see those pastoral scenes and imagine myself wandering those gentle hills. If only life could be that simple!

One simple pleasure we did enjoy in that kitchen was Mom and Dad making homemade root beer. They worked all day and set the bottles of root beer on the cellar steps to cool. Even after the last bottle was sealed, the sweet sassafras smell permeated our house for weeks.

On Christmas Eve, Mom and Dad planned to have some family and friends over to celebrate. We hung our stockings and they put us to bed early while reminding us that Santa wouldn't come until all three of us fell asleep. So we made haste by shutting our eyes tightly. We didn't want to delay him in bringing our presents. Mom and Dad must have been having a grand old time with their guests because the party got so loud that it woke us up.

Nancy was still fast asleep as Andi and I sleepily walked out of our bedroom. We tiptoed down the hall into the living room where we stood rubbing our eyes. Moments later, we were wide awake when we saw that Santa had already come! Happy screams rose from our mouths as we spied our coveted walking dolls and bulging stockings. Mom and Dad bolted out of the kitchen faster than Rudolph could fly.

They explained that they were all in the kitchen and must not have heard Santa sneak in and leave our gifts under the tree. Methinks that maybe more than root beer was involved that Christmas Eve, but they did manage to get us to buy the story and head back to bed, each happily dragging our new doll along behind us.

*Christmas Dolls: Andrea, Cheryl & Nancy.*

Like most women of her generation, Mom didn't work outside the house. But boy did she work! She worked so hard that sometimes she sweated through her cotton house dress, especially when she ironed our stiff organdy dresses on sweltering summer days. Each day was designated for a specific chore: *Monday - Laundry, Tuesday - Ironing, Wednesday - Floors*, and so on. Some of my earliest memories were seeing Mom scrub our linoleum kitchen floor on her hands and knees.

If Mom was caught up on her housework, she would allow herself an hour to watch *Queen for a Day* on the small black and white television set in the mahogany cabinet in the living room. I liked watching that show with Mom. Three women shared stories of their misfortune and the woman who told the saddest story won a washer or a refrigerator. If Jack Bailey had asked Mom, "Do you want to be queen for a day?" I'm sure she would have said yes. I wished that for her—that she'd get on the show and win prizes for being sad.

On Saturday nights, Dad occasionally took Mom out to dinner; Grammy and Grampa Smith would take the bus from Hartford to babysit. We loved those nights. Saturday night supper featured the same menu throughout New England: hot dogs, B&M baked beans, and steamed brown bread. In Connecticut, the hot dogs were always brown, but every August when we vacationed in Maine, we were treated to "red snappers", a Maine favorite. These hot dogs were indeed bright red, and the natural casing made a snapping sound when you bit into it, hence the name. Dessert was usually Jello or ice cream. If we were lucky, Grammy would arrive to babysit carrying treats in a white box tied with red string from the bakery near her apartment on Farmington Avenue.

Dad's mother, Mary Alice Smith (aka "Grammy Smith"), was born in 1898 in Haverhill, Massachusetts. She was gruff on the outside, with a big, big heart on the inside. Grammy Smith was probably my favorite person in the whole world. I firmly believed I wouldn't have survived my childhood and adolescence without her. I admired her independence and resilience. She wasn't one to put on appearances: she was a stocky woman who had her hair cut for three dollars at the barbershop near her apartment and usually didn't bother with makeup. If she was going out, she put on a little face powder and lipstick and that would be that.

She was a strong, self-reliant woman. No ice maker for her: when she needed crushed ice, she wrapped ice cubes in a dish towel, put them on the sturdy oak transition strip between her living room and kitchen floors, and whacked them with a hammer. Years later, when Nancy stalled out in Mom and Dad's car, which she wasn't supposed to be driving, Grammy saved her by driving her trusty push-button Valient to where Nancy was stuck, tying the stalled car to the Valient's back bumper, and towing Nancy home. She never did tell Mom and Dad Nancy's secret.

After supper, we'd all line up on the couch in the living room with Grammy and Grampa to watch television. Our TV was small, maybe 17 inches, and shows were only broadcast in black and white. There wasn't 24-hour broadcasting; all the stations signed off at midnight by playing "The Star-Spangled Banner." Grammy and Grandpa's routine never varied much: fish on Fridays, hot dogs and Lawrence Welk on Saturdays, Mass and pot roast on Sundays. *The Lawrence Welk Show* was a musical variety program hosted by the band leader of that name. Lawrence Welk had a strong German accent and started each number by counting, "And a one, and a two, and a one, two, three." Watching this high-production show must have reminded Grampa of the vaudeville shows he produced in Haverhill.

Sometimes we stayed up and watched part of the show, which aired from 8:00 to 9:00 p.m. All the women on the program wore matching chiffon-like dresses, and their big hair was perfectly coiffed. The men had slick hair and wore pastel-colored suits that matched the women's dresses. My favorite part was watching the Lennon Sisters sing, especially Janet Lennon, who was the youngest, but not much older than me. They were all a little too perfect and seemed way too sweet to be real, but Grammy and Grampa loved them and watching it together was fun.

Once winter came to Connecticut, the kids on Gilbert Road were itching to get out in the snow. Getting dressed to go out to play in the winter was an Olympic sport in itself. We wore one-piece snowsuits that zipped up the front. In addition, we put on scratchy woolen hats, mittens that shrunk when they got wet, and red rubber boots that zipped up over our shoes. Mrs. Dion next door loved "little Nancy" and knit special hats, mittens, and scarves for her. These getups were nothing like the high-tech snow gear of today, but they managed to keep us warm as long as we wore layers of socks and sweaters under them. Once we were outfitted, we played in the snow all day with no shortage of ways to pass the time. There was sledding, snow angel-making, snowball fighting, and constructing elaborate snow forts. My sisters and I spent hours in the snow drifts the plows left behind at the end of our driveway. We enlisted our friends and carved out intricate igloos together. Somehow, we never felt cold—it must have been a kid thing.

Sometimes I snuck off by myself to a secret snow fort I built in a lonely field beyond our neighborhood. There were rows of houses, then a tree line, and then the field. It's built up now, but back then it was quiet over there. A stream ran through the field near my secret snow house and I could hear the birds in the bare trees. I sat in there all by myself and dreamed. One day I scared myself: I fell asleep in my igloo and it was almost dark when I woke. I ran home under a cold, pink winter sky hoping my parents hadn't realized I was missing yet. I think I just needed alone time once in a while, even as a child.

*Kids at Site of New House.*

# CHAPTER. 2

# "*What a Wonderful World*"

## Louis Armstrong

### Newington, Connecticut, 1954 - 1956

No matter how bad the weather was, we walked to school. Moms didn't have cars back then. We marched from Gilbert Road, across Dowd Street, and down Neil Drive to "the school path." This kid-worn gravel path wound about a quarter of a mile through woods and fields that eventually led to New Meadows School. We trudged that path with our siblings or neighbor kids; the older kids looking out for the littles. Sometimes we'd stop along the path on our way home to capture pollywogs in an empty thermos or pick wildflowers for our mothers. In 2015, when I was back in Newington for a funeral, I located the old school path. It was exactly as I remembered it. For those few minutes while I walked the length of the path, I was a young girl again, reliving a happy time in my life. I feel nostalgic when I think that even after 70 years, kids are still using our old path—and, just maybe, stopping to pick flowers and catch tadpoles along the way.

*Cheryl on the old School Path in 2015—It's still there!*

Sometimes, when Mom was out of a necessity like bread or eggs, she gave me money in the morning and I walked home from school "the long way," through downtown Newington, so that I could stop at the A&P. She tied up the coins in a handkerchief and placed them in the bottom of my red plaid metal lunchbox. We still had milkmen back then, so milk was one thing people didn't often run out of. Empty glass milk bottles were put on the back steps and the milkman would replace them with fresh milk from his truck, waving when he saw us.

On a holy day, like Ash Wednesday, we walked home from New Meadows school "the back way" to go to Mass or get our ashes at Saint Mary's Catholic Church on Willard Avenue. One day, a girlfriend and I stopped at Saint Mary's on our way home to light a candle. We'd forgotten to bring hats with us, so we used bobby pins to secure facial tissues to our heads before entering the church. Another time, I wore a little chiffon scarf when we stopped at church to light a candle and leaned in too close. The candle caught the corner of my scarf on fire. I was shaking as my friend and I stomped the sooty square of silk onto the wooden church floor to put it out. We were more scared that a nun might see us than we were of starting a fire. We took rules about things like head coverings very seriously in those days. We took our fear of nuns very seriously as well.

One of my first girlfriends on Gilbert Road was Barbara Jean. Barbara Jean had white-blonde hair, while mine was dirty blonde. She was on the slimmer side, while I leaned more toward chubby. More than once, I found myself jealous of her first-grade beauty. Usually, we got along well and played well together, but occasionally Barbara Jean was my nemesis. We couldn't stay mad at one another for long though, especially being in the same class at New Meadows School.

Although we learned phonics, our teacher used the *Fun with Dick and Jane* basal readers to help us learn sight words and develop fluency. We loved reading the adventures of Dick and Jane, their little sister Sally and the family dog, Spot. In one story, Spot was chasing a bunny and their dad was building Spot a dog house. Excited by the story, Barbara

Jean and I each ran home, changed into our play clothes (you never wore "school clothes" to play in back then) and proceeded to create our own magical bunny hutch under the back stoop at Barbara Jean's house. Once we transformed ourselves into imaginary bunnies, we convinced Barbara Jean's mother to donate carrots. We spent the rest of the afternoon hopping around with carrot greens hanging out of our bunny mouths, until we got so tired we couldn't hop anymore.

On Saturdays, my mother occasionally took my sister Andrea and me shopping in Hartford; Nancy was still little and stayed home with Daddy or our neighbor, Mrs. Dion. I loved those days! We always dressed up to go shopping—Mom in heels and a hat, us in our Sunday best. My favorite part of the bus ride from Newington into Hartford was pulling the cord to let the driver know that we needed to get off at the next stop. Andi and I, in our stiff organdy dresses and patent-leather shoes, would clamor over each other on the plastic seat, fighting to be the first one to reach the cord and hear the *BZZZZ!* We were not exactly the epitome of ladylike bus riders at the time.

When we arrived downtown, we couldn't wait to get to the huge G. Fox Department Store on Main Street. It was a wonderland of revolving glass doors, steep escalators, and shiny elevators with serious-looking attendants in starched uniforms. We rode the elevator up and down, the operator pulling the big handle to start and stop the car. As he did, he called out what was on each floor: "Housewares, Appliances, Small Electrics, Dinnerware, Fine China!" The ride often ended on the 11th floor where we drooled over the Madame Alexander, Ginger, Tiny Tears, and Betsy Wetsy dolls on display in "Toyland," the December home of the G. Fox Santa Claus.

Even at my young age, the ninth floor was my favorite. It was the location of "The Connecticut House," a mockup of a full-size

New England Cape Cod style home right there in the store. As a kid, I couldn't imagine how someone had managed to get a real house all the way up to the ninth floor. After passing through the house's "porch," the home featured rooms outfitted with elegant furnishings, all available from Fox's, of course. I wandered through that house again and again until my mother finally had to all but drag me out.

Across from G. Fox was the J.J. Newberry Five and Dime store where Mom bought popcorn for the bus ride home. The smell hit us the moment we entered the store. For 15 cents, you received a foot-tall bag of salty popcorn overflowing with buttery goodness from the red and white striped cart. Sometimes we'd visit the nearby Mr. Peanut Store for hot salty nuts to accompany our popcorn. Mr. Peanut himself paced the sidewalk outside in full regalia, greeting shoppers. If we were lucky, it was a day when the store passed out a souvenir to each child. It was a plastic three-inch-tall Mr. Peanut whistle complete with top hat and cane. My sisters and I treasured those.

On the ride home, we had quite the armful if we had made both stops. As the bus rumbled along, Andi and I filled up on popcorn and peanuts, proudly blowing our Mr. Peanut whistles. Sometimes we were so distracted, we even forgot to fight about pulling the cord for our stop.

In the summer, the neighborhood kids spent a lot of time under the sprinklers, while the neighborhood moms - too hot for housework or ironing - sat in webbed aluminum lawn chairs, fanning themselves with their latest copies of *Woman's Day* or *Family Circle*. My girlfriends and I spread blankets in the shade and made pink, blue, green, and yellow flowers from pastel facial tissues. You could get all four in one box. Mom didn't want to buy them since they were more expensive than white ones, but I convinced her it was worth it. We used pipe cleaners from neighborhood fathers, twisted the tissue around them, and pulled out the edges to form petals. Once we each made enough flowers, we presented our bouquets to our mothers.

We spent a lot of time outside since most of us didn't have a TV yet. When we took a break from playing, we liked to dance. It was often to the soulful voice of Louis Armstrong emanating from Mr. Begley's study in the house across the street. He was Louis Armstrong's biggest fan and imitated his deep raspy voice to the delight of the kids on Gilbert Road. I knew the lyrics to most of his songs before I was seven years old, just from hanging around in the Begley's yard with their son, Jerry.

Unlike his father, Jerry emulated Elvis, doing his best to imitate his look and gyrating hips. When Jerry asked me to "play Elvis" together, it was goodbye, Louis Armstrong. We put Elvis on his dad's record player, and I donned my coveted black elastic cinch belt. We twirled to our version of the bop, music blaring from the Begley's window, which often drew the other neighborhood kids to join us.

We had more freedom in those days than most kids do today. On hot afternoons, we pedaled our bikes down to the Ma and Pa store on Willard Avenue for popsicles. We attached playing cards to the spokes of our bike wheels with clothespins to create a raucous symphony of flapping sounds announcing our arrival. The little market catered to housewives whose husbands took the family's only car to work but who had run out of bread or eggs. Like my mom, they would pile their babies in the carriage, hold the toddlers by the hand, and walk the three or four blocks to the store. These stores always smelled the same, an unlikely combination of old wood, dill pickles, and root beer. There was a rusty push-bar across the screen entrance door advertising Sunshine Bread on one side and Coca-Cola on the other. The old building had tin ceilings and two aisles dividing its display space. The wood floors were worn in the aisles and in front of the cashier, where jars of dill pickles and pickled eggs shared the counter with the antique cash register. Nearby shelves were lined with smaller jars of penny candy; my favorites were the red-hot fire balls, licorice whips, and Mary Jane's.

Just outside the screen door was a deep cooler filled with the holy grail of kiddom: red, purple, and orange popsicles. They cost five cents each, a pretty hefty sum at the time. There were no Good Humor bars in the case because the Good Humor Man still came through our childhood neighborhoods on summer afternoons ringing his bell and tempting us to spend what little allowance we had left. The old store sported a faded red and green striped awning across the front to help the freezer stay cold. We parked our bikes under the awning to keep the metal handlebars from burning our fingers on the ride home.

Even in 1954, 25 cents didn't buy much, so we looked for other ways of earning money. The most profitable was plucking Japanese beetles off of rose bushes, dropping them into jars of soapy water and charging the homeowners for the service. My parents had planted an extensive row of red rose bushes along the split-rail fence Daddy built around the front yard. Other neighbors had set out roses too: pink, white, and red climbers proliferated around the shiny new houses on Gilbert Road. We plucked the beetles, counted the unlucky corpses in our jars and charged the neighbors a penny for every 25 beetles we removed. There were hundreds of beetles, so we made pretty good money in the beetle business by kid standards. It wasn't until I was an adult that I realized that the whole beetle thing was a con invented by our parents to keep us quiet and out of their hair for hours at a time for only pennies.

*Newington House that Dad and Grampa built.*

Mom kept a copy of Dr. Spock's *The Common Sense Book of Baby and Child Care* on her dresser. While many parents believed in strict discipline, I had friends whose punishments were stricter than in our household. There was one infraction that required the harshest punishment of all in the Smith house: LYING. I can't remember what I lied about, but I sure can remember the punishment. I had to sit on the toilet seat in the bathroom with a bar of Ivory soap in my mouth until my mom said time was up. Looking back on this, the most dreaded of all punishments, reminds me of poor Ralphie in *The Christmas Story*, who was sadly subjected to the same fate, not for lying, but for using the F word. As Ralphie so poetically put it: "Over the years, I got to be quite a connoisseur of soap. My personal preference was for Lux, but I found Palmolive had a nice, piquant after-dinner flavor–heady, but with just a touch of mellow smoothness." (*The Christmas Story*, Warner Bros., 1983). Well, Ralphie, take it from Cheryl Dianne, you haven't really suffered until you've had a big bite of Ivory! To this day, if I even get a whiff of Ivory soap at someone's home, I feel nauseous.

If it was a serious offense other than lying, we had to miss out on something we were really looking forward to. One year, I missed the annual Fourth of July fireworks in Hartford. I sat alone at my bedroom window hearing the far-away booms. Unfortunately, I couldn't see much of anything over the two or three miles of treetops in between. Feeling sorry for myself, I sobbed at the unfairness I felt. "How come Andi and Nancy got to go?" I wailed. "They're not perfect!"

On rainy days, we kids moved indoors. Whether a ranch or Cape, each little post-war home in our neighborhood had a living room, dining room, kitchen, and bathroom with a couple of bedrooms upstairs or down a hallway. They were modest and efficient with no family room, and living rooms were usually more formal spaces reserved for "company." This meant that any indoor playtime was relegated to the basement, or what we called the cellar.

Most fathers painted their cellar cement floors, possibly in an attempt to make the space more cheerful. Ours were brick red. In winter, sometimes we brought down our bikes and roller skates–the adjustable kind you buckled over your shoes. We rode or skated around the kitchen staircase until we were dizzy. Everything went well as long as we avoided crashing into any of the mothers' cast-off furniture. There was usually a faded daybed we could relax on or a retired kitchen table, which was great for playing board games, making paper mâché animals, coloring, or making scrapbooks to donate to the kids at the Newington Children's Hospital.

Sometimes, my sisters and I hung blanket "stage curtains" from the ceiling beams and pipes and produced elaborate plays for whoever we could scrape together to watch. We made tickets, costumes, and scenery, while usually arguing with one another about every detail:

"The bad wolf should be red, 'cause he's mean," one would say.

"No, wolves are always brown, silly!" another yelled in response.

It's a wonder we ever got the play ready for opening afternoon. On the big day, our audience consisted mostly of neighborhood mothers, happy for an excuse to step away from their ironing boards for a few minutes, and their little kids, who didn't have much of a choice but to come with them.

My friend, Karen, had part of her cellar set up as a little school room. There were two real school desks and a bigger teacher's desk. Karen's school supplies included piles of used books and even a school bell. We played school there for hours, as we each took turns being the teacher. Being the teacher was the best because then you got to tell the other kids what to do!

# CHAPTER 3

# *"Que Sera Sera"*

## Doris Day

### Westport, Connecticut, 1957 - 1958

We moved to Patrick Road in Westport, Connecticut in 1957 when I was 10 years old and about to enter fifth grade. I was sad to leave behind the little red Cape I loved in Newington. Unfortunately, Dad was transferred—at that time, companies thought nothing of moving employees around as needed. The stay-at-home moms were expected to uproot their lives every few years as their husbands advanced. We had no choice but to pack, leave our favorite teachers and friends, and find new ones in unfamiliar places.

The maple kitchen table from Newington now sat under a big bay window at the far end of our new Westport kitchen. Sometimes I longed for my Wallpaper People from the old kitchen. I missed the stories they sowed in my imagination as I ate next to their farms and bridges.

My parents were thrifty and never hired anyone to do anything they could do themselves. Mom and Dad headed to the woods one day, found a young maple sapling, dug it up, and planted it themselves. Thank goodness our new car was a convertible! That newly planted little maple was the view we had out our kitchen's big bay window.

Mom was excited about our new "40,000-dollar house," as she called it, which left me feeling embarrassed. I imagined Great Aunt Elva in Virginia saying something like, "Well, bless her little heart. She's really walkin' in the tall cotton now." Mom did the same thing with clothes—never just a coat, but "my London Fog." Then there was our "3,000 dollar-car"—a royal blue 1959 Chevy Impala convertible with a white top.

Okay, I couldn't complain about the car—we all liked that car. It had huge bat-wing rear fenders and cat's eye taillamps. When the top was down, Andi, Nancy, and I loved to climb into the back seat. We felt like movie stars and as such, never went out without our sunglasses and 19 cent Westport five-and-dime chiffon scarves. We made sure to tie them around our heads in case our pixie cuts needed protection from the wind.

At the Westport house, I had my own room, which was painted blue. Andi and Nancy shared the pink bedroom next door. Color choices were courtesy of the Portsmouth Five and Dime. Mom didn't want us to damage her perfectly painted walls with posters, so magazine cutouts of my current idol, Fabian, were relegated to the sliding closet doors because Scotch tape didn't ruin their enamel paint.

My furnishings included my grandparent's old maple dresser, a low white painted table that held my record player with a rack of 45s, and a skirted desk that Dad made. Mom intended it to serve as both a makeup table and study table (I never used it for makeup, but I did a lot of schoolwork on it). My sisters and I played elevator in my Fabian covered closet, so deep we could all comfortably fit inside. Each of us took turns being the elevator operator—a game that likely came about from those Saturday trips to G. Fox's.

My big closet came in handy on other occasions as well. Our parents had cocktail hour most evenings when Dad got home from work, although sometimes Mom had gotten a head start. Sometimes the cocktail hour extended a few extra hours. When that happened, dinner was forgotten, and then the yelling started. Occasionally, it led to objects being thrown, and horrible things said. My sisters and I were often scared, not knowing what might happen. What if they got so drunk that Mom and Dad killed each other or, God forbid, one of us?

I kept a blanket and extra pillows in my closet. When it got really bad, I hid my sisters in there and snuggled with them under the blanket.

We sang so that we couldn't hear the raised voices: Grammy Boocock's "I See the Moon" or maybe a Grampa Smith favorite like 'Harrigan." From the inside, I slid the closet door open a crack and trembled as I listened for any sound. When I didn't hear anything, I looked out the small opening. It was dark and eerily quiet, so we knew that Mom and Dad were asleep. "We can come out now," I whispered to my younger sisters.

In our split-level Westport house, we no longer needed to play in the cellar; there was an official family room downstairs. We had years of fun in that room with its pine-paneled walls and French doors leading out to the pond. From the bus stop on weekdays, we rushed home to watch *The Mickey Mouse Club* and *American Bandstand* there. When we tired of TV, the brown and tan linoleum squares were laid out on the floor in a pattern that made for a perfect hopscotch layout! We knew which squares were in or out and stuck to it by sisterly consensus.

There was a large player piano in the family room, topped with stacks of aging piano rolls. Even though we all enjoyed playing, Andi got the prize for "Most Enthusiastic." She regaled us with songs like "Mississippi Mud" or "Let Me Call You Sweetheart" as her legs flew up and down on the pedals. We also had a record player, so we bopped to the music of Paul Anka, Bobby Rydell, Frankie Avalon, Bobby Vee, and of course, Fabian. When our Irish grandfather Smith came to visit, we used the whole 30 feet of family room space to practice the jig.

*Cheryl, Andrea, Nancy & friends celebrate a
birthday downstairs in Westport Rec. Room.*

The kitchen in our house on Partrick Road had turquoise appliances.
We had a wall oven, an electric stove top with push button controls,
and a refrigerator/freezer with aluminum ice trays. Of all the things we
made in that kitchen, my sisters and I loved making Jiffy Pop on that
stove the most.

As we shook the handle of the little foil pan, suspense built. With
each *POP!*, the lid expanded, forming a towering foil balloon full of hot
buttery goodness. As we broke open the foil bubble, the smell evoked
memories of Saturday matinees at the old Westport Theater and summer
nights at the Wells Beach Casino. After we salted the fat kernels and
dumped them into bowls, that only left arguing with my sisters about
who got the most.

On Sundays, Mom made a big family dinner at noon so we had
lots of free time to play outside or skate on the pond the rest of the
day. At dark, we went inside to make sandwiches and eat in front of
the TV, watching *Lassie* and *The Ed Sullivan Show*. Seeded bulky
rolls from the deli were loaded with roast beef, cheese, and pickled
onions. Only when Mom and Dad were going out to dinner were we
treated to Swanson TV dinners. We had to preheat the oven and wait
30 minutes for them to heat. Things were slower back then and we

learned to be patient; microwaves hadn't been invented yet. To our childhood palates, these little foil-wrapped wonders were well worth the wait. Each dinner came in a divided tin tray with turkey or meatloaf, corn, mashed potatoes, and a miniscule dessert. What more could a kid possibly want?

Christmas was magical during those years, especially because Mom and Dad made an effort not to fight during the holidays—at least not as much. Mom wrapped the front door with gold foil paper and a giant red bow like it was a present. Mid-December, our parents bundled us all into the Impala so we could visit the brightly-lit Knights of Columbus Christmas tree lot on Route 1 to choose the perfect tree. It was always a balsam fir tree, and Mom insisted there could be no bare spots. By the time we chose one, our feet were freezing.

My favorite part of Christmas was caroling with the neighborhood kids, crunching through the snow, ringing our jingle bells. When people heard us jingle jangle, they came to their doors smiling. Sometimes they sang along with us to the familiar carols the *Hartford Courant* inserted in the Sunday edition each year. A few even gave us hot cocoa or candy canes. We always seemed to pick the coldest night, so I wrapped my long green and white knit scarf around my neck two or three times to keep warm.

My sisters and I always hoped Santa would be good to us. We woke up early on Christmas Day and ran downstairs to look under the tree. There were skating outfits for each of us, hand sewn by Mom. Magic 8 balls, hula hoops, Barbie dolls, Mad Libs, board games, costume jewelry, records, fluffy slippers, stuffed animals, and clothes.

I often stayed up late reading the *Nancy Drew* books I got. It was fun to imagine myself as Nancy, driving around in my roadster convertible solving mysteries. My youngest sister asked for the same white stuffed dog every year. Thankfully Santa didn't disappoint, because by December, the previous year's dog was becoming worn. I often wondered what happened to dogs from years past.

When it snowed, my sisters and I headed to nearby Cypress Pond Road with our Flexible Flyers. We spent many hours sliding down that road, pulling the slush-coated sleds back up between rides. Our feet were covered with our warmest socks, sneakers, and our matching red rubber boots that zipped up the side so our feet would stay dry. Sadly, our woolen mittens froze quickly once they got damp, taking on the form of ice sculptures. We went sledding until dark or suppertime—5:30 p.m. sharp at the Smith house—whichever came first. I was jealous of my friends, Caroleen and Teddy, who didn't have to come inside until six.

On sunny winter afternoons, we rushed home from school, changed into our skating attire, and hit the ice. One year, Mom made us all black corduroy skating skirts with rick rack trim and bright red lining. We wore them with matching red tights and heavy skating sweaters. The Stunning Smith Sisters headed for the pond: me being the oldest and most serious, followed by the middle and most graceful sister Andi, followed by chubby little Nancy. She often hobbled through the snow as she screamed for us to "WAIT UP!"

When we wanted a bit more adventure, we skated through the woods around the edge of the pond, racing each other through its frozen paths. Andi would usually win. I'd get second place. Then later, sometimes much later, Nancy would appear. By then, she was wildly huffing, spitting, and cursing as few seven-year-old girls could. I think we lived as we skated, each finding our own way, in our own time.

My best friend at that time was Sandy Yoder. Sandy was a petite, serious-looking girl with short dark hair who always wore straight skirts, white socks, and loafers to school. Going to Sandy's house was always fun because, with her mother often at work, we got to do things we never would have gotten away with at my house. Her mother let us make copper enamel jewelry with her enamel powders and kiln in the basement; my nervous mom would never have trusted us to use a 2000-degree kiln. When we were sure Sandy's parents weren't going to arrive home unexpectedly, Sandy and I dragged her twin mattress up the stairs to their unfinished attic. We sat on it like a toboggan, rode it down the whole flight of stairs, and sailed across the dining room below. Luckily, we suffered no injuries in our reckless innocence!

For lunch, Sandy made us Campbell's mushroom or tomato soup, tuna sandwiches with dill pickles and onions, and her own beverage creation: equal parts ginger ale and a nonalcoholic Tom Collins mixer. I wrote in my diary that Sandy's mocktails were "actually quite good." Sandy also taught me that if you buttered a piece of bread before putting it in the toaster, it tasted like an English muffin when it came out. A most interesting and thrifty girl!

At recess, Sandy and I sat on a big rock at the back of the wooded Coleytown School playground and listened to Doris Day on her transistor radio while snacking on fancy little foil-wrapped wedges of cheese:

> *Que sera, sera*
> *Whatever will be, will be*
> *The future's not ours to see.*
> *Que sera, sera*
> *What will be, will be.*

I'm glad I didn't know what was in store back then. What a gift it was to have those few years of reckless innocence!

*In front of Westport House, Easter, 1958.*

# CHAPTER 4

# "*Here Comes Summer*"

## Jerry Keller

### Wells Beach, Maine, 1950s

Every August, Mom and Dad packed us into the Chevy and headed out for our two-week family vacation in Wells Beach, Maine. Our parents rode in the front while Nancy, Andi, and I squeezed into the back for the eight-hour trip alongside most of the luggage. With no air conditioning or seat belts, the ride became more unbearable as the hours ticked by. Andi and I bounced around and inevitably into one another.

The heat drove us all a bit crazy, until the back seat passengers started snapping at each other. "She touched me!" was met with "I did not!" From the front came, "Stop touching her!" More than once, Dad turned around from the driver's seat to say, "Don't make me pull this car over!" Other times, he just reached back and started swatting. If he reached you, you got it! It didn't matter whether you were guilty of something or not.

We knew we were finally getting close when we crossed the 10 cent bridge between Portsmouth, New Hampshire and Kittery, Maine. That was when we rolled down our windows for our first whiff of the ocean and screamed, "We're in Maine! We're in Maine!" until Dad had enough and threatened to pull the car over again. We firmly believed that Maine smelled different from New Hampshire.

A vacation tradition was to stop at El's Fried Clams in York. It was a little white wooden stand at the side of Route 1. You ordered at a linoleum counter and waited for the clams to be fried. The delicious clams and big paper tray of hand-cut French fries that accompanied them almost made up for the unbearable ride.

If we stood up in the back seat after 20 more miles, we could just make out the orange roof of the Wells Howard Johnsons, our first local landmark. The excitement in that back seat grew to a feverish pitch until a cacophony of female voices began repeating a chorus of "Are we there yet?" Dad turned right onto Mile Road where we spotted the clam flats that bordered the beach beyond.

A bystander would have seen three blond heads of varying sizes hanging out of the Chevy windows. Each set of nostrils tried to be the first to catch a whiff of the rotten egg odor of the marsh. "I smelled it first!" or "I smell the beach!" were yelled as the clusters of shingled summer cottages and the blue of the ocean beyond them came into view. The old wooden Casino in Wells Beach center was a sure sign that we'd finally arrived.

Once we escaped the heat of the Impala from Hell, we ran to our rooms to unpack our new beach clothes. These always included bright white sweatshirts, white sailor hats that came with built-in sunglasses, plaid Bermuda shorts and "clam diggers" (we call them "capris" now), white Keds, and cotton or knit bathing suits—some knit by Mrs. Dion—which unfortunately were like sponges when we got them wet. Once soaked, they tended to droop in all the wrong places.

The first cottage we stayed at was The Howgate on Webhannet Drive, which runs along the mile-long stretch of sandy beach. It was sided with gray weather-beaten shingles and surrounded on three sides by a wide covered porch that looked out to the surf. One of my earliest memories was of putting my baby doll to bed on that porch when I was probably three or four years old. Andi was a baby during those Howgate summers and Nancy and Joanne were not born yet. The Howgate was my favorite cottage, even though I always had an unexplainable fear of going down into its cellar.

*Our first cottage at Wells Beach, the Howgate.*

After the Howgate, we stayed for two summers on the marsh side of Webhannet Drive in a pink duplex cottage named Laura Lee. The mud flats behind the Laura Lee were great for clamming when the tide was out. Mom's sister, Auntie Doris and her husband, Uncle Donald, rented the other side of the duplex with their three children, our cousins, Dawn, Leslie, and Lisa Jollimore. They brought Mom's mom, "Grammy Boocock," up to vacation with us as well.

Like so many others, Lillian and Robinson Boocock, aka "Grammy and Grampa Boocock," sailed to America from Liverpool, England in 1924, when Mom was just three years old, seeking a better life. They left behind the mills in Bradford and Leeds, where Grammy Boocock had worked since the age of 13. They made their home in Haverhill, Massachusetts, where they had two more daughters, Marion and Doris. Grandpa Boocock, who fought in the British Cavalry in WWI, died unexpectedly in 1953. Grammy Boocock, who lived into her 90s, had tea every afternoon, never lost her English accent, and addressed each one of us as "Lovey."

At the Laura Lee, Grammy Boocock wore a navy and white polka dotted dress and straw coolie hat to wade through the beach grass in her bare feet looking for clam holes with us. We'd never seen her without her stockings before! Once we found a hole with sea water spouting out of it, we had to dig fast to get the clam. Those little suckers burrowed back down into the sand at the speed of light! If we got enough, Daddy would steam them in a big blue pot. When they were done, we'd crack them open and dip them in hot sea water and a little bowl of melted butter. Delicious!

Below the sea wall, there was an old metal two-seater swing set at the Laura Lee. It was firmly planted in the sand just at the water line. We waited for high tide so we could swing high and jump off into the salt water. Luckily, we timed it well enough that none of us got maimed or killed in spite of hundreds of near misses.

Many days, we walked the beach all the way to the Wells Beach Post Office to see if any of our friends from home might have written to us via General Delivery. We usually walked back empty handed. We looked forward to Beano night, when kids were invited to ride around adjoining Moody Beach on the old Wells fire truck to advertise the weekly Beano fundraiser. We were crammed on that truck like sardines in a can, but we zoomed along the beach listening to blaring sirens and feeling the wind whipping our hair—loving every moment.

When it wasn't Beano night, Mom and Dad often wanted to "take a ride" after supper. We didn't have air conditioning in the '50s, so "taking a ride" was often synonymous with cooling off before bed. Cruising in our bright blue '59 Chevy Impala with the top down, we felt like movie stars, each in a different color chiffon scarf to keep our hair from blowing around. Our rides were exactly the same each year. One evening we'd drive around Kennebunk Beach, through the Port and over to the Clock Farm and Goose Rocks Beach. On another hot night, we'd motor down to York Beach to watch taffy being made through the window at Goldenrod's Kisses and admire the view of Nubble Light. We visited the Indian Moccasin Shop in Wells to buy little beaded dolls and necklaces. One afternoon or early evening was always devoted to driving down to Ogunquit to stop at Perkin's Cove and walk the Marginal Way, a breathtaking trail along the cliffs overlooking the ocean. Mom and Dad had our caricatures done in Perkins Cove by the artist who always had his easel set up in the parking lot. If our chiffon scarves didn't do the trick, sitting for those portraits surrounded by curious tourists *really* made us feel like movie stars!

During those summers, we spent a lot of time with Auntie Doris and Uncle Donald and our cousins. One day, we were all body surfing when an obviously embarrassed Uncle Donald yelled over the roar of the waves, "I THINK I'VE LOST MY TEETH!" It seemed that while jumping the waves, Uncle Donald's upper plate had fallen out into the surf. That was a clear call to action for us kids.

"You need to help us!" we yelled. "Our uncle has lost his teeth! We need to find them!" Up and down the beach, from kid to kid, went the chant about Uncle Donald's missing teeth. Before long, there were about 50 kids with face masks floating at the edge of the waves looking for the missing choppers. Unfortunately, we were unsuccessful. Even so, the story of Uncle Donald's teeth has become the stuff of legend, told and retold around Labor Day campfires at Wells Beach to this day.

*Sisters at Wells Beach.*

# CHAPTER 5

# "*Mack the Knife*"

## **Bobby Darin**

Westport, Connecticut, 1959

The road over the hill from our house in Westport led to a large grassy oval surrounded by a split-rail fence. "The Green" was the school bus stop, ball field, lemonade stand, and general communications center for kiddom on Partrick Road. Next to The Green was "The Barn."

The neighborhood kids spent hours creeping through the ancient wooden barn, which we were convinced was haunted by its previous owners, the Tarkingtons. Although we never met them, my sisters and I conjured Mr. Tarkington up to be pretty scary. In my imagination, he had greasy white hair, old bibbed dungarees, and yellow teeth. We double and triple-dog-dared each other to go into the barn.

Fascinated, we looked through letters and penny postcards pulled from abandoned trunks, mildewed boxes of old clothes, and long-forgotten household and farm tools. It was our very own haunted playground any time of year. We never got tired of hiding behind its wide beams and sneaking up on one another.

Sometimes, we climbed the old ladder to the loft, laid down on the leftover hay, and told ghost stories. Occasionally, we fell asleep up there. I imagined the lives the Tarkingtons must have had in the ancient house next door to the barn. It was locked, which we know because we tried, but it still had tattered white curtains hanging askew in the windows.

In the fall, my sisters and I raked the bright oak and maple leaves that fell abundantly in our front yard into huge piles in preparation for one of our favorite fall projects: making leaf houses. Sometimes we made one big house with a room for each of us; other times we decided that we each needed our own house. No trespassing!

From above, our houses resembled the floor plan of a new home drawn on graph paper for prospective buyers. It showed the location of the rooms, closets, and hallways. Instead of pencil on graph paper, our walls were made of red, orange, and yellow leaves carefully raked into lines and squares on the brown grass.

Once the rooms were defined, we added leaf beds with leaf pillows to our bedrooms and leaf furniture for the living room. Assuming no sisterly fights were in progress, we visited each other's houses and hung out on a leaf couches. Sometimes we cooked up a bit of leaf soup together, imagining and pretending until the wind blew our houses away.

*Feb. 6, 1959*

*Dear Diary,*

*I have never had such a wonderful time in my life as tonight! Terry White brought me the most beautiful wrist corsage in the world. It cost (I think) about five dollars. Then he took me to the Boy Scout dance. During one of the first dances, when I was going under a boy's arm, my dress ripped. Since it was under my arm, it didn't show much. Linda taught us a circle dance which was sort of like rock 'n' roll. Terry bought us two bottles of soda and lots of popcorn. It was very good. I like Terry very much. I found out afterwards that the dance itself cost 50 cents each. Of course, Terry didn't tell me this. Later, Mr. White brought me home. Terry and I said goodbye on the porch.*

*Love, Cheryl*

My first date was Terry White, who took me to the annual Boy Scout Dance in 1959. For the Boy Scout dance, I wore a white dotted-swiss dress with a blue sash that Mom made and *real* stockings held up, I swear, by a garter belt. My hair was curled up tighter than a tick and I borrowed Mom's "diamond" earrings for the occasion. When the doorbell finally rang (as if my sisters hadn't been keeping watch from my parents' bathroom window and yelling, "He's h-e-r-e!"), there stood crew-cut Terry in his best suit. Poor Terry White was so nervous that he tripped over his own feet, descending red-faced into our ever-so-stylish sunken living room. I don't remember much about the dance, but I will always remember the smell of the first carnation I ever got from a boy. Even now, over 60 years later, the aroma of carnations transports me right back to that living room at 65 Partrick Road and the night of the Boy Scout dance.

As young teens, it was important to select just the right gift for each other's birthdays. The record shop was a favorite spot—45 rpm records at a dollar each were considered a respectable offering since it took four hours of babysitting to pay for just one. Some of our favorites at that time were "Teen Angel," "The Twist," "Puppy Love," "The Stroll," and "Devil or Angel" by artists like Bobby Vee, Paul Anka, Bobby Rydell, the Everly Brothers, and Frankie Avalon.

Other popular gifts were scarab bracelets or flip top leather purses, both pricey. There were also Magic 8 Balls and autograph dogs—white dachshunds that came with colored markers to collect signatures. My friends also loved Nancy Drew books as much as I did. If my budget for birthday gifts was tight, the Westport Five and Dime still sold little square chiffon scarves for 19 cents each—great to tie around our necks or ponytails.

My besties in Westport had fancy birthday celebrations, but Debbie Ashley's was the best. Although we drove by The Red Barn almost every day, I'd never eaten there. As was typical of high-end restaurants at that time, it featured colonial decor, flickering candles, pewter chargers, a big stone fireplace, white tablecloths, and the exposed beams of the farm building it once was.

I felt like royalty when the hostess led us to our table and I had definitely dressed for the occasion. After our main course but before dessert, we were each served a bowl of warm water on a small doi-ly-lined plate: a finger bowl. I'd never used a finger bowl before, so I just did what I saw Debbie do: dip my fingers in the water and dry them on the fresh napkin that was delivered with the bowl. Fancy indeed!

My next birthday was quite an affair. Mom decided on a daisy theme: she made party hats and decorations out of paper plates and yellow crepe paper. My sixth-grade girlfriends and I wore our best dresses and daisy hats. We partook of dainty little egg salad and olive sandwiches, followed by a daisy cake with lemon yellow sherbet. The only disappointment was that my pony, an ongoing promise by Grampa Smith, did not arrive from Ireland. Still hopeful, I was beginning to fear that his eternal promise might be a bit of Irish blarney.

Mom and Dad surprised me with an English bike for my birthday. They bought it secondhand from an older girl up the street named Judy, and I loved it. On summer days, Sandy Yoder and I packed peanut butter and jelly lunches before we set off on early mornings. Although we had no specific destination in mind, our regular meeting spot was always The Three Bears Inn. Over two centuries old, it was once a Stage Coach stop, general store, and post office. Our next stop after the inn was Al's gas station nearby to check the air in our tires. We were conscientious bikers.

Most of rural Westport still had narrow roads which began as dirt tracks in colonial times. Many of the old roads followed stream beds or ancient stone walls through miles of woods. They only had a scattered house or abandoned barn as punctuation. Sandy and I rode until we found a forlorn house to visit, an ancient graveyard, or a dusty barn waiting to be explored. We stopped there for our picnic lunch where we sat upon rocks by a stream or a stone wall or some long-forgotten dooryard. On those adventures, I felt so free, so brave, and so grown up.

On a hot summer morning, Mom and Dad packed the car with salads and desserts before we set off to see the Giannoni's. Their house was behind ours in Newington, and I was always fascinated by their two kitchens: one where a kitchen was supposed to be and one in the back of the garage. From Westport, their place in Newington was a little over an hour away on the Merritt Parkway and the Berlin Turnpike. Our favorite part of the ride was going through the "Big Tunnel" which ran under West Rock in New Haven. Whenever we drove through it, Dad removed his sunglasses and made the obvious announcement that "We're heading into the tunnel!"

We had so much fun eating grilled hot dogs and bowls of Mrs. Giannoni's spaghetti that we didn't want to leave. Neither did Mom and Dad, I guess. They both kept saying we'd leave after "one more drink" as the sun dropped lower, and the charcoal turned to ash in the grill. By the time we did finally leave, it was evening. Andi, Nancy, and I were lined up across the back seat of the Impala. Nancy was in the middle—on the hump—because Andi and I proclaimed that she had the shortest legs.

Dad drove and, by the time we got to the Berlin Turnpike, Mom was yelling that he was going to kill us all. A summer rain storm began; it was very dark. Patti Page was singing the "Tennessee Waltz" on the car radio. Mom kept telling Dad that he'd had too much to drink and screaming that she would go first if we crashed because she was in the "death seat." That's what Mom always called the front passenger seat: the "death seat." Not very comforting to the little audience in the back. The whole ride was punctuated by exclamations of, "Slow down!" "Fred, watch out, there's a truck!" or the best one, under the circumstances: "Fred, we've got the kids in the car." *And they're scared to death*, I might have added. Now that I'm an adult, I can't hear the "Tennessee Waltz" without a flashback to that rainy night on the Merritt Parkway when I thought we were all going to die.

# CHAPTER 6

# "*Little Sister*"

## Elvis Presley

### Westport, Connecticut, 1961

In January of 1961, Mom surprised us with another sister, and the Three Stunning Smith Sisters became Four. We voted to name her Joanne. Patricia came in second place, so that became her middle name. Her unexpected addition made for quite an age gap between us. I was 13 and in junior high school at the time.

Joanne was the immediate star of the Smith Family—Mom's blue-eyed flaxen-haired baby. We all adored her. As Joanne grew, she became even more attractive, with white-blonde hair and such pink cheeks that her nickname in high school was "Bunny." I think Mom saw herself in Joanne, the self she always wanted to be. Before long, the rest of us had left the nest and Joanne grew up like an only child. Mom and Dad doted on her, having more time and expendable income than when they raised their first three daughters.

Instead of hot dogs, B&M beans, and brown bread on Saturday nights, Mom and Dad could afford to dine out, and they took Joanne with them. Mom liked to joke about Joanne preferring smoked baby clams, ceviche, and other delicacies not found on most children's menus. At that age, the older three "Stunning Smith Sisters" were certainly well fed, but we'd never eaten a smoked baby clam nor heard of ceviche.

Andi, Nancy, and I rarely ate out at restaurants growing up and "fast food" was not yet heard of. Occasionally, Mom and Dad took us to an old-school Italian restaurant near the Saugatuck railroad station in Westport where we were welcomed by the tomatoey whiffs of "gravy" combined with the pungent smell of garlic. The interior decor featured dark wood, red checked tablecloths, and dusty plastic grape vines. Joanne never got to share the somewhat-decadent ambiance of the Arrow Restaurant with us, but truffle tagliolini may have been more to her taste than meatballs anyway.

When she came along, Joanne was welcomed, not only by me but by her other sisters, Andrea and Nancy.

Andi, aka Andrea Jean, was born in June of 1950, two and a half years after me. Even when we were little, I felt protective of her, likely due to Mom's frequent reminder, "Watch out for Andrea!" It was often the last thing Mom said as we headed out on the School Path. No matter the season, I remembered Mom's words and followed them dutifully. As the sister closest in age to me, Andi was the yin to my yang.

If Andi had red Keds, mine were navy. She had the flowered pink and blue Junior Miss lunchbox; mine was a bold red tartan plaid. She slept in the pink and green bedroom; mine was blue and white. For Andi and I, when our yin and yang were balanced, all was right with our world. We were best friends. When it was out of balance, jealousy took over. Occasionally we were known to scream childhood obscenities in which we called each other butthead, stupid, or chicken butt while trying to pull each other's hair.

In our family, I was seen as the controlling, perfectionistic, stubborn, self-righteous older sister—who, in the blink of an eye, could turn perfectly sensible situations into crises of gargantuan proportions. Ironically, outside of our family, I was known as the strong one, the one you could confide in, the one who always knew the right words, the one who could handle anything. Except, sometimes, herself.

While Andi was the pleaser in our family, one of my superpowers was being able to make Mom crazy with hardly a sound. Andi was more laid back. She learned early how to mold herself into any shape to keep the peace at home.

Andi was clearly Mom's favorite—until Joanne came along. In our tend-to-be-chubby family, Andi was the thin one, the smart one, the one who was good at everything. She was salutatorian and Homecoming Queen. My other sisters and I just tried to keep up. What the rest of us did, she did faster and better—winning art contests, playing the piano, and looking beautiful. Sometimes I wondered if Andi hid her emotions behind her many activities and accomplishments.

*Andi, Cheryl & Nancy with new sister, Joanne, 1961.*

Nancy Ann Smith was born in September of 1952, making her the third of the Stunning Smith Sisters. I was almost five and Andi was two and a half when Nancy came along. We lived in the Newington house that Dad and Grampa built. Since Nancy and I were farther apart in age than Andi and I, we didn't compete with one another. She was the baby until Joanne came along, so we all doted on her until she was displaced.

Nancy was the shortest of the Stunning Smith Sisters, with a chunky build and light brown hair, while the rest of us were blond. She was cursed with what the family referred to as "Grammy Smith's feet," meaning enlarged bunions which required foot surgery when she was six. Nancy was never very athletic but always tried to keep up with the rest of us.

One Easter morning, we were all dressed up in our church attire and hats. A wobbly seven-year-old Nancy, wanting desperately to be like her older sisters, all but fell out the front door on a pair of plastic dress-up high heels with elastic straps. Nancy compensated for her lack of grace with humor. She was popular and outgoing, always making people laugh. Over time, I realized that Nancy often used laughter to cover sadness. I loved her to the moon.

Our Grammy Smith and her four sisters were the "Stunning Parker Sisters," born in the late 1800s and early 1900s: Mary Alice (our grandmother), Helen, Dora, Ruth, and Eunice. If their antics in old age were any indication, they must have kept Haverhill, Massachusetts hopping when they were young!

I found it uncanny how our personalities seemed to mirror theirs. I, being the oldest, was the "responsible one," just like Grammy Smith. I was the protective older sister, the problem solver, sometimes the overly-bossy one, the one who would hammer ice.

Andi always reminded me of Aunt Helen, who only I was old enough to have met. I remember her as kind and quietly efficient. I have distant memories of sleeping under an electric blanket, which was a wonder to me at the time, on the unheated third floor of Aunt Helen's house in Haverhill when I visited with Grammy Smith.

I never knew Grammy's sister, Ruth, as she died in her 20s. Grammy Smith and Aunt Helen took in her two young children.

Nancy always reminded me of the second youngest Parker sister, Dora. She was the life of the party, the one who always kept everyone laughing. Aunt Dora had a great recipe for turkey stuffing. It advised the holiday cook to, "Stuff the bird with popcorn and 'cook until its ass blows off.'" That was Aunt Dora, and that was Nancy too.

In the transtemporal worlds of the Parker sisters and the Smith sisters, my sister Joanne evokes memories of Grammy's sister, Eunice. Aunt Eunice, the youngest Parker sister, was a lovely lady with stunning white hair. Having worked for years in a fine jewelry store, she was always impeccably dressed and bejeweled. When she spoke, she addressed each of us as "Dear." Mom and Dad lived with Aunt Eunice in Middletown, Connecticut when I was born. I always felt especially close to her.

Someday, the Stunning Smith Sisters may learn to celebrate each other's differences, together by choice, as friends and sisters. That was how I pictured us one day—old and gray and delighting in one another's company. Any childhood competition would have been left in the past, while we, like the Parker sisters, each came into our own.

*Parker Sisters: Dora, Helen, Eunice, and
our grandmother, Mary Alice.*

# CHAPTER 7

# *"See You in September"*

## The Tempos

### Wells Beach, Maine, 1960s

Once Joanne came along, instead of squeezing five of us in the car for the long ride to Maine, there were six. In addition to his passengers and the food and luggage for two weeks, Daddy lassoed a huge old black and white TV set to the trunk for us to watch at the cottage. At the size of a small refrigerator, it could hardly have been called a "portable" TV. When Joanne was a baby, it was my job to hold her in the back seat, but by 18 months, she sat in a little plastic contraption that hung between Mom and Dad in the front.

There was no turnpike in the '50s and early '60s, so it took all day to drive through Connecticut, Massachusetts and New Hampshire on old Route 1. Andi, Nancy, and I squeezed into the back for the eight-hour trip. After settling the inevitable sisterly arguments about who would have to sit in the middle with her feet on the "hump", we set out for Maine. As we got closer, we began our annual chorus of "Are we there yet?", to which our parents would reply, "Look out the windows; we'll be there soon". This was never particularly reassuring to the tired and cranky back seat passengers.

Upon arrival, we went straight to our rooms to unpack. Our luggage contained our usual vacation attire, but once we reached a certain age, we also tucked in something special for Saturday night dances at the casino. We planned what we were going to wear to the casino as carefully as a general might plan an upcoming military operation. A blouse with white linen shorts usually won, matched with new white sneakers (and no socks of course).

Other than the summer we all got those trendy but ever-so-unflattering pixie haircuts (which led us to wear sailor hats everywhere), we suffered in our rollers at the beach on the days before casino nights. And we daydreamed, wildly anticipating the big night when we might just meet *him, the one*, this year's summer love. I envied my summer friend, Eileen Hawkins, whose slim figure and tan skin looked great in her bathing suit. I saw myself as chunky and ashen white—not a sexy look for Wells Beach when you only had two weeks to snag a beau.

Life's Dream was the cottage we called home during the '60s. It was a brown bungalow right on the ocean, with its own swing set and shuffleboard court along the sea wall. Andi and Nancy shared the big front bedroom upstairs with its two Victorian beds looking out over the ocean. Being the oldest and a teenager, I got the smaller upstairs bedroom all to myself. Joanne slept in Mom and Dad's room. It smelled of salt air as we slept beneath the weight of quilts with the windows open on cool nights. I loved hearing the soft roar of the waves breaking as I fell asleep.

One Saturday in 1961, it was rumored that Freddie "Boom Boom" Cannon would be at the casino that night. The news flew up and down the beach via the teen grapevine, increasing the excitement with each retelling. By the end of the afternoon, there was word that Frankie Avalon was going to join him. This called for even more advanced feminine preparation than usual. Clothes were tried on and rejected, sneakers replaced with red leather flats borrowed from Aunt Ann, and my standby Cutex "Pink Pearl" lipstick tissued off. Instead, I swapped it out for a sexier red, secretly snagged from my mother's stash.

When we arrived at the casino, our hands were stamped before we rushed up the creaky flight of wooden stairs to the dance hall. The casino had huge barn-style windows that swung out all along the sides so we could hear the surf and smell the popcorn while listening to Paul Anka, the Everly Brothers, Johnny Mathis, and the Platters. Below the dance hall was a little sundries shop with a soda fountain that provided a place to hang out and look cool when the chances of being asked to dance were beginning to look slim.

*The Casino.*

When you were lucky enough to be asked, the Wells Beach Casino became the most romantic venue in the world. Amongst the colored spotlights and sea breezes, a boy, likely just as nervous as we were, danced with you for a few short minutes. From moments such as these, teenage dreams were woven! The only disappointment was that neither "Boom Boom" nor Frankie came by that evening. We reluctantly decided they must have had other plans.

In the summer of 1962, I fell madly in love twice in just two weeks. My first love was with the TableTalk pie kid. I sprayed my hair, snuck more of Mom's lipstick, and made sure I was ready and waiting to run to the door when I heard the chant, "The pie man's here! The pie man's here!" as the pie truck bounced down Webhannet Drive. We never ate so much pie as we did that summer: coconut, blueberry, custard, apple, strawberry rhubarb (dad's favorite) and Boston cream were eagerly purchased by yours truly in the cause of true love.

By the second week of vacation, the pie man having shown little interest in inviting me to the dance, I set my sights a little lower: the teenage trash man. As the huge Town of Wells trash truck rumbled down Webhannet Drive, I coyly offered up our weeks' worth of garbage in hopes of pulling off a coveted invitation to the dance. Sadly, in spite of all my efforts (and all my trash), I was still dateless come Saturday night. Reluctantly, I went to the dance on the arm of my younger sister Andi.

Two weeks is not much time to snag a boyfriend. How I wished that Mom and Dad had rented the cottage for three weeks instead of two—surely I would have had more success.

Even if my love life was disappointing, at least the days at Wells Beach were never boring. We slathered on the Coppertone, grabbed our transistor radios, and filled our time with swimming, sunbathing, and visiting our regular haunts. We walked to the Sunny Surf Market for Italian sandwiches. Souvenirs were procured for our friends back home at Pop's Shell Shake, and we hoarded postcards at Parent's Market. We went to the arcade near the casino and played skeeball, saving our tickets to win valuable prizes like miniature China dogs held together by golden chains.

We dreaded rainy days at Wells Beach because that inevitably meant the unavoidable trip to Gonic, New Hampshire to buy wool. Mom made most of our clothes back then and she'd load up on fabric for the winter at the Gonic Woolen Mill. It was always about 95 degrees and humid in the mill when Mom draped us in layer after layer of the hot, scratchy stuff. Somehow, August and wool just did not go together well. We did get some great clothes out of the deal though. One year it was matching ponchos, another it was skirts and vests that you could "mix and match."

Unlike today where we can wear jeans everywhere, girls were not allowed to wear pants to school or church, so we each had multiple categories of clothes. There were "school clothes" (plaid dresses with full skirts, nylon slips, black and white saddle shoes, red tights), "play clothes" (worn out or too-small school clothes and a pair of dungarees if we were lucky) "church clothes" (our best dress, hat, white gloves, patent leather shoes) and "party clothes" (see church clothes but forget the hat and gloves).

After a day in Gonic, we prayed that it would never rain again in Maine; any stray cloud might give Mom the idea of taking us back for more wool. We all preferred those sun-soaked days on the sand, which thankfully came more often than not.

# CHAPTER 8

# *"Sherry"*

## The Four Seasons

### Vestal, New York, 1961 - 1962

We were happy in Westport. My sisters and I had friends, forts, and a pond. I was doing well in school. I'd even made Center on the Bedford Junior High girls' basketball team. So, during the summer of 1961 at almost 14 years old, the last thing I wanted to hear was that we were moving to New York State. It was as terrifying as being told we were moving to the moon. I hated the thought of starting my first year of high school as the new girl, especially in some little Podunk town far from everyone and everything I cared about. Where in the hell was Vestal, New York anyway?

Dad, who was mostly self-taught, was brilliant! He could finish the *New York Times* Sunday Crossword in under an hour. Show him something once, and he could often figure it out. Yet, while other engineers were getting advanced degrees, Dad was overseas fighting the Germans. Whenever it was time for a company to downsize, he was often among the first to go. Reluctantly, Dad had taken an engineering job at Ozalid in Binghamton, New York. None of us wanted to go, but he was determined to provide us with a middle-class lifestyle and educational opportunities he didn't have.

Everything we owned was loaded into a moving van, and we followed in two cars. This meant that the Death Seat was sometimes unoccupied. Seemingly forgetting Mom's nickname, Andi and Nancy spent most of the ride jumping around arguing about who would get the prized front seat. The drive through Deposit, New York was depressing with barely anywhere to stop for a break on narrow Route 17. It was a scorching hot summer day, and we were all glued together with sweat. Unfortunately, I was also glued to Joanne, which is why I wasn't fighting for the front seat. As the oldest, it was my job to hold her in the back seat, as well as feed, change, and entertain her. I loved my baby sister, but I really didn't enjoy this particular assignment.

I expected worse, but as it turned out, Vestal wasn't that bad. As a suburban town just outside of Binghamton, new neighborhoods were springing up along the Vestal Parkway. Our brand new white split-level house was on Sequoia Lane, part of a hillside neighborhood that looked out over the Susquehanna Valley. At night, the lights sparkled from Endicott and Binghamton below, which I'll admit was a beautiful sight.

On our first morning in Vestal, the neighborhood paper boy, Jerry, came to the door to see if we wanted delivery of the *Binghamton Gazette*. Well, of course we did! He was a hunk! Unfortunately, a bit of teen research revealed that our gorgeous Italian paper boy already had a girlfriend named Kathy. Since Jerry was already spoken for, and they both lived in our neighborhood, Kathy and I became friends.

For some reason, Kathy called me "Sherry" instead of "Cheryl," and the name stuck. For the two years we lived in Vestal, I was Sherry, a name I didn't really like—until the fall of 1962, when the Four Seasons recorded "Sherry" and it became a number one hit overnight. Now I didn't mind being Sherry quite so much after all!

As luck had it, Kathy happened to have a brother named Eddie. Although on the short side, Eddie was handsome, with beautiful eyes and a great sense of humor. When he sat at a piano, he could play popular songs by ear. I was totally enchanted.

It didn't take long to figure out that if I stood at just the right angle on my parents' bathroom toilet seat and looked out the window with Dad's binoculars, I could see into Eddie's kitchen window at the bottom of the hill. I spent hours standing on that toilet just waiting for Eddie to walk into his kitchen for a Coke. Suddenly, Vestal was becoming a lot more interesting!

Once I began Vestal High School as a freshman, there were Friday night football games and dances to keep me busy. The school was huge, so there was always something going on, plus I made sure to reserve some time for Eddie-watching. However, once I met Lana—a girl my age who lived right across the street—I found out that she was also in love with Eddie. That's when she became my nemesis.

Visiting Lana's house was weird. I thought her parents must have been rich because their home decor was so over the top, dripping gold and crystal everywhere, even in Lana's room. Their home was like a miniature Trump Tower right there on Sequoia Lane, except that every piece of furniture in the house was slip-covered in clear plastic. On hot days, when I was sweating, I had to work hard not to slide right off.

Lana also played the piano. I really needed to sharpen my piano prowess if I was going to hold onto Eddie. He was definitely a boon to the music scene on Sequoia Lane. All of the girls in the neighborhood pulled out their mothers' old sheet music to impress him. Music aside, when I got my braces off that year, I was sure I finally had Lana beat for good. I was all smiles! Ironically, a recent Facebook search indicated that Eddie eventually became a successful oral and maxillofacial surgeon, so I guess those nimble piano fingers were put to good use!

Sophomore year at Vestal High School seemed to fly by in a haze of both intense fear and first love. The Cuban Missile Crisis was a confrontation between the governments of the United States and the Soviet Union, when the Soviets deployed nuclear missiles in Cuba, only 300 miles from Miami. From October 16th to 28th of 1962, we all worried that we were going to die. It was all we could think about in school and out. It was even scarier to see that our parents were worried; they watched the news constantly. Apparently, it was the closest the Cold War came to escalating into full-scale nuclear war. And all of us, young and old, were terrified.

That same fall, Eddie invited me to the Homecoming Dance, much to Lana's dismay. I felt sophisticated in the white satin skirt and black velvet top my mother had made me. I appreciated Mom doing that for me, even though most of the time I was convinced that she hated me. At the time, I didn't know how much worse it was about to get.

I really enjoyed school that year, especially Biology. Dissecting the frog was my least favorite part, however, convincing me that a career in medicine was not in the cards for me. I loved English and read a lot. Maybe if I became an English teacher I could at least avoid amphibians. Piano practice (this was war!), homework, listening to Bob Dylan, and movies in Binghamton with girlfriends took up the rest of my Sophomore year. Although I was never an Elvis fan, the number one movie in 1961 was *Blue Hawaii* and we couldn't wait to see it. The nearest theater back then was in Binghamton, so parents had to drive us and pick us up, but we still felt pretty adult shopping and going to a movie in the "big city" by ourselves. In fact, hearing the song from the movie soundtrack, "Can't Help Falling in Love," almost made me an Elvis fan. Almost; not quite.

Then, my world fell apart again.

After all of that, Dad accepted a new job in Connecticut. Once we sold the Vestal house, we would be moving back to Westport.

# CHAPTER 9

# "The End of the World"

## Skeeter Davis

### Westport, Connecticut, 1963 - 1964

As autumn approached and our Vestal house still hadn't sold, my parents faced a dilemma. Dad had to start his new job in Connecticut, but they didn't want to uproot the entire family partway through the school year. Well, except for me. The plan was for Dad to rent a place in Westport until the rest of the family could make the move. Taking on the responsibilities of a single parent all week long, Mom wanted Dad to relieve her by commuting back and forth on the weekends. I thought that was bad enough, until they announced part two of the plan: I was going too. They wanted me to live with Dad in the rental and re-enroll at Staples High School in Westport for my junior year.

I worried about what it would be like to be back in school with friends I knew years ago who were now teenagers. Would they remember me? Would they accept me now? Where would we live? Would I have to share a room with Dad? And now that I had almost snagged my heartthrob, Eddie, what would I do without him? What about all the other friends I'd made in Vestal that I'd be leaving too soon? Mom would lose her built-in babysitter; I was expected to occupy toddler Joanne when I got home from school most days to give Mom a much-needed break. But maybe Mom considered that a good trade for getting rid of me—I wasn't exactly her favorite child.

This meant that I would have a foot in two separate worlds, Vestal and Westport, but I would belong in neither. During the week, I would be Cheryl; on weekends, after the six-hour ride back to Vestal, I would become Sherry again. That wasn't too much to ask of a 16-year-old, was it?

Instead of renting a house or apartment in Westport, Dad rented two rooms in the home of an elderly lady named Mrs. Beecroft, who I came to love. Her home was in the neighborhood of Saugatuck at the end of a wooded dirt lane. My room was at the front of her house, small but comfortable, and Dad's room was across the hall with a bathroom in between. Facing the woods at the back of the house was the kitchen, which looked out onto Mrs. Beecroft's rows of birdfeeders.

I felt safe at Mrs. Beecroft's. There was no cocktail hour, no yelling, no fear. It was quiet. When I got home from school each afternoon, Mrs. Beecroft had a cup of hot tea waiting for me. I enjoyed watching the birds, and she had lots of books lining the shelves of the living room walls. I hadn't realized how stressed and scared I'd been in my everyday life—until I wasn't.

My sisters and I had always been afraid to have friends over in case Mom and Dad were drunk, fighting, or both. We were in the habit of opening the door a crack and loudly announcing their presence ("I HAVE DEBBIE WITH ME!") to avoid any potentially embarrassing situations. Even with the rule of, "Whatever happens in this house, stays in this house," we were afraid that someone would find us out and not want to be friends with us anymore.

There was none of that at Mrs. Beecroft's. I came home from school, had my tea, and maybe a homemade cookie. Then, I enjoyed quiet time to study or read in my room until Dad got home. I think I could have happily stayed with Mrs. Beecroft, her birds, her books, and her tea in her quiet house forever.

Dad's arrangement with Mrs. Beecroft included her providing our breakfast each morning. We also had kitchen privileges if we decided to prepare dinners there. However, we mostly ate dinner out. Dinner plans often included Dad's coworkers Dorr and Mrs. Twain ("Mary"), who I briefly knew as a substitute teacher at Staples High School. Her daughter Jody was in my class, and I thought it was cool that they lived on a boat in Saugatuck Harbor. Sometimes we ate supper on their boat and I hung out with Jody while the adults hoisted the cocktail flag.

I hated the weekend trips back to Vestal. Going from the peace of Mrs. Beecroft's to the craziness of our house was a difficult transition. To make things even more difficult, Mom insisted that Dad and I stay for Sunday dinner. That meant that we went to bed in Vestal early on Sunday night before getting on the road Monday morning by 2:00 a.m. Then, we drove to Westport; I slept in the back seat already in my school clothes. Dad dropped me off at school by 8:00 a.m. before he headed to work. He must have been exhausted, working all day after driving most of the night; I know I was and I had at least gotten a little sleep. It all felt icky to me; strange and embarrassing. I kept my nomadic lifestyle a secret from my friends in both worlds, convinced they would think I was just plain odd.

It was finally Friday! This particular afternoon after class, instead of the long drive back to Vestal, Dad was going to drop me off at the train station to visit Grammy Smith in Hartford for the weekend. I was looking forward to spending time with Grammy; she was always willing to listen, always empathetic, and always kept my anxious secrets.

Grammy and Grampa each had their own humble little apartment. Grampa Smith drove Grammy—the serious, responsible one—crazy! While she was raising three boys during the Great Depression, Grampa was performing in Vaudeville—and maybe drinking away a little too much of the grocery money. Being both Catholic, divorce was out of the question. Their solution was to live apart, and when we visited them in Hartford we stayed with Grammy.

In spite of their unusual living situation, Grammy and Grandpa ate Sunday dinner together, traveled together, and often visited their grandchildren together. It wasn't odd to us because they never legally separated. It worked for them, and we didn't know any differently. We just thought that that must be how all grandparents lived. We never questioned their love for one another because it was clear to see. Unlike Mom and Dad, we never heard yelling and arguing between Grammy and Grampa.

Eating at Grammy Smith's was always a feast. A survivor of the Great Depression, no matter whether she had a lot or a little, she could come up with a meal. Grammy's dinner menu always included meat, potatoes, a vegetable or three, and bread and butter. If there was a salad, it would be iceberg lettuce with a slice each of tomato and onion, with apple cider vinegar as the dressing (and she always had a cruet of vinegar on her table). Grammy did most of her cooking in her well-worn pressure cooker. That thing scared the hell out of me with its rattling and hissing and hot steam bursting out of the glass knob on top. Grammy's specialty of the house was pot roast, which she made in the pressure cooker almost every Sunday. Even today, when I smell pot roast, it brings me right back to that tiny kitchen in Grammy's apartment in Hartford.

Like Mrs. Beecroft's, Grammy's humble apartment was a place where I felt safe and loved and maybe even a little bit spoiled. All that week, I looked forward to seeing her for the weekend. Little did any of us know that would be the day the world stopped.

It was the last period at Staples High School. The date was Friday, November 22nd, 1963. The principal's voice came over the intercom. His intonation sounded strange and our usually raucous the-week's-finally-over homeroom got very quiet. He hesitated and then announced that our popular young president, John Fitzgerald Kennedy, had been shot in Dallas.

He was dead.

No one moved. No one spoke. We were solemnly dismissed and I went to wait for Dad outside on the steps of the cafeteria. When he pulled up, I could see the sorrow and maybe some fear in his eyes. I was crying. I managed to ask if I was still going to visit Grammy. He told me the trains were running, and he'd already spoken to his mother who was still expecting me. I couldn't think of anyone else I'd be happier to be miserable with.

Dad dropped me at Saugatuck Station with my suitcase, and I boarded the train for the hour and a half ride to Hartford. I had taken the commuter train many times before to both New York City and Hartford. There was always a certain hustle and bustle among the passengers, as well as passing conversations. On this day, the train ride was different.

The train was full of commuters and weekend day-trippers, but no one was talking. Except for the drone of the wheels on the tracks, the train was almost silent. Many people were crying, even some men; I tried not to look at them so they wouldn't be embarrassed. I focused on looking out the window, trying to hold back my own tears. When the train pulled into Hartford, Grammy and Grampa Smith were waiting for me on the platform. We hugged for a long time and quietly headed for the Farmington Avenue bus that would take us to Grammy's apartment.

From Grammy's apartment window, you could see usually-busy Farmington Avenue, a major thoroughfare through Hartford. Not that weekend. The street was almost empty of cars. Businesses were closed; churches were full. Like most Americans that November, Grammy, Grampa, and I stayed in front of the television grieving. The President's funeral was declared a National Day of Mourning, so there was no school. I watched the funeral with Grammy all day. I didn't remember the train ride back to Westport, or whether or not we had school on Tuesday. I was too swept up in the national grief that consumed us all. I will never forget.

# CHAPTER 10

# "She Loves You"

## The Beatles

### Saugatuck, Connecticut, 1964

By December of 1963, our Vestal house finally sold and we were in a Saugatuck Beach rental that would go through June of '64. Saugatuck is part of Westport, so at least I would still go to Westport schools. I realized I was sadly getting good at saying goodbyes as I left my friends and Eddie—which I'm sure pleased my nemesis Lana immensely. Thankfully, Mom's decorating talents made the rental look cozy for the holidays.

Grammy and Grampa Smith and Grammy Boocock all came to visit. It was wonderful to have them there, a welcome distraction from our family's most recent uneasiness. On Christmas Eve, Grammy Boocock sang her sweet rendition of "Silent Night" while Andi played the piano. I savored it, and we had a happy Christmas in spite of ourselves.

*Silent Night.*

At least we all *appeared* to have a happy Christmas. What we didn't realize was that mom had been secretly seething underneath her cheery holiday exterior. She and Dad had simply been pretending that everything was okay while the grandparents were with us. As soon as the tree came down, so did all hell.

Mom suspected that Mary Twain might be more than a friend to my dad. She was furious. Her rage was scary; we didn't know what she might do. She was desperate for someone to blame. Sadly, that's where I came in. Apparently, my assignment when I moved back to Westport with Dad, which Mom hadn't bothered to read me in on, was to babysit my father and rat him out as required. (Secret agent, Cheryl Dianne Smith, reporting for duty!) I never knew I was supposed to be working undercover. But as I confessed earlier, I clearly was the world's most naive high school junior because I never saw or even thought that there was anything to report. I was 16; I knew about sex; I just never thought about either of my parents actually *having* it. If I hadn't been Mom's least favorite before, she certainly resented me now. I couldn't convince her that I hadn't seen anything suspicious. But alas, she was sure I was in on it. She took every opportunity to remind me of my disloyalty, and not gently.

At eight o'clock on Sunday night, February 9th, 1964, America tuned in to CBS and the *Ed Sullivan Show*. But this night was different—73 million people gathered in front of their TV sets to see the Beatles' first live performance on US soil. "I Want to Hold Your Hand" had just been released and automatically became the number one hit in the US and the UK. My sisters and I had been waiting all week to hear the Beatles sing it. Our rental house had a cozy little TV room behind the kitchen and that was where we gathered awaiting the Beatles. We almost missed it. There was a commotion in the kitchen; Mom was hitting Dad over the head with the telephone. (*She loves you, Yeah, Yeah, Yeah, Yeah...*). Back then, there were no lightweight cell phones; this was the heavy receiver of an ever-so-fashionable harvest gold wall phone. It turned out that dad did not need stitches, so we did get to see the Beatles after all.

The Beatles had some heavy competition from our house. They had barely finished the last "Yeah, Yeah, Yeah" when Mom grabbed her car keys, hollering that she was going to drive the car off the Saugatuck Pier into Long Island Sound. How does a 16-year-old girl who already feels as if she let her parents down deal with that? If Mom died, would it be my fault? For being an unsophisticated dork? Late that night, Mom came back. Alive. I think I knew even then that the memory of the Beatles long-awaited appearance on the *Ed Sullivan Show* would always be associated with trauma for me.

That night was typical of how our lives were: up one moment and then way down—and scared—the next. From pure joy to pure terror; a constant roller-coaster ride. I walked in the door after school never knowing what I might be walking into. How I missed coming home to Mrs. Beecroft and her peaceful cup of tea!

My dad was Catholic. One of the saddest days of all was when Mom got her revenge for her suspicions about Mary Twain by embarrassing Dad in front of us, his children. She loaded us into the Impala, Dad in the passenger seat and the four of us girls crowded together in back. As she drove into Saugatuck, we turned onto Riverside Avenue, passed my school, and stopped in front of Assumption Catholic Church, where we had always attended Mass. Dad got out of the car, crossed the street, and went into the church by himself. Usually, Dad took us to confession with him, but not this time. Mom told us to stay in the car. Not a word was spoken. I'll never know if Daddy actually made a confession that day, or if he even needed to. Maybe he just sat in the darkened church and cried, knowing that his daughters had seen him beaten down like this.

One night in late February, when Dad hadn't come home, Mom decided she was going to go look for him, and I was told I would be joining her. She made Andi stay behind to watch Nancy and Joanne. Mom told me to get in the car "since this was my fault." As she drove, I was torn between wanting to find him and worrying about what Mom might do if we did. She drove past every restaurant and bar in town looking for his car. We didn't see it, which meant there was only one place left to look.

Mom drove to Mrs. Twain's small house near Long Island Sound, where she lived when it was too cold to live on her boat, and parked in the driveway. Next to Dad's car. Mom ordered me to get out of the car and go get my father. I was afraid and didn't want to get out, but I was even more scared of what Mom would do if I refused her. What if she drove the car into Long Island Sound and killed us both? I trembled as I made my way up the icy driveway in the dark. My hands were shaking as I knocked on the kitchen door. When there was no answer, I tried the handle. It turned.

I looked back at my mother watching my every move from the car. I took a deep breath and crept in. The house was quiet and I didn't know my way around. But I knew that Dad must be there somewhere, maybe sleeping on the couch or in a guest room. I didn't know and I didn't want to know. I was ashamed and scared and just wanted to get out of there. I stood in the dark kitchen, yelled as loud as I could, "MOM IS OUTSIDE!" and headed back to the car as fast as I could. That was where my memory of that night ended. I didn't know when or how I got home, nor how my dad got home, but I did learn one lesson that icy night: always expect the other shoe to drop.

# CHAPTER 11

# "*Moon River*"

## Andy Williams

### Guilford, Connecticut, 1964 - 1965

In the Spring of 1964, it became clear that Mom could no longer live in Westport. So our family moved again, this time to Guilford, about an hour from Westport. The move was Mom's way of ensuring that she would never run into Mrs. Twain. She still assumed the worst and only seemed interested in making Dad feel the hurt she did. With Dad's job still in Westport, he now needed to commute back and forth on I-95, the busiest stretch of road in Connecticut, at rush hour every day. And I would have to enroll in my third high school in three years.

We moved into a new yellow four-bedroom Colonial on Sparrowbush Lane in a neighborhood called "Sunrise." In the center of the neighborhood was a large green on which the association planned lots of family events: cookouts, picnics, Halloween costume parties, and Christmas caroling. It all seemed so normal, at least compared to life at our house. Mom and Dad didn't take us to most of these events, because Mom was always sick on those days. Sometimes my sisters and I walked over by ourselves or with Dad. I was afraid everyone must have thought our family was weird. They were right.

I liked Guilford. Settled by Puritans in 1639, Guilford was an idyllic New England village. In the town center was the historic town green, used by the early settlers for grazing cattle and sheep. By the 1960s, the Guilford Green hosted many weekend events: fairs, petting zoos, antique shows, and farmers markets. It was a perfect little town and I enjoyed walking there, especially to the library. I loved the quiet among the stacks, the smell of the books. No one was yelling there. On my way, I passed a few old chestnut trees that had survived the chestnut blight. They reminded me of waiting for Grampa at his bus stop so many years ago. I was no longer six years old, but I still came home from the library with pockets full of chestnuts and arms full of books.

Besides the chestnut trees, the green, and the old library, Guilford was the home of Checkerberry Soda. Frank F. Douden invented it at the turn of the last century as a way to attract customers to his store. It worked; we all clustered around the old marble-topped soda fountain at Douden's Drugstore after school. Guilford residents couldn't get enough of the top-secret recipe that included the bright pink syrup of the wintergreen berry mixed with vanilla ice cream. Because we moved so often, I didn't have the lifelong friendships my parents had made growing up in Haverhill, but at least I had memories of afternoons drinking the best ice cream soda I'd ever tasted. The original drugstore is gone now, as is Mr. Douden. Although many have tried to duplicate it, the original recipe for checkerberry soda remains a well-kept secret.

In September of 1964, I started my senior year as the new girl yet again. At Guilford High School, I worked to assimilate and make friends. While it was getting old, I was good at it by now. I joined the drama club, played Antigone in the senior class play, and even had a boyfriend. Duncan was a nice guy about my height, which was short for most boys his age. He had ginger-colored hair and lived with his mother in a historic house facing the Guilford Green. He was smart, talented, and popular. Duncan dressed preppy but had an artistic side, which I liked. His taste in music included the blues, especially Nina Simone.

Inspired by the music and signs of our times, I went into a pseudo-hippie phase. I became active in the Civil Rights movement and traveled to New Haven with my new friends, Meg and Kathy. We hung out together, marched in protests, collected books for Selma, and spent hours in deep philosophical discussions on the steps of the library. Although I still listened to the Beatles, my musical tastes were broadening to include Pete Seegar, Peter, Paul and Mary, the Mamas and the Papas, and my very favorite, Bob Dylan.

*Moon River Guilford, CT.*

As I lived through the events of the last few years, I started to see Mom a bit more clearly. I couldn't justify her behavior, nor my dad's actually, whether he did or didn't. But I could see how low her self-esteem was. As much as she blamed me for the unhappiness in her marriage, a lot of that came from her own insecurities. She didn't think she was pretty enough, smart enough, or well-dressed enough to even make it to a simple Fourth of July cookout on the Sunrise neighborhood green. Even though I didn't appreciate her unexpected mood swings, I was starting to see that Mom was only human. She was doing her best with what she had at the time, just like the rest of us.

One minute, Mom hated me; the next minute, she used her sewing prowess to make me a beautiful aqua dress for the prom. It was chiffon and floor length, embellished with a long green velvet-stemmed rose Mom hand stitched down the length of the skirt. I think the gown was something she might have liked to wear if she had more confidence in herself. It didn't make up for the way things were between us some-times, but I still appreciated the work my mother put into making that dreamy dress for me. I wore it when my heartthrob Duncan escorted me to our Senior Prom. We danced the night away to songs like "I Got You, Babe" by Sonny and Cher, "My Girl" by the Temptations, "I Can't Get No Satisfaction" by the Rolling Stones, "Yesterday" by the Beatles, and of course "Moon River," the prom theme by Andy Williams. Songs of a generation.

Graduation loomed, and I worried about college since Mom and Dad had never discussed it with me. Good grades were expected, which I had delivered—but instead of the college tours most families plan and enjoy together, I had to hitch rides with friends, or sometimes Duncan drove me. We visited the University of Connecticut, Boston University (in a blizzard!), Salve Regina, and Russell Sage. I applied to all four, using the money I earned waitressing at Maple Shade Dairy Bar on Route 1 to pay the application fees. I was getting good at figuring things out by myself, possibly due to watching self-sufficient women like Grammy Smith.

When I had to get to work at Maple Shade Dairy Bar, I walked, cutting through back yards, trooping down the big hill from Sunrise to Route 1. I must have looked like the flying nun, with my apron ballooning behind me as I ran through people's back yards in my shiny white waitress shoes. It was embarrassing, but Mom and Dad never thought of driving me. It was just assumed that I'd get around on my own. In fact, I wasn't allowed to get my driver's license until just before graduation and unlike many of my friends, there was no car in my future. The first time I was allowed to drive alone was in Daddy's blue 1953 Ford, with standard shift on the steering column. The distance? No more than a mile from Sunrise to the hairdresser the afternoon of my senior prom, and the same distance back. No "little deuce coupe" for Cheryl Dianne!

With three high schools behind me, I chose to attend Russell Sage College in Troy, New York. My future seemed bright on graduation day—June 18th, 1965. I was looking forward to being a Sagette. When I visited, I fell in love with the small all-girls liberal arts school founded in 1916 by feisty suffragettes who believed that women should have access to a college education. I felt delighted by the thought of being on my own in a city, being a part of the sense of the tradition that Sage represented with its blocks of old brownstone buildings. I was excited to proudly wear one of the blazers upperclassmen wore—red, blue, gold, or purple. If I did well freshman year, I would be presented with a blue blazer as part of the Blue Angels Class of '69 in the spring.

# CHAPTER 12

# "*Monday, Monday*"

## The Mamas and the Papas

### Troy, New York, 1965 - 1966

September 1st, 1965 was the first day of fall semester at Russell Sage and the start of my freedom. It was a steamy late-summer day for early autumn. I was sweating in my hand-sewn wool suit, full slip, and nylon stockings while I found my way to McKinstry Hall. Loaded down with almost everything I owned, I pushed through the double doors and struggled up the lobby stairs. I walked down the hallway on the first floor to find my room. My tall, thin, brown-haired nursing major roommate with a familiar name, Nancy, had already moved in.

Nancy had me on the cool factor before she even began to unpack. Her deep voice complimented the two cartons of Parliament 100s she unpacked. In addition, she had a closetful of Villager and John Meyer skirts and sweaters I only wished I could afford. My wardrobe consisted of knockoffs from stores like Zayre's and Bradlee's, a few skirts I sewed myself, and one "real" Villager sweater I saved up all summer for. Women were required to wear skirts on campus—except on weekends, when pants needed to be covered by a full-length trench coat outside of the dorm.

Our earthly possessions hastily deposited in our little McKinstry 1 dorm room, Nancy and I found our way to the opening convocation. We were now both sweating in wool suits, stockings, and kitten heels. The venue was a huge church in downtown Troy, where we were welcomed by Dean Virginia Harvey and instructed on campus expectations.

As we sat in our own convocation, our parents were perspiring at a separate meeting in the campus auditorium. Mom later informed me that President Cotter assured parents that one of the college's goals was producing women with the social skills necessary to be "successful executive wives." I assumed this was why we were expected to host frequent teas for faculty and required to take a half semester each of sports like golf, tennis, swimming, and modern dance. I signed up for fencing; it felt like tapping into a defiant streak I didn't know I had.

While the staff and our parents may have planned to train us up as Stepford wives, I didn't come to Russell Sage to learn how to pour tea. When we next saw our parents, they wouldn't recognize the genteel daughters they dropped off. We found fun little ways to flaunt the rules. We sometimes shrugged off the "no pants" rule by rushing off for an 8:00 a.m. class with just a nightgown underneath a knee-length trench coat. Or even less for the really daring among us.

We were a new generation with our own ideas that may not have aligned with those of our parents. While some of our bookshelves and sheet music may have had similar titles—works by Robert Frost, Mark Twain, Khalil Gibran, Harper Lee and songs from *West Side Story* and *South Pacific*—we also had our own favorites in popular culture. I adored poetry, including Maya Angelou, Toni Morrison, and Sylvia Plath. I read Elie Wiesel, James Baldwin, S.E. Hinton, Betty Friedan, and J.D. Salinger.

Even though I loved some of the musicals of my parents' generation, I especially liked listening to the LPs from more recent ones like *Funny Girl* and *Bye Bye Birdie.* My sisters and I had played these songs for hours on the upright piano in our living room, and one song that stuck with me was "An English Teacher" from *Bye Bye Birdie.* The song was about a young woman aspiring to become the wife of an English teacher. Except, I didn't want to be the *wife* of a masters-level Phi Beta Kappa English teacher; I wanted to *be* the Phi Beta Kappa English teacher. I had known that since my junior year of high school, and I enrolled as an English major at Russell Sage. Pouring tea definitely was not in my plans.

I reveled in the freedom that college offered. No more dreading the inevitable parental arguments every evening, no more sheltering my sisters in the closet, no more being scared whenever I was at home.

I was free from that fear, free to have quiet, free to come and go. I was free to unleash my scholarly side, free to occasionally indulge my hippie side, free to take long walks without announcing my destination, free to decide if I wanted to go to Mass on Sundays or not. Freedom was a powerful narcotic to 17-year-old me, who had developed significant anxiety after years of tumult at home. I was no longer in a place where I was always on alert, where I was always ready to fight or take flight. At Russell Sage, I felt safe.

I made some good friends freshman year in McKinstry Hall. Across the hall was another Nancy, and nearby were Jan, Elin, Susan, Betsy, Toni, Alix, Maxine, Sarah, Joyce, and so many more. Almost 60 years later, I remember them still.

*Jan, Nancy B., Cheryl, Nancy S. – Russell Sage, 1965.*

I took basic freshman courses my first year and did well, except for my first semester class in Logic with the illogical Dr. Hetco. He lectured, on and on and on, oblivious to the sheer number of girls who fell asleep in his class. "Learning style be damned" seemed to be his motto. I studied voraciously for that class, praying to under-stand Aristotle and the four kinds of syllogisms. I got about as far as, "All dogs are mammals, Fido is a dog, therefore Fido is a mammal," before ending up with the only C+ of my college career. I was devastated. Apparently I'm not very logical after all.

I loved my survey of English Literature class with Dr. Russell Barker so much that I've saved the two thick red volumes that were required for that class, full of highlights and marginal notes. In Spanish I, Dr. Perez-Lopez christened me "Carolina;" I assume that "Cheryl" just didn't translate. My schedule was rounded out with Biology 101 and Art History, both of which I loved, and P.E., which I didn't.

The Russell Sage campus is compact, covering about four blocks in Troy, a once-proud city trying to recover from years of urban decay. Troy is noted for its Victorian architecture; the classic brick rowhouses along elm-shaded First Street, remnants of Troy's wealthy industrial past, were now spacious dorms. Many of the "houses" had a theme. French House and German House were especially popular, as practicing the title language was encouraged for residents of each. The rowhouses were quirky, with big formal parlors and warrens of tall-ceilinged bedrooms on the three floors above.

Other remnants of the Victorian age on campus were the many little vine-covered buildings hidden in overgrown courtyards among the brownstones. One of those buildings was the Little Theatre, where the members of the Sage drama group, *Box and Candle*, performed. That's where I made my freshman college theatre debut as the White Rabbit in *Alice in Wonderland*. My role required me to leap around the tiny stage in a fuzzy white rabbit suit, dragging a huge pocket watch. A 20-pound paper mache rabbit head with big ears and wire-covered eye holes completed the ensemble. At least I had very few lines to learn: "I'm late, I'm late, for a very important date" being my sole soliloquy.

At dusk on November 9th, 1965, the fall of my freshman year, one of the biggest power failures in history occurred. All of New York state, portions of seven nearby states, and parts of Canada were plunged into darkness. Lasting about 13 hours in the Troy area, the blackout impacted 30 million people in eight states. There was no warning, so at first there was both annoyance and anxiety in McKinstry Hall. We had no cell phones and since our radios ran on electricity, information was sketchy. When we eventually heard that the blackout covered the whole Northeastern United States, people began to worry. Was the US under some kind of attack? By Russia? By aliens? How long would we be in the dark? And the scariest thought of all: Were the RPI guys at this very moment storming down the hill under the cover of darkness, to launch a major panty raid on McKinstry Hall? None of those catastrophes happened, but the Great Northeast Blackout will always be a vivid memory of my first year at college.

The blackout seemed especially formidable because we didn't have the technology to monitor it. In fact, we had no technology at all. There was one pay phone in the lounge of each floor of our dorm, shared by all 50+ young women who had to line up to use it. There were no cell phones. If a call came into the phone in the lounge, whoever happened to pick it up would politely say, "Just a moment, please," put her hand over the speaker and scream: "PHONE CALL FOR CHERYL!" (or Nancy, or Elin, or Jan) in a voice that could probably be heard all the way up the hill to RPI.

Making phone calls was difficult and we had to pay for each one, including long-distance charges outside of Troy and Albany. Out of necessity, we still engaged in the now all-but-lost art of letter writing. I loved receiving letters. I rushed to my mailbox after class every afternoon to see if something had arrived for me. An envelope from Mom and Dad usually contained a short note and a check: my 25-dollar monthly spending money. Somehow, between that and a part-time student job at the college library, I managed to stretch my money to meet my day-to-day needs. The only extravagance I bought freshman year was a sterling silver cuff bracelet I saw in the window of a jewelry store in downtown Troy. By scrimping and saving, I was able to purchase it as a Mother's Day gift for my mom. I had it engraved with her initials "ABS" on the outside and "Love, Cheryl '66" on the inside. My mom passed away in 2014. I treasure the few happy memories Mom and I had together and still wear that bracelet in remembrance of them. I know she tried to be a good mother in spite of her demons. My favorite letters were from my father's father, Grampa Smith (Arthur William Smith, 1900-1977). He wrote lengthy missives full of family lore, funny stories, and Irish blarney. His letters reflected his personality and I treasured them.

As prehistoric as it may sound, we lived without TVs, mini-refrigerators or microwaves in our rooms. Microwaves didn't even exist yet. There were a shared refrigerator, stove, and TV in the lounge on each floor. I don't think portable TVs existed yet either; most were heavy cabinet models with small screens. We used hot water out of the tap in our room to make instant coffee or ramen noodles before early classes or during all-nighters. The Sanka was lukewarm but it was all we had. When we got sick of all the chips and candy, we smoked. Everybody smoked back then. I started sharing Nancy's Parliaments and got hooked. Smoking was cool. It was only years later that we realized how dangerous it was.

Since we didn't have computers, our home page was the Sage library and our Google was the card catalogue. Doing research involved copious hand-written note cards, books, periodicals, yellow highlighters and micro-fiche. If we were lucky, a photo copier that produced shiny dark images was available at 10 cents a page. We simply didn't know what we didn't have. Technology for college research wouldn't be embraced until later, by our sisters in the classes of the '70s and '80s. Nancy and I did have electric typewriters, which we used for final copies of papers. We wrote our first drafts by hand from the rubber-band-encased piles of notecards we'd accumulated at the library. We took class notes by hand as well, in full size spiral bound college-ruled Russell Sage notebooks, one for each class. On exams, we hand wrote our answers in "Blue Books." All of our required texts were purchased at the little college bookstore in the basement of Sage Hall. Just one of the required texts I hauled to class three times a week, Jansen's *History of Art*, weighed over eight pounds!

In the basement of Paine Hall was the well-loved "AR." It was probably December by the time I figured out that AR stood for "Aluminum Rail," the rail you slide your tray along when purchasing food in a cafeteria. The AR was the campus hangout, where you could grab a hot coffee, or if time permitted, stuff yourself into one of the old Formica-topped wooden booths to catch up with friends. It looked as if it had not changed much since the first classes graduated from Russell Sage; you could almost hear those bygone student voices if you listened closely enough. We could relax in the AR. It was our *Cheers*.

My social life was pretty limited freshman year. The Mixers up the hill at RPI with all the beer and groping got old pretty fast. During the week we studied, drank cold coffee, and danced in our nightgowns (often with our hair in rollers) to the music of *The Mamas & the Papas, the Righteous Brothers, the Beatles, the Stones* and Bob Dylan. That fall, we were lucky enough to get tickets to see *Diana Ross & The Supremes* in concert at RPI–my first real concert. We sang along from the bleachers as they regaled us with some of their early songs like "Baby Love," "Where Did Our Love Go?," "Stop in the Name of Love," and "You Can't Hurry Love."

Spring at Russell Sage was the time to celebrate Rally Day, a competition among the classes and a fine excuse to party. The tradition started when the college was founded, and some of its customs, like the daisy chain, were outdated, even in the 1960s. But Rally Day was a day away from lectures, labs, papers, and blue books; that part of the tradition more than made up for some of the silliness of the rest. Each class had a name and a class color which rotated every four years. I was class of '69, a "Blue Angel," and our "sister class" was the class two years behind us, 1971, christened the "Red Devils." I was relieved that I wasn't in a graduating class signified by an even-numbered year or I would have ended up as a "Golden Horseshoe" or "Purple Cow"! Just before Rally Day, freshmen received their much-coveted Sage blazers in the color of their class. I still have my blue one, although it no longer fits quite like it did in 1966. We were proud to wear our blazers and often did. Now, on rare occasions when I meet another Sage alumna, we find ourselves trying to stuff our no-longer-young selves into our blazers and giving in to the urge to sing, *R-A-double L-Y! D-A-Y! Spells RALLY DAY!*

# CHAPTER 13

# "*Beyond the Sea*"

## Bobby Darin

Kennebunkport, Maine, 1966

As spring of 1966 arrived, I started thinking about summer plans. I didn't think I could take another summer at home listening to my parents argue. Since I loved childhood summers in Maine, I wanted to return. It was a rite of passage for college students to take summer jobs at the big hotels along the Maine coast, and lodging was usually provided on site as part of the pay. That would provide me the income I needed as well as the independence I desired.

Wally Reid was a legend in Kennebunkport, Maine. When I first met him, he was in his late 40s—a tall, balding, distinguished-looking man with military bearing and a very slight lisp. Wally had been a decorated pilot during WWII, retiring with the rank of Colonel in 1975. He and his wife Virginia owned and operated an old inn on the Maine coast called the Arundel. And he insisted that you pronounce it the "correct" way: *a-run-DEL*, not *a-RUN-del*. He was a stickler on that. Wally Reid was formidable; larger than life. It was to him that I wrote in the Spring of 1966, with my very brief resume enclosed, applying for a summer position as a waitress at the Arundel.

It was exciting when Mr. Reid's letter arrived in my McKinstry Hall mailbox offering me a position. The letter was very formal; you might have thought I was applying to be Secretary of State rather than a seasonal waitress. The pay was minimal but housing was included, I could keep my tips, and I would be in Maine for the summer. It was perfect. I accepted and sent a formal letter in response on my best Crane's stationery. I would start in May of 1966 and live on the third floor of the Somerlyst with the other female employees.

I was already familiar with the Arundel complex, located at the mouth of the Kennebunk River where a rocky breakwater marks its intersection with the sea. Somerlyst was one of the three larger buildings that made up the complex, and it was connected to the Arundel's main building by a wooden walkway. Across Ocean Avenue was the third building, once a separate inn, called the Green Heron. In addition, there was an antique Cape on the property where Mr. Reid lived with his wife and children.

The Green Heron featured a breakfast room looking over a salt-water cove with guest rooms above. It was famous for Virginia Reid's homemade breakfasts. She was a tall, plain scarecrow of a woman with disheveled brown hair and beautiful skin that was almost translucent. Virginia Reid was a tireless worker and a prodigious baker. She was known as a mother figure, not only to her own six children, but to the summer staff as well. Virginia Reid was a rock for anyone who needed her.

The Arundel was a red gambrel with a wraparound porch populated with worn wicker rockers that invited guests to enjoy the view. I loved to sit on that porch, close my eyes, and breathe in the moist sea salt air. The waves beyond the breakwater whispered in the distance; their white noise daring a tired waitress to indulge in a nap. Hinges squeaked as the heavy green screened door slammed to announce the arrival of each guest. The building's main floor contained the dining room, cocktail lounge, living room, library, and kitchen. Guest rooms on the second and third floors were wallpapered in vintage floral patterns punctuated by tall windows whose billowing white curtains foretold of the sea breezes beyond.

Between the Arundel and the river was a huge oak tree whose leaves lent cool shade to the cocktail lounge and living room on humid summer days. The only deciduous tree on the riverfront, it seemed out of place there—but at the same time, perfectly placed. On my short walk to work each day, I'd look up and daydream about who planted it and when, and why they chose that exact spot. That tree was my summer talisman, still there all these years later. I'm glad some things remain just where they are.

On my first day at the Arundel, my parents dropped me off in front. I had no car. If I needed to go into "the Port," I walked. The little town square was less than a mile up river from the Arundel via Ocean Avenue. I hauled my things up to the third floor of the Somerlyst and met my roommate, Pam. Pam was a year older than me and a bit more sophisticated. I liked her. She had worked summers in the Port before; maybe she could show me the ropes. We had a plain front corner room with iron beds that faced the river in one direction and the Yacht Club and Kennebunkport in the other. The best thing about our room was the fire escape for the building that ran from one of its two windows. It was located on the side of our room facing away from the office and the owners' home. In other words, if we snuck out at night, Wally Reid couldn't see us.

Sandy Kennebunk Beach was directly across the river from The Arundel. Necessity being the mother of invention, the Reids had already solved the problem of how to get their houseguests over to the beach and back without needing a car or dealing with the heavy traffic on Ocean Avenue. Their son Bobby had a rowboat, and for 10 cents per person he rowed the guests back and forth. During the Vietnam War, Bobby became an Air Force pilot like his dad, so local friend Mike Marceau took over the service. Many of us took the ferry to Kennebunk Beach between lunch and dinner while we had a few hours off. The 20 cent round trip was a deal.

*The Arundel "Ferry" to the Beach, 1966.*

On my first day of work, I met the rest of the staff. Chef Kelly and his wife—whom we called Cheffy and Mrs. Kelly—were a good-natured, middle-aged couple. She was a sweet Irish lady who drove us to Biddeford once a week, the nearest city with downtown shopping. Chef Kelly's two sous chefs were named John Goddard and Bob Underwood. I would get to know them well since I volunteered to come a half hour early each evening to make the salads for an extra two dollars a week.

John was a stout young man in his 20s with a high-pitched voice and a round, boyish face that made him look younger. He had recently graduated from the Culinary Institute in New Haven, Connecticut. Like most chefs, John could be a tyrant in the kitchen, but he was a good friend after work. He would occasionally invite me to ride on the back of his scooter to the Viking in Ogunquit which featured "make your own" ice cream sundaes.

The highlight of every trip to Wells or Ogunquit was waving to "Smokey," who was an institution. He was an old heavy-set black man who lived in the woods between Route 9 and the ocean near Kennebunkport's line with Wells. There was a dirt road on the left that went up a hill and disappeared into the trees. He spent much of the day and night standing there waving to everyone who passed. Even now when I take Route 9, I expect to see Smokey, though he passed away many years ago. The memory of Smokey is always there though, waving at those of us who remember.

The other sous chef that summer was Bob, who was only a year older than me. He was from Worcester and majoring in Food Service Management at Muhlenberg College in Pennsylvania. He was a tall, heavy-set guy with dark hair and hazel eyes. He seemed kind. I liked him right away. His parents were regulars at the Arundel, staying there for two weeks every summer. Eschewing a scooter, Bob drove a black and white '57 Chevy.

Mr. Reid was a perfectionist, and we all worked hard that summer. The waitresses wore traditional white uniforms with white tie-up shoes. Filled mostly by houseguests, the small dining room was from another era, like the inn itself. It had burgundy and blue floral wallpaper, white tablecloths, and heavy flowered restaurant china. It was located away from the water in the back of the building, which I always thought was odd since people came to Kennebunkport to see the ocean—but it had always been that way, so that's the way it stayed.

Instead, the ocean view was saved for the living room, card room, and bar, which were the areas the houseguests spent most of their time in. The tiny bar with just four tables was presided over by a dour, balding Scandinavian bartender in his 30s named Nils. He was quiet, and I wondered if maybe he saved his talking for the few regulars at the bar. The drinking age in Maine was 21, making the majority of the college waitstaff too young. When a guest ordered a drink with their dinner, it was Nils who delivered it to their table.

We had a few transient visitors for dinner each evening, but Mr. Reid concentrated his efforts on the houseguests he could count on year after year. When Mr. Reid first used the word "transient," I wasn't sure what he meant. I pictured homeless people storming the flowered dining room for food. I hadn't realized the word had a different meaning in restaurant lingo. Transients were those who weren't staying on site and came to the inn just to eat dinner.

There were quite a few frequently-yelled kitchen phrases I learned as well. It was quite common to hear "Order up!" or "We're 86 on the prime rib," but my personal favorite was, "Get your ass in here; the food's getting cold!" While Mr. Reid focused on the regulars, the waitstaff did our best to impress the transients because they left better tips. One of the best nights at the restaurant was the night we served 100 meals, or in restaurant lingo, "broke 100" in the Arundel dining room.

While the Arundel library was intended as an amenity for the guests, Mr. Reid let me use it, for which I was immensely grateful. It felt snug and safe, and when I had time off (outside of a beach day), you could usually find me there. You entered the small windowless room from a landing between the first and second floors. It was lined on all sides with bookshelves, and two old upholstered reading chairs were the only other furnishings.

Sometimes I believed I would have been an academic in another life. I found solace in reading, research, and teaching—a side of me I keep hidden from most people. Maybe it partly had to do with my generation's search for meaning and reasons for the things that happened around us we didn't understand. Perhaps all young people try to find answers in their own way.

That summer, I found some answers among the large number of books on the Bahá'í Faith in the Arundel's collection. I read them all. I was brought up Catholic, but many Bahá'í principals appealed to me on a spiritual level. Among them were the unity of all races and elimination of prejudice, the equality of women and men, universal education, the elimination of extremes of wealth and poverty, and the harmony of science and religion. I didn't become a member of the Bahá'í faith, but it did cause me to do a lot of thinking.

At work and in my free time, I enjoyed getting to know Bob Underwood better. We took day trips to Brunswick or Boothbay Harbor, went to auctions, and a few times we went out to dinner. One evening, Bob took me to Vallee's Steak House at the old Exit 8 in Westbrook. He wore a sports jacket and tie while I wore a typical '60s above the knee A-line dress with white hose and flats. No one went out to dinner in jeans, t-shirts, or shorts in 1966, although we could feel that change was coming.

# CHAPTER 14

# "*Devil or Angel*"

## Bobby Vee

Troy, New York & Amherst, Massachusetts, 1966 - 1967

By my second year at Sage, I was happy to be taking more classes in my major: Chaucer first semester and Shakespeare the second. I learned to read texts in Old English and recited obscure lines of British poetry from memory. I loved it all. I also loved my second-year biology class with the legendary Dr. Geneva Sayre. I enjoyed it so much that I gave serious consideration to changing my major. The structure of DNA had recently been discovered by Watson and Crick, and Dr. Sayre made adenine, cytosine, guanine, and thymine sound almost romantic.

I definitely did not like the modern dance class I had to take to complete my P.E. requirement. However, I will never forget the instructor. The appropriately-named Mr. Bushey spent the class leaping across the gym in his body-hugging leotard and tights, much to the delight of his 25 teenage female students.

In spite of the climb, I loved living in my little turret room on the fourth floor of German House. I had previously been in a triple and even though I had great roommates, I needed more alone time. The little single suited me perfectly. I had a view of the statue of Russell Sage's founder, Emma Willard, and much of the rest of the campus from my desk. My room felt cozy and safe and, when Spring came to Troy, it was close to the little stairway to the roof, where we basked in the sun to get an early start on summer tans.

My social life improved sophomore year because I had started dating Bob Underwood the previous summer in Kennebunkport. Bob was at UMass in Amherst and sometimes I would go there, usually by bus; other times he would gas up his black and white '57 Chevy and drive up to Troy for the weekend.

*Bob's '57 Chevy - Kennebunkport.*

By mid-semester of my junior year, we were both getting tired of commuting. Not only was it exhausting, but it left me little time to catch up on course work, which was intensifying as I got deeper into my major. Weekend after weekend, we talked about how to make it work: needing to be together and needing to be apart at the same time. After a lot of discussion and a lot of thought, love won out. Bob and I decided to get married.

It was late autumn of my junior year and the Russell Sage calendar still included "Intersession," a long break in January. I decided to complete all of my first semester exams and withdraw from Sage when grades closed. I planned to transfer to UMass to join Bob and finish my degree. At the time it seemed like a good decision; looking back, not so much. I would miss the little hidden garden in the French House courtyard. I'd miss afternoons spent working on the college newspaper. I'd miss the Little Theatre, the A.R., and informal concerts by the Sagettes. I'd miss the nights in the dorm when we grabbed "microphones" and belted out Smokey Robinson tunes in our pajamas. I wanted to graduate with my sister Blue Angels, but I was young and crazy in love.

With mixed emotions, I withdrew from Sage between semesters in 1968 and moved with Bob to Northampton. I felt bad leaving Bob's sister Carolyn, who had started at Russell Sage as a freshman that year, following in my footsteps. She joined the Red Devils class of 1971, our sister class, and I was her Blue Angel big sister. I also knew that I disappointed my parents, who worried that leaving Sage meant that I might never actually finish college; I would be the first in our family to do so. They didn't realize how determined I was to get my degree. I was sad that being with Bob meant leaving the small all-girls campus I had come to love. I knew that transferring to a huge university like UMass Amherst could never offer me the close relationships with students and faculty that I cherished at Sage. I left a little piece of my heart at Russell Sage.

UMass was a shockingly different world from Russell Sage. The campus itself was huge, with high rise dorms and a much more diverse student population than Sage. At UMass, the turbulence of the late '60s had already arrived. There were almost constant demonstrations for equal rights, civil rights, gender equity, and peace. Students were actively challenging the status quo and demanding change. The students at UMass were female *and* male, young, old, straight, gay, Black, Asian, tall, short, and everything in between. Some were traditional, others were counterculture. There were scholars and revolutionaries among both students and faculty. The students had long ago foregone Sage-style skirts and sweaters for jeans and t-shirts, peace signs and tie dye. Many t-shirts expressed radical political views, some quite graphically. The odor of pot was in the air. Bill Cosby was working on a masters at the School of Education, while in the huge UMass gym, aka "the Cage," Julius Irving set basketball records for scoring and rebounding. I had some challenging classes at UMass with engaging and demanding professors. I took everything from Astronomy (in a real planetarium!), to History of Russia, Sociology, and the Bible as Literature. Just being at UMass in 1968 and '69 was an education in itself.

Social change occurred rapidly between 1965 and 1969 in America. Students were angry about a lottery that sent brothers and friends to a faraway country called Vietnam to die for no reason we could justify. The Black Power movement had largely overtaken the more patient Civil Rights movement. Women were asserting themselves and studying to enter formerly all-male professions like medicine and law. Russell Sage was changing as well. The turmoil of the '60s could no longer be avoided, even in an academic microcosm like ours. Sage women demanded an end to the "no pants" rule, and jeans took the place of Villager skirts. Rules about campus etiquette and visits from males relaxed as well; no one had to yell, "Man on the floor!" anymore. To President Cotter's dismay, it was the end of "in loco parentis" on campus. Sage students were definitely not planning to pour any more tea!

# CHAPTER 15

# *"Little Deuce Coupe"*

## The Beach Boys

### Kennebunkport, Maine, 1967

In the summer of 1967, after finishing my sophomore year as an English major at Russell Sage, I returned to the Arundel. Bob was also back for a second summer in the kitchen. He brought with him his best friend from high school, Bruce. Mr. Reid hired Bruce to work in the kitchen with Bob and John, who we had both worked with the previous summer. It was nice to have Bob close by so we could see each other more often.

That summer I was joined by my sister Andi, who would also be a waitress at the Arundel. Mom and Dad had just purchased a house on Holland Place (now called Dutcher Lane) in nearby Kennebunk Beach. They planned to renovate it from a summer cottage into a year-round home. It was a big, brown chalet-style home with a wide side porch and mullioned windows. A separate garage was connected by a covered breezeway. In order to help Dad with the renovations, we made the tough choice of money over independence. By staying with our parents, Andi and I could keep more of our tips. However, that brought us the challenge of transportation.

As usual, it was up to me and Andi to figure out how to get to and from work, since our parents never considered driving us. Sometimes we were lucky enough to catch rides with one of the few Arundel employees who had a car, but mostly we walked. We'd head from the beach up Boothby Road to Route 9, over the bridge from Kennebunk to Kennebunkport, and up Ocean Avenue to the hotel.

The walk from Holland Place took about an hour; 45 minutes if we hustled. That got old real fast, so we came up with an idea. We'd pool our tip money to buy a car for the commute. After we located an old tan Ford sedan that we could get for 50 dollars, it became apparent that we knew nothing about cars. However, this one met our only requirement at the time: it ran. That meant it could, theoretically, get us to and from work. Being desperate, we each contributed 25 bucks and bought it.

We sailed through Dock Square with the windows down, our blonde hair blowing in the sea breeze like ladies out for a jaunt. Although the condition of our car might have revealed our meager fortunes, no one could see our shiny white uniforms and clunky waitress shoes. The Smith sisters were having a luxurious week of traveling in style, until our life as wannabe summer people ended rather abruptly.

Exactly a week later, the car started to hiss and puff through its final mile before dying completely. We managed to drive it as far as Jim's Service Center only for Jim to pronounce it dead. He said he would take it off our hands to sell for junk parts. Without transportation, we had to find another solution.

Andi was good friends with Deidre, the Reid's daughter, so the family invited her to live with them for the rest of the summer. However, I had to rely on my own two feet to get to and from work. I alternated walking and riding my rusty old English bike.

Unfortunately, I was no longer able to imagine myself as a preppy teenage beauty breezing through Dock Square. Instead, I must have looked like Almira Gulch from *the Wizard of Oz*, riding through the Port with my white apron flapping behind me. All I needed to complete the image was a dog named Toto.

*The Arundel.*

Andi and I convinced Grampa Smith to spend a week as a guest at the Arundel. Sadly, despite his outgoing personality, his recent surgery left him with scarring he felt self conscious about. He had been a smoker his whole life and it finally caught up with him when he developed mouth and throat cancer. While a visit was an exciting prospect, his surgery had made chewing and swallowing difficult and he hesitated due to having to eat with others in the dining room.

Andi and I solved the problem by reserving a tucked-away table in a quiet corner of the dining room that was once a hallway. The table was in front of a window so Grampa could enjoy the view. When he finally arrived, he carried a small brown leather suitcase and wore his usual white shirt, jacket, and tie.

Slowly, Grampa became less embarrassed by his mouth and made friends with the other guests. Many of them were close to his age, and they were all fascinated by stories of his years in vaudeville. When

Grampa shared his sadness over not performing anymore, it gave Andi and me an idea. What if we helped Grampa put on one last vaudeville show here at the Arundel? Mr. Reid okayed the idea, and with very little encouragement, Grampa was on board.

The show was to be held after dinner on the last evening of Grampa's stay. We promised him we'd prepare the dining room for the show and procure whatever props or instruments he might need. Everyone on staff knew about Grampa's last show and offered to help. We put up signs around the hotel announcing the event, and the guests were excited.

On the day of the performance, guys from the kitchen moved tables aside to make an open area for Grampa's "stage." We got sand from the beach for his famous sand dance, borrowed a tambourine, and set up a record player in a back corner of the room. He didn't have his tap shoes, but his black leather brogans would have to do. Chairs were arranged for the audience, which quickly filled the space. In fact, we had to bring in extra chairs from the living room to accommodate the crowd.

When Grampa was ready, Andi and I introduced him and shared a little background about his history in vaudeville. Then it was Grampa's turn. He was in his glory! First, he waxed emotional—being Irish after all. Grampa told the guests how thankful he was that his granddaughters had given him this opportunity to put on one more show. And then, he was off.

His routine included songs like *Harrigan* and *In the Shade of the Old Apple Tree*, tap dances, tambourine work, some jokes, and stories. Then it was time for his grand finale—the sand dance—in which Grampa spread a bucket of sand on the wooden floor and tap danced on it. As Grampa danced, the sand made a brushing sound timed with his footwork. I'm not sure we mentioned that last bit to Mr. Reid before the event.

The show was over and the applause died down. Grampa was a rock star! We were so proud and happy to see him in his element and loving every second. He said he'd never forget his last show. I knew I wouldn't either.

*My Grandfather Smith doing his Vaudeville act.*

One evening after work, Andi and I took the last ferry across the river to a late-night beach party, out of curiosity more than anything. However, we hadn't given any thought to how we were going to get home so late at night. There were lots of summer hotel kids, lots of beer, probably some pot, and after awhile the party seemed to be getting out of hand. We realized the attendees were not all college kids. Some older guys we didn't recognize were being a little too friendly. That made us nervous, so we decided to start walking home.

Like a knight in a shining black '57 Chevy, Bob Underwood drove up and stopped for us. He heard we had taken the ferry over to the party and wanted to make sure we were okay. It was nice to see a familiar face! After he drove us home, I decided I was going to marry that guy one day. He was kind, ambitious, and protective. I needed that.

In 1967, love was in the air everywhere. As Bob and I were becoming more serious, Bob's best friend and now coworker, Bruce, had begun dating Carolyn. Her father owned an inn and restaurant on Ocean Avenue called the Port House. Carolyn was known for the brand new burgundy Mustang convertible in which she rode around the beach, courtesy of her dad. And Pam, my original Arundel roommate, was dating Kennebunk heartthrob Denny, who was said to throw the best garage parties over in the Port.

Music that summer fit the theme. The Beatles topped the charts with "All You Need Is Love," "Strawberry Fields," and "Penny Lane." Van Morrison recorded "Brown Eyed Girl," Lulu sang "To Sir with Love," and the BeeGees released "Massachusetts." It was a good year to be young and in love, especially in Kennebunkport.

# CHAPTER 16

# *"Chapel of Love"*

## The Dixie Cups

### Kennebunkport, Maine & Amherst, Massachusetts, 1968

When Bob and I sprung news of our marriage plans to our parents at Christmas, it wasn't met with cries of encouragement from either side. Upon hearing of our engagement, Grammy Smith, as predictably blunt as ever, asked right out loud if I was pregnant. I was not, and I was grateful to get that little nugget out into the open before the family phone tree had time to organize itself.

My parents liked Bob very much, but they were not happy I was leaving Russell Sage to finish my BA at the University of Massachusetts. That was the hardest part of the decision for me as well.

Bob's family, especially his father and paternal grandfather, were concerned I was Catholic. They were devout Episcopalians who carried some outdated ideas about Catholics. His father was also concerned about our finances and insisted we present him with our proposed budget. It looked good to us. Bob and I believed we could make it if we were careful.

However, Bob's father tripped us up with one line item we did not include. We hadn't planned for "contingencies." We had enough to get by with us both working part-time jobs, but only if we had no unexpected expenses. That didn't satisfy Bob's father, who, we later would learn, was absolutely right.

Bob and I wanted to marry at St. Martha's Catholic Church in Kennebunkport, but that presented a major stumbling block in the person of Father Kelly. If Wally Reid was a legend in Kennebunkport,

Father Kelly was a force of nature. Not only was he old-school, he had a reputation for being just plain mean. I'm not sure if anyone had ever seen him smile.

Dad had a private sit-down with the good Father and convinced him to allow our marriage with only one pre-Cana meeting instead of the usual three. Dad reportedly said something to the effect of, "I have taken my daughter to Mass every Sunday of her life, I've made sure she received all the sacraments, and now you are telling me you won't marry her in the Church? I can't accept that." I sensed Dad wasn't smiling when he said that, and his face may have been on the beet red side. Apparently, it worked. Our wedding was set for January 27th, 1968 at St. Martha's between college semesters.

That meant we had just two weeks to plan a wedding! Relatives were called; flowers were ordered. Mom and I drove to Burlington, Massachusetts to buy fabric and trim for our dresses; the Maine Mall wouldn't open until the next year. Ever frugal and even within this narrow timeline, Mom was determined to sew them. And she did. There was a simple long white wool dress trimmed in satin for me and a similar one in turquoise for my sister Andi, who was my only bridesmaid. Nancy, who was now 15, would be the flower girl.

Bob and I had a simple Catholic wedding on that sunny but cold winter's day. Dad booked the Hofbrau House in Ogunquit for a buffet reception after the service. My parents really came through for me! While most married couples left for their honeymoon with cans and streamers trailing behind the car, we pulled an orange U-Haul stuffed with everything we owned. After spending our 12-hour honeymoon Saturday night at the Sheraton Boston, we headed for Northampton to move into our first apartment before classes started at UMass the next day.

Our little apartment was in an older building on Green Street in Northampton; it reminded me of Grammy Smith's little flat in Hartford. I swore I could even smell pot roast in the hallway! Our rent was 75

dollars a month—a stretch for us at the time. We were near Smith College and close to downtown, so I could walk to get anything we needed. Wanting to cheer the dreary little place up a bit, I traipsed to the Woolworth's downtown, splurged on two yards of yellow check gingham fabric, trudged home and hand sewed curtains for our bedroom. I realized how spoiled I was to have always had a sewing machine nearby at home. We had no TV until we received one from Mom and Dad Smith a few weeks later as a surprise wedding gift.

Spring semester of 1968 was a bit rough financially and logistically. We scheduled most of our classes in the morning so we could both work in the afternoon and evenings. Bob was a line cook, and I was a waitress at the James H. McManus Ice Cream Shop in Amherst. It was a restaurant similar to Friendly's with a counter and booths, hamburgers, fries, and frappes. After my shift, Bob would stay on to cook dinner while I ran to the ladies' room and emulated Clark Kent, quickly swapping out my tan McManus uniform for my turquoise-checked Howard Johnson one.

Somehow, I managed to get from Amherst to the HoJo's in Northampton with only Bob's trusty '57 Chevy between the two of us. I always made it to Howard Johnson just in time for the dinner rush and stayed until closing at midnight. Once, when I walked, I was running late, wearing my turquoise waitress uniform, and feeling about as far from preppy as one can get in a five-college town. It seemed that everyone driving by was staring, and the story I told myself was that they were looking down on me. I wanted to yell to each driver, "This isn't what it looks like! I'm smart! I read books! I go to UMass! This isn't who I really am!"

Along the way, I made eye contact with one young woman in big sunglasses driving a high-end new car. I vowed to myself that someday, somehow, I would be her. Except I would be kind enough to stop and offer the pitiful waitress on the side of the road a ride. Our crazy schedule really got to me sometimes, but I knew we would never ask our parents for help. We just kept moving ahead, finishing up one day, and getting up the next day to do it all again.

A great deal changed by the summer of 1968. I was now married and still taking classes at UMass. When we were out for the summer, Bob and I were back in Kennebunkport for a third year, but no longer at the Arundel. Bruce and Carolyn were engaged, and her father offered us all jobs at his restaurant and inn, the Port House. Bob was offered the position of head chef and couldn't resist. I accepted the hostess position, Bruce was a sous chef, and Carolyn cruised around in her Mustang and was busy planning her wedding to Bruce. In May, when the hotel was about to open, we moved into our little room on the third floor, above the two guest floors. Carolyn and Bruce inhabited the attic.

The country was in a state of unrest, still reeling from the April assassination of Dr. Martin Luther King. I had hoped for a busy but quiet summer in Kennebunkport. That wasn't going to happen. On the night of June 5th, as we watched our little TV after a busy night in the dining room, a news bulletin came on. Robert Kennedy had been shot in Los Angeles. He was dead.

Carolyn and Bruce ran in to find Bob and I just staring at the TV. It seemed impossible—first John, then Martin, now Bobby. These were the dreamers who had given hope to a generation tired of racial injustice, the draft, and the deadly lottery that accompanied it for the war in Vietnam. Then they were gone and hope seemed dead.

August brought the Democratic National Convention to Chicago and riots to the streets. While we were distracted cooking and serving lobster dinners at the Port House, the world around us changed. The lyrics on the radio went from "I Want to Hold Your Hand" to an anti-Vietnam song that asked what we were fighting for. "Fortunate Son" by Creedence Clearwater Revival became the rallying cry of a generation. The summer of '68 was different from past summers, and even we could see it from Kennebunkport. The world had changed, and so had we.

# CHAPTER 17

# "*Leaving on a Jet Plane*"

## Peter, Paul and Mary

Kennebunk Beach, Maine
London, UK
Brimfield, Massachusetts & Somewhere in Connecticut
1968- 1971

Although Nancy and I were five years apart, when she became a teenager, we became closer as sisters. While she was a sophomore at Kennebunk High School, I was away at college. Dad was busy renovating the big brown cottage on Holland Place in Kennebunk Beach and Mom was pinching pennies. That meant that whenever Nancy and I needed to talk on the phone, we had a time limit. Because we had to pay by the minute for long distance calls back then, Mom only gave us three minutes to catch up, which was definitely not enough time.

Andi was a freshman at the University of Maine in Orono, having graduated from Kennebunk High School as Salutatorian of the class of 1968. Andi was Mom and Dad's daughter who did it all perfectly. In the fall of her senior year, she was declared Homecoming Queen while continuing to get straight A's in her courses. She had also inherited Mom's artistic talent, successfully competing in local art shows. She was beautiful, with long blonde hair and blue eyes.

Andi had barely unpacked at UMaine when she fell in love. Mom and Dad made it clear they were opposed to their perfect daughter embarking on a serious relationship at such a young age. Andi had always been the peacemaker in the family and Mom and Dad didn't expect rebellious behavior from her; Nancy and I were usually the "naughty ones." "Who was this guy anyway?" Mom and Dad wondered. That fall, suspicion abounded down in the Kennebunks.

Nancy had just turned sixteen, and she knew something was up with Andi and her boyfriend. Much like the title character of my favorite series of detective novels, Nancy became an expert at listening through closed doors when Mom and Dad were on the phone. Nancy filled me in as best she could in our three minutes. Meanwhile, Andi and "that boy" taunted our parents on weekends by driving by the house but never coming in. Ever the placid pleaser, Andi found her voice in college, and it was a passively defiant one.

"That boy" was named Brendan. He and Andi had been an item for a few months when my parents called to say that Dad was going on a business trip. They said that he was going to London and taking Andi with him. Odd. In all of Dad's career, he had never been on a business trip farther than Baltimore, Maryland. It was the middle of the academic semester and Andi and our parents hadn't exactly been on good terms of late. But off they flew.

Dad came back a week later, but Andi remained, staying with Mom's Uncle Gilbert and his wife in London. Nancy and I were told that Andi wanted more time to explore London and visit more of Mom's family there. It didn't really make sense. We were especially confused because it didn't align with the whispered phone calls Nancy had become an expert at eavesdropping in on.

*Andi, London, 1968.*

My parents barely clung to their middle-class status by saving money wherever they could. Mom sewed jar rings on the underside of rugs to keep them from slipping and sewed our clothes instead of buying them at Young Sophisticates. Dad mowed his own lawn, fixed his own car, and even hung his own sheetrock. How had they suddenly come up with the money to fly Andi to London for three weeks? Typical of the secrets that have helped destroy our family, Nancy and I were kept totally in the dark. Whatever happened during that time was a secret our parents took to their graves.

Andi left UMaine and married Brendan by the ocean in Ogunquit, Maine in June of 1969. Although she was a beautiful bride, my parents were worried. With Andi's "I come last" people-pleasing personality, she managed to marry a young man who took complete control of her life. While Brendan continued his education at Worcester State, Andi left school. She became a full-time waitress at Friendly's, and they moved into a single room in Worcester, Massachusetts with a shared bathroom down the hall.

The one bright spot was that Bob and I had moved to Worcester that summer after I accepted my first teaching job at Worcester's North High School. I'd just graduated with a degree in English from the University of Massachusetts at Amherst. It was wonderful to have Andi nearby, and I was happy to watch over her as Mom instructed. However, as I watched, I started to notice just how financially dependent on Brendan Andi had become.

I only realized the extent when I unexpectedly stopped by after school one day. Because their room had no kitchen, meals consisted of leftovers Andi brought home from Friendly's, often eaten cold. There was nothing personal in their single room. As soon as she got home from work, Brendan would count Andi's tips and pocket them along with her meager check. Brendan decided how every penny she earned would be spent.

After that visit, I started stopping by after school to visit and bring Andi little gifts—a lipstick, an Italian sandwich, a Clinique bonus gift or some socks. These made Andi happy, but they annoyed

Brendan. After months of this miserly behavior, Nancy and I christened Brendan with the moniker "Nickelnose."

Later in Andi's marriage to Nickelnose, they went into the antique business part time. By then, they had managed to move to a historic saltbox home in nearby Agawam Massachusetts. When we arrived for our first dinner at their new home, we noticed that *everything* was priced. The bottom of our dinner plates had little white stickers on them as did the silverware, their cookware, and linens. You could purchase the chair you were sitting on if you had the 50 dollars the string tag on the back requested. Once dinner was over, you could even buy the table it had been served on if you were so inclined. Apparently Andi and Brendan would use the "antiques" during the week and then, on weekends, pack them up and take them to antique shows to sell. Even though it appeared that Andi lived better now, she still didn't have much of her own. Everything in her home, except possibly her toothbrush and underwear, was "inventory." My beautiful sister appeared even more nervous, anxious, and self-deprecating than ever, always scampering about trying to please Brendan.

Ironically, it was shortly after that first dinner that my husband and I decided to go into the antique business with Andi and Brendan as a sideline to our "real jobs." We had a large basement in which Bob liked to build and refinish furniture in his spare time. We even had an aging green van which we used as our car. We had always enjoyed going to auctions and I loved antique pottery, linens, toys, and ephemera so we thought, "Why not?" It would be a good excuse for me to spend more time with Andi and we might even make a little profit. We shared the idea with Andi and Brendan and they were in. Business cards were printed and "Four Peddlers' Antiques" was soon in business.

Our first major show was the big one: Brimfield! Dealers and collectors came from "the City" and all of New England to buy. Andi, Brendan, Bob, and I, the aforementioned "Four Peddlers," arrived at Brimfield before dawn on the first day to set up our adjoining sites. We planned to do what most "Brimfielders" did: sleep in our vehicles. Inside our van, we packed warm sleeping bags, extra blankets and pillows, soap and towels, fresh water, a grill and charcoal, lighters, candles, and enough food for three days. Andi and Brendan arrived in their car, with one bag of food and meager sleeping and cooking supplies. Their car was a Camaro—not a vehicle known for comfortable overnight accommodation.

The Peddlers did well on the first day, selling quite a bit of merchandise. By dinnertime, we were hungry and tired. We'd agreed that, to keep it simple, each couple would just "do our own thing" for meals. Since my husband was a chef, he lit the grill and cooked rib-eyes, baked potatoes, and garlic bread. We opened a bottle of "Two Buck Chuck" and dined by candlelight on a maple drop-leaf table that had not yet sold. It was pretty romantic, actually. Until we looked next door. There were the other two peddlers sitting in the front seats of the Camaro with the doors open eating peanut butter sandwiches out of a paper bag. And so, the weekend began: two peddlers sharing wine under the moonlight after a full-course dinner and two other peddlers shivering all night in the front seats of a Camaro having dined on peanut butter. Needless to say, the discrepancy in our accommodations began to wear on Andi and Brendan and, by the time the sun started down on the last day, Peddlers One and Two were barely speaking to Peddlers Three and Four. Not a prodigious start to our business plan.

*Cheryl - The Four Peddlers.*

By the summer of 1971, Nickelnose was gone. But so was Andi! Nancy and I understood that she and Brendan were going through a divorce and that Andi was living in a "cult" with a group of friends somewhere in rural Connecticut. Andi was always a bit naive and trusting and our parents were worried about her. After no one had heard from her for some time, Nancy and I began to worry too. We assured Mom and Dad that we would find her.

Nancy and I packed enough clothes for two or three days, drove to Connecticut, and started our search. Having read almost every *Nancy Drew* book in publication, we were confident in our skills as amateur sleuths. We learned that there was a cult in the Norwich area, so we decided to start there. We didn't have the internet yet, so our research consisted of driving the back roads using paper maps of the area, stopping at country stores or gas stations and asking if anyone had heard of a nearby cult or seen a woman who met Andi's description. As we slinked around and conducted our interviews, Nancy and I were beginning to think of ourselves as quite the detectives.

The first day brought us no luck. People had heard rumors of a cult but had no details that would help us with our search. On the second day, Nancy and I came up with a new idea: we'd ask priests and ministers at local churches if they were aware of any religious cults in the area. Who better to know? We started with the Catholic churches, telling and retelling our story about our poor lost sister who had been brought up Catholic and who may have gone astray and joined a cult. When needed, we embellished our sad appeal with how worried our parents were about her and begged for their help.

On the third stop, we lucked out. The priest knew of a nearby King's Chapel and suggested we check it out. Armed with the directions the priest had given us, we found it. Andi was there! She wasn't wearing white robes, sandals, and flowers in her hair; just jeans and a UMO t-shirt. She said she was living with friends. She was surprised to see us and couldn't understand why we were there. She said she never thought that anyone would be worried about her. That was Andi, always floating above the rest of us, not quite tethered to everyday life. A dreamer, she seemed unaware of the effect her choices might have on others. Andi's decision-making process was childlike; she quite literally never gave long-term consequences a thought. Hence, a rushed marriage (I should talk!), rushed divorce, and now the cult. Sadly, there would be more.

Driving home, Nancy and I couldn't stop talking about Andi, the priest, the cult, our detective work, and the sheer number of weird things that seem to happen in our family. Doesn't everyone have to drive to Connecticut to rescue their sister from a cult? The more we thought about our little caper, the funnier it became. That was how it often was when Nancy and I found ourselves involved in these crazy escapades. The stress would ease, the worry would resolve, and the hysterics would begin. Once we started laughing–snorting actually–we couldn't stop!

"Do these kinds of things happen in normal families?" we asked each other. I think we knew the answer to that one. Neither of us ever suffered under the delusion that our family was completely functional.

*Andi on Swing, Searsport Shores*

CHAPTER 18

# *"My Girl"*

## The Temptations

Rochester, Michigan, 1975 - 1976

It was 2:00 a.m. when we got to Niagara Falls. We could hear the falls before we saw them. The parking lot was deserted and the eerily-lit falls were ominous at this hour. Having picked up coffee to go, we stopped on the American side to switch drivers and give three-week-old Kristen a bottle. Three-year-old Robert was asleep in the bed we made for him out of sleeping bags, pillows, and his well-worn yellow blanket. The cargo area of our brown 1973 Chevy wagon was so big he could stretch out. Kristen's car bed was positioned where I could reach her if she woke.

We decided to make most of the trip overnight so the kids could sleep through the longest part of the ride. None of us had seatbelts; they came along later. I wonder why we never worried back then about our children becoming flying objects in an accident? We thought we had done all we could to make them safe on the long trip from Connecticut to Michigan. At Niagara, we were about halfway there.

Married with children of my own, I didn't think to question the fact that, like my father, my husband had a job requiring us to move every couple of years. Neither Bob nor I had ever lived outside of New England and moving to the upper Midwest was an adventure. We liked Rochester, a community with a New England feel. It had a real downtown, rural areas bisected by tree-lined dirt roads, and new subdivisions. It was located in suburban Oakland County, about a 30-minute drive north of Detroit. We knew we had a few things to get used to—like remembering to order a "pop" when we wanted soda, or asking where the "bubbler" was when looking for a water fountain.

But those adjustments seemed minor and we were excited to see what life was like in a different part of the United States.

We flew to Detroit a couple of months before to look at houses. The one we chose was only a short ride from Oakland University in Pontiac, where Bob would be Food Service Director. We bought the model home, professionally decorated in ultra-'70s style. Although Colonial on the exterior, the inside of the house featured bold-patterned wallpaper in the popular color combinations of the day: orange and yellow, and brown and white. Having grown up in conservative New England, I would never have chosen such graphic designs and bright colors, but I found that I liked them. They made me happy. It was as if the house gave me permission to go a little wild, to break out of "what Mom always did" and find my own style. I was ready to part company with my antique spinning wheel and vintage coffee tins, cream-colored curtains tied back with ball fringe, and dark pine furniture adorned with heavy pewter tankards and brass candlesticks. No more Currier & Ives prints in dark frames for me; I experimented with big, bright canvases, even if our budget limited me to reproductions. It was refreshing to start over.

After over 14 hours of driving, we arrived at our new home at 929 Briston Drive in the late morning. The moving van pulled up soon after and, tired as we were, we were anxious to get settled by Thanksgiving on the very next week of that year, 1975.

We enrolled Robert in Red Barn Nursery School three days a week. I loved that little school; it reminded me of home. It was in a small white farmhouse next to an old red barn. To get there, you drove part of the way on a not-yet-paved section of Mile Road. That stretch of road ran through a beautiful wooded part of Rochester; I could have been back in Connecticut! There were arts and crafts in the little kitchen, farm animals, a garden, and, on special days, hayrides around the farm. Often, parents were included. I remember those as halcyon times; my now-grown son, not so much. He remembers being removed from the hay wagon for throwing hay. I was on the same hay wagon and have no memory of that. Maybe it did happen that way but, since this is my memoir, I'm pronouncing the hayride memories happy ones.

Oakland University, where Bob worked, was a short ride down one of Oakland County's remaining dirt roads from the newly-opened Silverdome, where the Detroit Lions played. In the summer, the team practiced at Oakland and it was Bob's job to keep them well fed. He got to know the players and occasionally was given tickets to an upcoming home game. I'd never been to a professional football game and was overwhelmed by the vast silver roof, the huge crowd, the noise, and the excitement. Growing up in a family of all girls, I'd never understood football. All I knew the first time I went to a game was that each team was headed for the opposite goal posts and that, at half-time, they changed sides. I also knew that when the other Lion's fans cheered, I should too. (Unless, of course, the Lions were playing the New England Patriots, in which case my plan was to just keep quiet.)

The most exciting game we attended during our brief two years in Michigan was in Ann Arbor. It was the BIG ONE: the University of Michigan versus Ohio State. It seemed that the whole state was one big fan club that weekend, with homes and businesses decorated in blue and maize. We attended a pregame party at the home of one of Bob's co-workers and everything there was blue and maize as well: the streamers, the balloons, the food, the towels, and even the toilet paper! I could only assume that over the state line in Ohio, scarlet and gray toilet paper was in short supply that weekend.

July 4th, 1976 was cause for celebration in Rochester, Michigan and across the United States. It was the much-anticipated bicentennial. I tore a recipe out of *Women's* Day for a bicentennial cake that I couldn't wait to make. It was rectangular, covered with white frosting and decorated with blueberries and strawberries to form the stripes and stars of the American flag. We invited a few neighbors who had children about Robert's age to a cookout on the new brick patio Bob and I built behind our house. The weather was beautiful; the wading pool was out and there were hamburgers and hot dogs on the grill. While Robert played with his young friends, Kristen was holding court in her little baby seat on the patio, being the center of attention as babies always seem to be. She was already almost nine months old. She had her dad's coloring, with brown hair and beautiful brown eyes. Robert, on the other hand, had blondish hair and blue eyes, favoring my side of the family. That night we listened to the fireworks from the patio after finishing off every bit of my American flag cake. Two days later, our world changed forever.

It was a Tuesday. I came home from grocery shopping and was unloading the groceries. I placed Kristen on the carpet in the family room with some of her toys. She'd just learned to sit up on her own the month before and I could see her playing from the adjoining kitchen while I put the groceries away. Robert was at nursery school.

And then, Kristen wasn't playing anymore. She had fallen over and was having what we then would have called a grand mal seizure. I'd never seen a seizure but had watched enough TV shows and read enough books to know what one looked like. Her lips and fingertips were taking on a blue cast and there was saliva drooling from the corner of her sweet baby mouth. I was no longer thinking; adrenaline was in control now. I grabbed Kristen, who was still seizing, and ran next door with her, banging on the neighbor's front door. I didn't know these neighbors well but I did know that the husband was a policeman. In my frenzy, I figured he would know what to do. When he opened the door and saw what was happening, he took Kristen from me, laid her down on the rug in their front hall and started to give her CPR. In the meantime, his wife called the ambulance. This all felt unreal, like it was happening to someone else. Here was my previously healthy little girl who had had an Apgar score of 10 at birth and had met all her developmental milestones having a tonic-clonic seizure. How could this be?

I remember riding in the back of the ambulance while the EMTs attended to Kristen. It seemed as if the ambulance wasn't going fast enough; many cars didn't pull over quickly. I was terrified. By the time we arrived at Crittenton Hospital in Rochester Hills, Kristen's seizure had stopped and she was awake. As she was carried in, we were directed to an exam room in the ER.

That's when I first learned the importance of parents as advocates for their children. After examining her, the young doctor on-call in the ER determined that Kristen had not had a seizure. He said that if she had, she would be asleep now, in what I later learned was called a "postictal state."

"How could this be?" I asked. "I saw a seizure, my neighbor saw a seizure, the EMTs saw a seizure."

He insisted that we must have seen what we thought was a seizure but was not. Maybe it was a behavior, some kind of temper tantrum? I was frightened and frustrated at the same time. I was angry that this male doctor was questioning what I'd seen with my own eyes and talking down to me. No, I wasn't in the medical field, but I did have a college degree and teaching experience; I knew how to report observations professionally.

"Well, she's fine now," the doctor said. "You can take her home." By then, my husband had arrived at the hospital. No cell phones at that time; I'd called him from the hospital pay phone when we arrived. Like the doctor, he had not seen the seizure either.

We took Kristen home and called both sets of her grandparents, partly to inform them but also, I think, to hear their voices. We were scared and needed their comfort. We assured them that there was no need for them to come out; Kristen was fine now. We'd keep them posted.

Call it mother's intuition, but for the days following, I knew we were not done with this "thing," whatever it was. I kept waiting for the proverbial other shoe to drop. I didn't want Robert upset, so I tried hard not to let my anxiety show. But I was worried. I remember having coffee that week with another mother from the neighborhood, Barbara O'Reilly, and sharing with her that I had a feeling that whatever this was, it was going to happen again. And it did. But this time it was much worse.

On the following Tuesday, July 13th, Kristen started seizing again. Only this time, the seizure didn't stop. I called an ambulance and by the time we reached Crittenton hospital, she had been seizing for 30 minutes and still was. This time, there were no questions about what I'd seen; the doctors saw it for themselves. And they couldn't stop it. Kristen was in what I now know is called "status epilepticus," a life-threatening condition where seizures come one after another so that they actually look nonstop. After long periods of status, the heart can give out and brain damage or death can occur. When the doctors at Crittenton couldn't stop the seizures, they decided to send Kristen by ambulance to St. Joseph's Hospital in Detroit, where she continued to seize on and off for five more hours. On the way, I remember watching the EMTs bag her to keep her respirations going. I was afraid that my baby was going to die before we got to Detroit. Finally, at 5:00 a.m. the next morning, a combination of phenobarbital, Valium, and Dilantin stopped the seizures and Kristen slept.

But the damage was done. Brain damage had occurred, as we would slowly observe over the next few months when she failed to make typical developmental milestones. Kristen's development had slowed significantly.

I was even angrier now. Had the doctor at Crittenton believed that she had a seizure the first time I brought her in, she may not have had to endure those hours of status. She might not have suffered the brain damage that has significantly affected her life every day since. I think of the proverbial chicken and egg and my anger lessens a bit. What caused the initial seizure? Was the brain damage the result of whatever caused the initial seizures rather than the effect of them? We might never know.

It was frustrating not to have a name for what was happening to Kristen. After the events of the 13th, the doctors used the term "seizure disorder." I didn't know what that meant. When I researched the term at the Oakland University library, there was little to go on. Finally, I came to one medical text that did list "seizure disorder" in the index. But it went on to say, "see Epilepsy." Epilepsy? Did Kristen have epilepsy? None of the doctors had used that word. I was confused.

When I got home and told Bob what I'd read, he was confused too, and worried. He had a good relationship with his family's doctor back in Massachusetts, where he'd grown up, and decided to call him for his opinion. Anxious to hear what he said, I listened on the other phone. Suddenly, everything became clear. The doctor said, "Nowadays we use the term 'seizure disorder' instead of 'epilepsy' because that word has such negative associations for people." We finally knew. Our daughter had epilepsy.

After that phone call, I was determined to learn all that I could about epilepsy. We didn't have home computers or smart phones back then so I spent as much time as I could at the library. I also wrote away to the Epilepsy Foundation of America for information. The more I learned, the more I understood about why the doctors at Crittenton proceeded as they did, although I still wondered why they didn't suggest further testing. I learned that a single seizure does not epilepsy make; the term refers to conditions involving *repeated* seizures. And it doesn't include seizures babies may have because of a high temperature; those are called febrile seizures. I was frustrated that the doctors did not explain all of this to me, that I had to do the research myself to finally understand what we were facing. Kristen had epilepsy. The monster now had a name. We could handle that. And we would fight it.

We were in Michigan for another year. Kristen continued to have seizures and multiple hospitalizations. A variety of medicines were tried but her seizures persisted. She was still not walking when we packed to move again. This time, we headed back to New England, where Bob would manage the food service program at the University of Vermont in Burlington. I was surprised when I realized how much I would miss Michigan and the friends we made there. All in all, it was a good experience, but sadly overshadowed by what we then knew: our beautiful daughter would always have special needs.

Our little family was moving again. This time to Vermont.

# CHAPTER 19

# "Like a Rolling Stone"

## Bob Dylan

Essex Junction, Vermont
T'aint Town, Kennebunk, Maine, 1977 - 1979

Bob and I bought a split-level home in quiet Essex Junction, a suburb of Burlington, Vermont. I called it a backwards split-level because the house was positioned so the front door faced the woods. The back deck was shaded and faced the street.

We enrolled Robert in a private kindergarten in Essex Junction. I was surprised to learn that Vermont did not have public school kindergartens yet. While Robert was at school, I took Kristen to appointments at Mary Hitchcock Hospital, which was affiliated with nearby Dartmouth College. The hospital was across the Connecticut river in Hanover, New Hampshire.

Kristen was one of the first patients started on the newly approved seizure drug, Depakote. Prescribed by her pediatric neurologist Dr. Emory, we hoped it would reduce the frequency of her seizures. Kristen's special needs meant she required both physical therapy services in Burlington and occupational therapy services at our home. It was during one of her physical therapy sessions that she finally took her first step, to the accompaniment of cheers from the staff and tears from me. At three years old, she was delayed, but she was walking!

One of the most difficult things I had to do during our time in Vermont was count seizures. I was asked to wear a little silver counter on my finger at all times in order to record the seizures Kristen had each day. Every night I was to write them down for the doctor and therapists—what kind, how long, her recovery time. That and trying to meet the needs of both of my children nearly consumed me. I was always on high alert, listening or watching for a seizure, while trying to devote some time to Robert as well. As with every other posting with his company, Saga Food Service, Bob worked long days and was frequently not home to help. I often wonder if this is the time that my anxiety disorder first developed. Coupled with the guilt I felt for having to put Robert, my first child, second so much of the time just to keep Kristen alive, I was barely holding on.

Bob and I spent a year and a half in Vermont before we became "flatlanders" again in late 1978. Saga assigned Bob to the position of Food Service Director at Maine Medical Center in Portland, Maine. Although we were just beginning to build a life in Vermont, I didn't have a choice, nor did the kids. At least if we had to move, Southern Maine was where we always wanted to be. Although it was a 40 minute commute to the hospital, we chose to move back to Kennebunkport, where we had first met all those summers ago at the Ar-un-DEL.

I decided that, now that we were back in Maine, it was time to put my kids before Saga Food Service. Robert would be enrolling in Kennebunk for his second half-year of Kindergarten in January and I was done moving him around. I was ready to keep the promise I had made to myself years ago: that my children would not have the interrupted education I had. I attended three high schools, never having time at any one to make lasting friendships. My children deserved to know the security of staying in one place. While Robert briefly started kindergarten in Vermont, this was the last time I wanted him to be the "new kid." I hoped both Robert and Kristen would graduate from Kennebunk High School having made lifelong friends.

We rented a small house in Kennebunkport until we were ready to buy. When the first day of school arrived, Robert, dressed in red plaid pants and a little navy blue red sox jacket, couldn't wait to go. But the school bus didn't stop for him. I had enrolled him in kindergarten and spoken to the Cousens school secretary, Mrs. Rose. We lived on Route 9, and she had all of our information, so why hadn't the bus come? When I called Mrs. Rose to find out what happened, it turned out that she had assumed we lived somewhere else entirely.

As I explained in more detail where our house was, Mrs. Rose replied, "Well, why didn't you say you were in 'Taint Town?" Our house was across the river on the Kennebunk side, meaning we weren't technically living in Kennebunkport as we thought. It was in the middle of the two or, as the locals say—'t'aint Kennebunk and 't'aint Kennebunkport." Hence the name "T'aint Town." Once we figured out the local place names, we were all set; the next day, the bus stopped.

After our lease on the winter rental in Lower Village (aka T'aint Town) expired, Bob and I purchased an antique house in Kennebunk on Cat Mousam Road. I loved the 1820s Cape Cod farmhouse. It had a chicken barn out back, a huge yard, and the clever play-on-words name of the road made me chuckle. Someone back in the day had a sense of humor.

The day we moved in, I sat in the backyard beneath the big pine tree. My mind reverberated with the sentiment: "I'm home." Since those long-ago days on Wells Beach, my heart knew that someday home would be in Maine. The house needed work, but we were young and optimistic. During all the moves—from Massachusetts, to Connecticut, to Michigan, to Vermont, I kept asking myself, "Are we there yet? Will we ever be home?" We had finally made it!

My sister Nancy was married now, to a blond outdoorsy young man named Philip the Third, who everyone called Kip. They had recently purchased their first home—a small raised ranch in Wells. Since we now both had homes in adjacent towns, we saw a lot more of each other. With Andi in Arizona and Joanne at college in Boston, Nancy and I were the only two Stunning Smith Sisters in Maine. We revived our sisterly bond and relied on one another as we hadn't in many years.

Nancy was still teaching at Wells Elementary School and I had recently started teaching at Scarborough High School when she became pregnant with her son, who she named Ken. Ken had the blondest hair ever and was the light of Nancy's life. He was all boy: he built "miles" of roads and bridges in the dirt piles in front of their house in El Pond with his vast collection of Tonka trucks. He and his friends, Brian and Scott, played there by the hour. Every fall, Ken canvassed the neighborhood, carrying a cardboard suitcase almost as big as he was, full of Tom-Wat fundraising materials. When opened, the case spewed out everything from potholders to pretzel sticks, candy to candles, stationery to soap. He was so adorable when he came to the door with his oversized case that people couldn't resist purchasing something they didn't need to benefit the elementary school band.

Ken is a huge part of Nancy's story because the two of them were so close. They had to be. When Ken was still an infant, Nancy's husband fell "in love" with a young woman he met at work, leaving Nancy to raise Ken on her own. It was a struggle financially but Nancy made it work, becoming everyone's favorite Mom for all the cookies and brownies she baked for the neighborhood kids. She taught school, raised Ken, shoveled snow, mowed the lawn, and still managed to roast a turkey every week to donate to the fundraising suppers for the school band. Nancy lived with white plastic lawn chairs as her dining area seating for 18 years to make sure that Ken always had everything he needed. During that time, Nancy and I held each other up through numerous challenges, from seizures to heartbreaks, divorces to financial set-backs.

Unfortunately, in our family, when something good happens to one of us, we are always on alert, waiting for the next crisis. This time, it was Nancy's turn. My heart broke for her and yet I was in awe of her resilience. That doesn't mean that she never had horrible *I don't know how I can keep doing this* days; she did. But she persevered. She leaned on her many friends. She kept trying. She never forgot to laugh. And she got through it.

And Andi? Now divorced from Brendan, she met a nice-looking Irish guy named Tim at her new insurance job in Hartford. He had also been married and divorced. When they became serious, our family was regaled with stories of how awful Tim's ex-wife was, how she caused the divorce, and how she hardly ever let him see his two children. Mom and Dad felt bad for "poor Tim" and welcomed him into our family. Not long after, Andi shocked us all with the news that she and Tim had flown to Kissimmee, Florida and eloped. They were already married!

As before with "Nickelnose," Andi deferred to her new husband, who found new ways to abuse her. Unlike the financially controlling behavior of Brendan, Tim's abuse was much scarier. He verbally and emotionally wore her down. Except the more she complied, the meaner Tim got. At one point there was a gun involved, and our Uncle Ed, who lived nearby, stepped in. Our dad's younger brother and an Army veteran, he picked Andi up and brought her to stay with his family where she'd be safe. However, like so many abused women, Andi returned to Tim a short time later. As so often happens, he assured her that he had "changed" and it would never happen again.

Our family had only recently become aware of the danger Andi was in, which Tim seemingly did not appreciate, especially whenever we intervened. Abruptly, Tim decided he would start his own insurance business and move closer to his parents, who retired to Arizona. He and Andi would leave Connecticut and start over in a new place; that would fix everything. In a matter of weeks, Andi found herself 2,500 miles away from home, where she knew no one, and with no access to her friends or family to support her. We all knew this didn't bode well for Andi, but there was little we could do. She believed and loved him.

These were fragile years for both of my sisters. Given our history, I was afraid to contemplate what might happen next.

# CHAPTER 20

# *"Leavin' on Your Mind"*

## Patsy Cline

### Kennebunk, Maine, 1982 - 1985

In the hope of gaining more insight into Kristen's condition and finding more resources, I accepted an invitation to join the Board of Directors of the Epilepsy Foundation of America in 1982. Officially, I would represent the New England states; unofficially, I wanted to make sure parents like me had a voice at the national level. It was an honor to serve on this board for twelve years. I was especially grateful to the "Epiladies," as we called ourselves, a group of amazing women with whom I shared meals and hotel rooms when we traveled for EFA board meetings and national conferences. I became especially close with a social worker from Johns Hopkins in Baltimore named Diana Pillas and an entrepreneur from Atlanta named Jeanne Cahill.

*The Epiladies – Diana, Jeanne, & Cheryl.*

Diana was seven years older than me—a stunningly beautiful woman, tall with auburn hair and Greek coloring. She dressed in bold outfits, sported big hoop earrings, and lots of bangle bracelets. Diana's mother and father once owned a Greek restaurant in Baltimore. A visit to Diana's house always included a homemade Greek dinner, complete with lamb, souvlaki, and baklava, and accompanied by a glass or two of Ouzo or Retsina. *Opa!* Diana was one of the smartest, kindest people I ever met. Social work was the perfect career for her as people were naturally drawn to her optimistic and caring nature, the way she talked and listened, as well as her hugs.

Jeanne and I were 15 years apart, but she was so beautiful, vibrant, and talented that you'd never know it. As a petite woman with graying blondish hair, a trim figure, and a stunning sense for fashion, Jeanne led a fascinating life. She was born into poverty in rural South Georgia and later became an icon of Democratic politics and a close friend of Jimmy and Roslyn Carter. Jeanne was always full of surprises. On one visit to Atlanta, Jeanne took us to the Carter Center, pulled out a key, and showed us into President Carter's private office.

It was now 1984. Bob and I were leaving behind our little antique Cape on Cat Mousam Road for a home under construction in River Bend Woods, a new development in Kennebunk, closer to the beach. The River Bend house had more space, a beautiful "Good Morning" staircase, a real garage, and it didn't require all the work of the old house—which we were looking forward to. We loved our old house but never seemed to have enough money or time to complete all the renovations. Bob had recently won national recognition for his work at Maine Medical Center and except for Kristen's recent broken arm, we were happy. Or at least I thought we were.

It was an unusually hot Labor Day for Maine that year. While the rest of the state was likely at the beach, for some reason I chose to iron on that sweltering afternoon. I was determined to iron every piece of clothing in the pile that had been nagging at me for weeks. Very few women I knew still ironed; my sisters didn't even own ironing boards. I knew I should just take the clothes out of the dryer the minute it stopped, but by the time it was done I was usually onto something else.

So, there I was, sweating, spraying, ironing, and putting clothes away instead of taking my kids to play in the waves. Did that make me a bad mother? I wasn't sure. I worried about that. I tried to be more of an easygoing and come-what-may kind of mother. I really did. But I felt tense, always waiting for the next emergency with a child who had unmanageable seizures. I hated that for all of us. I wished I could have been the kind of mother who could just leave it all behind and sit on the beach for hours relaxing with my kids. That just didn't seem to be in my DNA.

As the oldest child, I was brought up to be the responsible one. Sometimes that felt like a curse. Why had God given me all of that responsibility, and the child with intractable seizures to boot? Did He think I could handle it? Did He think my son—who missed out on things like beach days because Kristen had more seizures when she was hot—should have had to handle it?

The kids were playing and I was still ironing when the phone rang. It startled me.

"Hello, is this the Underwood residence?"

It wasn't a voice I recognized. "Yes, I'm Cheryl Underwood. Can I help you?"

"This is York Hospital. We're trying to reach Robert Underwood. Is he at home?"

"No, he's away on business," I answered.

"When will he be home? We really need to speak to him," said the serious male voice.

"He's at a conference in New Orleans and won't be home for three more days."

"It's important. It's regarding his brother. Can you please contact him and have him call us as soon as possible?"

I said I would and wrote down the number and extension.

As cell phones didn't exist yet, I spent the next 15 minutes trying to reach my husband at the hotel number he had left for me. After I explained the urgency of reaching him to the hotel operator, I was told that Bob wasn't there. I called the hospital back, and upon hearing that Bob was not available, they asked if I might be able to reach another relative of Richard Underwood. Now I was getting scared. I asked what this was about and the person on the phone, who now identified himself as a physician, said that due to confidentiality requirements he could only speak with a blood relative. Apparently saying that I was Richard's sister-in-law wasn't good enough.

I hung up and attempted to reach Rick's father on Cape Cod and Rick's sister Carolyn at the Breakwater, the hotel she and her husband Ron owned in Kennebunkport. I knew it well; it was formerly the Arundel. There was no answer at the senior Underwood's home—someone else who wasn't ironing on this beautiful afternoon. The front desk at the Breakwater informed me that Bob's sister Carolyn and Ron were out on their boat. Of course. They weren't ironing either. Hot, scared, and frustrated, I called the hospital.

"Hi. This is Cheryl Underwood again, returning your call about Richard Underwood. I've tried Rick's brother, sister, and father. No one is at home. I'm afraid that, if this is urgent, you're stuck with me. I'll do what I can to help."

There was a long pause. "Mrs. Underwood, I'm sorry to have to inform you that Richard is deceased."

"What? That can't be! He's only 24!" I choked out.

"Again, I'm very sorry. Richard was caught in a riptide at Wells Beach earlier this afternoon. He drowned. The ambulance brought him here, but it was too late for us to save him. I'm sorry. We need to know what the family would like us to do with his body."

I was usually good in emergencies, the strong one. I was deter-mined to hold it together. My children were home. No one was around to help me. Every family in Kennebunk used Bibber's Funeral Home, and I was sure that Bob's family would want to as well. I told the doctor and asked if I should call Bibber's. He repeated that he was sorry and assured me the hospital would handle it.

Next, I needed to shut off the iron and find someone else who wasn't at the beach to stay with Robert and Kristen. I needed to tell my sister-in-law Carolyn in person, without the kids with me. I wasn't ready to tell my son, who loved his Uncle Rick, and I was thankful my daughter Kristen wouldn't understand. I finally reached my cousin and godson Brian and his wife Lynn, who must have been the only two other people in Kennebunk not at the beach. They were devastated to hear why I needed them but assured me they'd be right over.

Trembling and crying, I drove to tell Carolyn; I was barely able to see the road and unaware of my surroundings. I was in shock. Carolyn's pastor, who I'd already called, would meet me at the Breakwater, where I arrived safely and very luckily didn't hurt someone on the way. He was there when I arrived and we waited together for Carolyn to come up to the porch. It was one of the most difficult moments I've experienced, watching the pastor tell Carolyn. Afterward, I hugged her because I couldn't think of what else to do.

The rest is a blur. I don't remember driving home. I don't remember calling Bob in New Orleans to tell him his little brother was dead or telling Rick's dad; I think Carolyn did that. I do remember Bibber's calling me later to let me know that Rick was there. Somehow, I had to pull myself together and make dinner for Robert and Kristen. Then, I had to figure out how to tell Robert what had happened to his favorite uncle.

Had I known then what I know now, I might have answered the doctor's questions differently. Here's how our conversation might have gone:

"This is York Hospital. We're trying to reach Robert Underwood. Is he at home?"

"No. This is his wife, Cheryl. He wants me to think that he's at a business conference in New Orleans but he's really having an affair with one of the other attendees. At this very moment, he's probably on a sailboat in Lake Pontchartrain with her before they go back to the hotel for a nice dinner and a hot night of sex. He left me alone with the kids on this steamy holiday weekend. He thinks I don't know about it, but someday I will. Right now it sucks. How can I help you?"

When I was young, New Year's Eve was fun: getting dressed up in silver shoes and dancing until midnight. I hadn't yet lost enough, gone through enough struggles to be wary of New Year's. Being a person who needs structure, predictability, and routine, I simply don't do well with the uncertainty accompanying the holiday. Over the years, through all the ups and downs, the gains and losses, I could no longer find the excitement I once had.

On New Year's Eve 1985, I was outwardly stressed about little things. I thought about what to wear or whether Kristen would behave for the babysitter. Yet, my anxiety went much deeper. I agonized about unnamed threats that might loom in the upcoming year. I wasn't sure if I wanted to make first tracks into the new year.

Bob was away again. He said a group of his colleagues from Maine Medical Center invited him on a hunting trip in Northern Maine and that they would be gone for five days. It was odd that Bob was so anxious to go because Bruce, our host for our "Gourmet Group's" New Year's Eve dinner this year, had been his best friend since high school. For me it would be just another holiday alone with Robert and Kristen.

I arranged for the babysitter so I could go to the Gourmet New Year's dinner for a few hours. We started our Gourmet Group in 1979 when a number of us were new teachers at Scarborough Junior High School. The group was made up of four couples who took turns hosting dinner once a month; it later grew to five or six. Bob and I had been in a similar group in Michigan and really enjoyed it. Over the years, our little group has sampled the cuisines of dozens of countries, ridden on skis, in sleighs, haywagons, limousines, trains, and wheelbarrows, been to ball games and concerts (oh, Elton John!), and dressed in ridiculous costumes. We've celebrated the births of our children and cried through deaths and divorces. We've dined with each other, laughed with each other, but always looked out for each other. I wasn't looking forward to going to Gourmet solo, but these were my closest friends. The Gourmet group was like family; it still is.

*The Gourmet Group, 1988.*

While I waited for the babysitter to arrive, I went through the stack of mail that had accumulated on the kitchen counter: junk mail, bills, and a few late-arriving Christmas cards in red envelopes. I started opening the Christmas cards. The bills could wait. As I read the address on the envelope in my hand, I froze. It was addressed to Rob. Was that my Bob? If so, why wasn't it addressed to both of us? I looked at the envelope again. It was postmarked Chicago. Who did we know in Chicago? Then I read the note:

*Dearest Rob,*

*I am so happy that you and Carol are getting this time together. I loved the beautiful Christmas tree you helped decorate while you were here. I hope the two of you are having a wonderful time at The Balsams.*

*Happy New Year!*
*Betty*

It was at that moment that I knew Bob wasn't hunting. He was with "Carol." He'd gone to Chicago on what he told me was a business trip earlier in December. Is that when they decorated the tree? And who was Betty? I had spent all of these weekends and holidays alone, working full time, taking care of Robert and Kristen. I'd been counting seizures, sitting in ERs, being a Boy Scout mom, and handling Rick's death, all without my husband. I was too stunned to think, so I just stared blankly at the wall and waited for the babysitter. I didn't want my children to see me crying.

I arrived at Bruce and Carolyn's shaking and in tears. Someone placed a glass of wine in my hand. Hyperventilating, I spilled the whole story. The Christmas card that wasn't meant for me, the Christmas tree in Chicago, the Balsams—all of it. Then Bruce took charge. He called the Balsams to see if Bob was registered. I listened in on the upstairs receiver. The hotel desk answered and Bruce asked. "Yes," they told him, "Mr. *and Mrs.* Underwood were registered, but they were not in their room at the moment. Would Bruce like them paged?" Bruce thanked them and hung up the phone.

My marriage was over.

# CHAPTER 21

# *"All Alone Am I"*

## Brenda Lee

Kennebunk, Maine
Jackson, New Hampshire, 1986

In the new year, my husband of 18 years left me. He filed for both a divorce and an annulment in the Catholic Church. The irony was that Bob, who now went by "Rob," was Episcopalian, not Catholic like me. However, if he and Carol (who apparently was Catholic) were going to wed in the Church the following December, he needed our marriage annulled. My Church sent me a letter informing me that my marriage had never been valid. There had been no sacrament, because they said that I hadn't fully understood the commitment of the marriage covenant. I was shocked and devastated. Bob and Carol married in the Church—at the expense of my Faith.

The annulment was humiliating and demeaning; worse than the divorce. I was reminded of the book by Sheila Kennedy, *Shattered Faith*. She had been through the same hypocrisy and was willing to fight it. I, on the other hand, was defeated. They claimed I didn't understand the commitment to which I had been faithful for 18 years. They claimed I didn't understand the commitment of children when I'd been the sole caretaker of our two children, one with unmanageable seizures. The annulment was just another gut punch in a year that landed me one gut punch after another.

That year, it was hard to breathe.

I couldn't afford to remain at our new house in River Bend Woods. The kids and I would have to move. Again. I purchased a smaller, older house in my own name. It was a raised ranch in an established neighborhood on nearby Woodside Drive in Kennebunk. I didn't like the house much, but it was all I could afford. It was outdated to say the least, with gold appliances and olive-green shag carpeting that I would never be able to replace on my income from Village Greetings. At least it was safe. Robert would still be near his friends, and it was within biking distance of the beach. I kept my promise to myself to live in such a way that my kids didn't have to change schools like I did.

Being unable to afford to hire a mover, I did the move myself. After working during the day, I waited until Kristen was asleep for the night. I instructed Robert to listen for her while he did his homework. I felt guilty for putting that burden on him at such a young age; I simply didn't know what else I could do. Load after load, night after night—with the help of whatever friends or family I could enlist, I moved. I hauled two or three loads to nearby Woodside Drive in my car, alone in the dark, ensuring that I was quick. If Kristen had a seizure, Robert was smart and knew to dial 911, but he would need me. He didn't deserve to have to bear that kind of responsibility alone.

When I got back from one of the nightly moving trips, our dog Whiskers just lay down on her bed in the mudroom and died. It was that quick, that unexpected, that untimely. She hadn't even been sick. I left Robert to listen for Kristen yet again, so I could rush Whiskers to the local veterinary hospital. It was already too late, I knew. We loved that dog. Losing Whiskers broke Robert's heart even more—he'd already lost his dad, his Uncle Rick, and now his dog. I was starting to feel like Job. At least he got it all back and then some, so maybe there was hope for me yet.

My sister Nancy helped get me through many of those dark days. Nancy *and* my psychiatrist, Dr. Collins, because it was all becoming more than I could handle. On top of everything else, I still owned a business: the local Hallmark shop, Village Greetings. There were still orders, inventory, employees, payroll, and taxes to manage. My customers expected me to be smiling when I waited on them.

I was committed to continuing to enjoy ski trips with my now-teenage-son, Robert, after I was divorced. As usual, every time I tried to do something good, I was pulled back into the mire that had become my life. One weekend, I arranged for a local couple, who I had interviewed and background checked, to stay overnight with Kristen so that Bobby and I could get away to Whitney's Inn in Jackson, New Hampshire to ski. I owed him that. He'd been through hell these past few years too. He loved to ski and, with his Dad gone, he had few chances to go.

Although it had snowed, we arrived at the inn in time for me to have a cocktail in the bar while watching Robert shovel off the little skating pond just outside the window. It made me sad to watch him out there in the cold all by himself, but that emotion was soon replaced by happiness as I watched him glide around the pond under the lights.

Just as Robert and I finished breakfast the next morning, the front desk notified me that I had a phone call. It was from the babysitters. They said they were LEAVING! Kristen's behavior had been totally out of control and they "couldn't do it anymore." They were in Kennebunk and we were hours away in New Hampshire. Kristen couldn't safely be left alone—ever. I talked them into staying for one more hour while I figured out what to do.

Once again, Nancy saved me. She was at my house to care for Kristen a half hour later. It looked like a war zone when she arrived: she reported lamp shades askew, food and toys strewn everywhere. I knew Kristen acted out because she was scared; she wanted "Mommy." But what about Robert's needs? We headed home shortly after breakfast and needless to say, he lost out again. I felt guilty no matter what I did. I tried to be resilient, but I just couldn't seem to find a balance.

With the divorce and annulment, the move, the dog, the store, my children, the ski trip from hell, finances, and seizures to worry about, I could see no way out. The usually strong, resilient me had finally had enough. One Saturday night, when Bob and his girlfriend Carol had taken Robert and Kristen for the weekend, I hit bottom. After all I'd done to raise them and keep them safe, another woman was enjoying this beautiful weekend with my children. I was jealous of her–she was pretty, with long brown hair, nice clothes, and an important job. Meanwhile, I felt like an ugly duckling, barely holding things together, missing work to see to Kristen's needs, not eating–I was down to 100 pounds–and unable to find time to care for myself. I felt hopeless. Bob had the money and could afford to sue me for the children; I had nothing but a heavily mortgaged store, an ugly highly-mortgaged raised ranch with olive green shag carpet, an old car which still wasn't paid for, and a dead dog. I saw no way that I could meet Kristen's increasing medical needs and work at the same time. I saw no way that I could afford to send my academically gifted son to college, even with Bob paying half.

Bob had rented a place at Kennebunk Beach and had the kids for the whole weekend of the Fourth of July. I'll admit that I drove by his rental when he wasn't around to check it out. I even peeked in a window once, but I instantly regretted it. There on his dresser was a framed 8x10 photo of Carol. That quick stab of pain was what I deserved for being nosy.

As darkness descended that July night, Woodside Drive was quiet. I sat on the orange plaid living room couch and listened for the far away booms of the fireworks at the beach. Then I went to the front window to try and see the flickers of rockets over the treetops. I sighed. Why were holidays always sad for me? Then it hit me that this was how I felt over 30 years ago in Newington. It was the night everyone else was having fun at the fireworks, but I was a little girl being punished. Why, as an adult, did I still feel as if I was being punished?

I put myself to bed that night after taking the whole bottle of Lorazepam that had been prescribed for my anxiety. I loved my children to the moon and thought maybe Bob was right that they would be better off with attractive, successful Carol and well-off "Rob" than with me. Exhausted and aching with hurt, I just wanted to escape.

I woke up in the emergency room at Southern Maine Medical Center with Nancy and my parents standing over me. Thankfully, Nancy and an old Arundel friend, John Goddard, had stopped by to check on me and when I didn't answer the door, let themselves in and called an ambulance. I must have been out for a while as my parents, who lived in Andover, Massachusetts had driven all the way up to Biddeford before I woke up. The only thing I remember is the ER doctors asking if I wore contact lenses.

I was admitted to the hospital under the care of Dr. Collins. I just wanted to sleep. After four or five days of little progress, he looked me in the eye and said, "Cheryl, if you don't get it together, Bob Underwood is going to take your children." That was all I needed to hear. That was the turning point. I was determined that Bob and Carol were *never* going to take my children from me. Not after all we'd been through together.

I was so glad that Nancy and John checked on me that evening. I know that martyrdom is not a solution. It's a permanent fix to a temporary problem. I was ashamed of having ever considered it. I never wanted to hurt my parents and children in that way; I was just too scared and exhausted that night to think of options. Now I know that there are always options. Life is too precious. I should have reached out instead.

When I got home, Nancy was my savior. Somehow, she always found time for me, her big sister. I don't know how she did it with everything else on her plate. Nancy helped me with Kristen when the seizures overwhelmed me, babysat when I needed a break, told me stupid jokes to make me laugh, and listened to me cry hour after hour as I retold every detail of Bob's betrayal ad nauseum.

When she wasn't helping me out, Nancy taught school, raised Ken alone, shoveled snow, and still managed to roast a turkey every week to donate to the fundraising suppers for the school band. During that time, Nancy and I held each other up through numerous challenges. I don't think I could have made it through without her.

It's difficult to explain what it's like to parent a child with special needs. Some days are hell, especially with sensory and emotional overload often ending in meltdowns. When Kristen was young, I could only use the vacuum cleaner when she was at school, and I couldn't use cleaners containing bleach or ammonia. The sound of the vacuum and the smell of the cleaners would overwhelm her. But while it can be hell dealing with the fallout, it likely starts because Kristen is trying to escape her own hell in those moments. She reacts atypically to touch, smells, and loud noises.

I, like so many parents caring for a child with significant disabilities, struggled to hold the rest of the family together while just barely hanging on myself. The emotional needs of Kristen's brother Robert, a great kid, a high achiever, an Eagle Scout, sometimes got lost in the confusion of seizures, meltdowns, trips to the ER, and the unpredictability of our lives. I know that this has taken a toll on him, especially since he, like me, is the oldest, which comes with its own sometimes-unspoken responsibilities. Bob had breaks—his many late nights at work, golf outings, and frequent business trips—Robert and I didn't. Sometimes I wonder if part of the reason Bob left was that he could no longer cope with the stress and limitations that having a child with a disability placed on our lives: no willing babysitters, no romantic weekends away, no travel, always being on alert for seizures. Kristen couldn't help it, I could barely handle it, and Bob couldn't handle it at all. When he chose to leave, he divorced both of us. I had to find the strength, the resilience to get through this alone.

In addition to her epilepsy, Kristen was diagnosed with obsessive-compulsive disorder. Sometimes it was about the order of things. Kristen stacked up the DVDs she wanted to watch in the order she planned to watch them. Other times it was about collecting things.

She had difficulty resisting the urge to collect money, business cards, wallets, tea bags, math books, mints, and... ants. She knew just how things needed to be in her world; disrupting that order would lead to a meltdown. Kristen didn't choose these behaviors; they chose her. It broke my heart to watch her struggle every day.

One day, Nancy and I were shopping in Bradlees, and I told Kristen that she could pick out one item to purchase. She chose a math workbook. When we got to the register, Kristen insisted that she pay with her own money. She opened the coin portion of her pink My Little Pony wallet and out marched a contingent of ants determined to make their way across the counter toward the cashier.

I never knew quite what to expect when Nancy and I took Kristen out, but this was a new one. My cheeks were burning as customers gathered around to look, whispering things to the effect of, "Oh my God, those are real ants!" Meanwhile the cashier turned on the flashing light at her register, which I assumed meant she was calling for management backup. Hopefully a SWAT team wouldn't be next!

I fished a tissue out of my purse, corralled the ants into it, and squished them before I tossed the whole colony into the plastic waste-basket beneath the register stand. Kristen started crying. Apparently, these were not just collectibles, but her tiny friends. Everyone was staring, the light continued to blink, and the store manager was running in our direction. I handed the cashier a few dollars for the book and thanked her. Then Nancy and I dragged Kristen away from the scene of the mass insecticide as fast as we could.

Probably our most memorable shopping trip with Kristen occurred at Walmart. We had just checked out, and I asked Nancy if she would keep an eye on Kristen while I ran to the nearby ladies' room. Cell phones were just coming on the market then, and at the front of the store was a Verizon booth, similar to the booths often seen at street fairs or farmer's markets. There was a desk in the middle, a folding fencelike structure around the edge, and a bright yellow canopy over the top.

When I came out of the ladies' room, I heard a commotion. A portion of the Verizon booth was down, and the canopy had fallen onto the salesman's desk. I just knew Kristen had something to do with this before I even saw Nancy pulling Kristen out from under a piece of the canopy. Nancy was using her teacher's voice saying, "Kristen Underwood! You're too big to do things like this!"

Nancy explained later that as soon as I went around the corner to the restroom, Kristen spotted a big pile of business cards, one of her very favorite collectibles. Since they were out of reach on the salesman's desk, she dove over the fence to get them, taking part of the canopy with her.

When I approached to survey more of the scene, the young Verizon representative looked stunned. He was sitting at his desk staring straight ahead, as if he still hadn't been able to make sense of what had just happened. Heck, I don't blame him. It's not every day that a young woman in her favorite flowered dress jumped the fence and dove into your display, leaving you pinned to a desk with part of a canopy resting on your head. Red-faced and embarrassed, I rushed Kristen out to the car. I didn't think I would be laughing about this day any time soon.

Thankfully, the next couple of years were quieter. I was teaching Robert to drive in my red Ford Escort, which was a stick. The first few days of "Mom's Driving School" were spent bumping and jerking our way around Woodside Drive, until he finally got the hang of it. Kristen liked her new pink room. She spent hours sitting on the olive-green shag carpet, playing stories on her little portable record player. She loved Batman and Robin for all its otherworldly sound effects. Kristen also loved Sesame Street records, and she was particular about the order in which she listened to them. While Kristen was entertained, I scrubbed, painted, and wallpapered. Woodside Drive was beginning to look like home.

There were still some emotional times as we coped with changes and losses. Kristen was having multiple seizures a day, some long enough that I would have to call 911. I learned my lesson about driving her to the hospital myself. In an attempt to keep her safe while I was driving, I rear-ended another car in front of the Kennebunk Post Office.

An officer ran over from the police station across the street and saw Kristen seizing in the back seat. He had me pull my car over and put Kristen and I in his car. Then he sped the three of us to the hospital with his siren wailing. For me, it was just another day.

Once Bob moved to Chicago, he didn't see Robert and Kristen often. When they did visit, flying them there was a nightmare with Kristen's disabilities. I needed to pack up all of her medications and instructions, and that in and of itself was a huge job. And what if Carol couldn't handle her behaviors? In spite of my worry, I would get her on the plane and belt her in. Unfortunately, that meant that Robert was stuck with the responsibility of caring for his sister during the flight.

What if she needed to use the bathroom? What if she had a seizure? What if her behavior became out of control? What could I expect her brother to do then? One time, Kristen acted up before the flight even took off. The flight attendants asked me to follow them down the jetway. Then they asked me to remove Kristen from the plane. Life was a little better in some ways, but it was still far from easy.

The three of us—Robert, Kristen, and I—had our first Christmas alone in 1986. We went to a local farm, cut down a big tree, and decorated it with some of the Shiny Brite ornaments I had hung on the tree as a child. If I tried really hard, I could overlook the ugly carpeting by thinking of it as grass, sunning itself under the tree in all its olive-green ugliness. Nancy, Ken, Mom, and Dad came for Christmas dinner. After the tumult of the past two years, this was the most peaceful Christmas I could hope for. I was thankful for a much-needed quiet, holy night.

CHAPTER 22

# *"Call Me Maybe"*

## Carly Rae Jepsen

Kennebunk, Maine, 1987

By the spring of 1987, we were back in a routine–school for the kids and Village Greetings for me. I purchased the popular Kennebunk gift and card shop in the summer of 1984. With Kristen having such frequent seizures, I could no longer continue teaching at Scarborough High School, which was 40 minutes away from her school. I loved teaching English, but it wasn't fair to my students to be summoned to leave school to meet Kristen's medical needs as often as I did.

I purchased the shop by reluctantly taking an early withdrawal from my teachers' retirement account, my only asset. Village Greetings was perfect because it was near our home, Kristen's school, her doctor's office, and the hospital. Even better, if I did need to run out unexpectedly, there were two older responsible ladies to cover for me; both Charlotte and Louise had worked there for years.

Charlotte and I were working in the store late one afternoon in March of 1987 when the bell on the door jingled. In walked an attractive man about my age wearing gray dress slacks and a navy Members Only jacket. He was medium height, with curly dark blond hair and a great smile. Needless to say, he'd barely made it to the card rack before I swooped in to ask if I could help. I hadn't been dating since Bob left two years before and I wasn't looking. Between my kids, my home, seizures, finances, and the store, I had quite enough on my plate.

Men were in and out of the shop all the time, and I didn't know why this particular guy drew me in as he did. When he replied to my "Hello,"

I realized I even loved his soft, kind voice. He told me he was looking for a card for his girlfriend. Darn it! But then he told me she'd just broken up with him. *Ooh...* I showed him Easter cards, "thinking of you" cards, funny cards, and sad cards, selecting only the ugliest ones with the sappiest messages on purpose. Unfortunately, we didn't have one that said, "Sorry, but I just met someone else." I would have definitely shown him that.

I asked him if he'd like a cup of coffee from our "coffee corner" near the register before I realized that today's pot was empty. I suggested he come back for coffee another day. He said he just might, and if he did he would bring some coffee to share, maybe an exotic blend. At the register, he paid Charlotte, took one glance back, smiled, and left.

I ran to the glass front door as I yelled a stream of questions to Charlotte, "Do you know him? Is he from Kennebunk? Have you seen him before?" Thank goodness there were no other customers in the store while I was behaving like a crazy woman. Charlotte was a plain spoken, gray-haired "Maine-a" woman in her 60s who'd lived her whole life in Kennebunk. She knew everyone. Charlotte joined me at the door so we could see if the car he got into had Maine license plates. It did! That was promising. We could work with that.

I was in love. At first sight. I didn't believe in that before, but there was no other way to explain how I felt. My head was spinning, and Charlotte made me sit down. I hoped he would actually come back someday. I felt a mix of happiness and sadness. I was happy that I had finally met "him" but sad that he was gone. I also realized that I didn't even know his name.

Kristen's seizures became more frequent over the next few days, and she went into status epilepticus. Status is a type of seizure longer than five minutes, more than one seizure in a five-minute period, or not returning to a normal level of consciousness between episodes. After long periods of status, the heart can give out and brain damage or death can occur. It's a medical emergency. Kristen was rushed to our local hospital in Biddeford before she was sent to Boston City Hospital for further evaluation.

Finally, she was transferred to the Kennedy Memorial Hospital for even more evaluation. I had to leave Kristen in the hands of the hospital staff overnight because Robert was home alone. Then I commuted each day from Maine to Boston to be with Kristen and meet with her doctors. It was a stressful time and a hellish schedule, but I had no choice.

Since I was unable to be at Village Greetings to keep an eye out for "the coffee man," as we had begun referring to him, Charlotte and I hatched a plan. We decorated an empty Maxwell House coffee can with bright green paper and glued a pink flamingo to the front. The flamingo was likely wishful thinking since we were having a cold, rainy spring in Maine. Inside the coffee can, I placed a note for the coffee man, just in case he returned while I was in Boston. I left the can in the capable hands of Charlotte. She knew what to do!

*Hi!*

*Just my luck—you finally bring the exotic coffee,*
*and I'm at the hospital with a sick child.*
*I'm sure Charlotte will love it. (Lucky her!)*
*Hope you stop back again—it was fun!*

*Cheryl Underwood*

Of course, when he did come back, bringing with him his promised pound of exotic grind, I was at the hospital in Boston. Charlotte knew how much I hoped to see this man again. With my permission, she gave him my address and phone number, and she told him a little bit about Kristen and what I was going through with her epilepsy. Needless to say, I was hoping he would call me, maybe?

On a rainy Tuesday evening in late March, I pulled into the driveway at Woodside Drive after the long commute from Boston. As I thought about what I would make Robert for supper, I noticed something on the front stoop. It was an Easter Lily and, after the lousy day I'd had, it made me smile. I sat on the front stoop, ripped open the floral envelope, and read the message. "I hope your daughter is okay," signed, "The Coffee Man." I sat on those wet steps crying. I don't know how long. Nice things just didn't happen to me very often.

When he finally called, I learned that his name was Hank. I liked that name, it was strong. He was from Portland, a "Munjoy Hill Boy" who grew up in Portland's iconic Little Italy. He asked me out and I accepted! On the following Saturday evening, the night before Easter Sunday, he would pick me up at 8:00 p.m. We'd go to Hu Shang in Portland for Szechuan food and maybe some dancing after.

Our first date involved a lot of tap dancing on my part to make it work. Kristen was moved back to Southern Maine Medical Center in Biddeford where she would stay through Easter. Before my date, I needed to help Kristen color eggs, our Easter tradition. Feeling anxious with both guilt and anticipation, I headed to the hospital a few hours early wearing the red knit dress I had chosen for the date. My canvas L.L. Bean bag contained a dozen hard boiled white eggs, an egg coloring kit, and a bottle of vinegar.

When I arrived I found Kristen awake in her bed, tugging at restraints. I'd never given the hospital permission to restrain her and I was upset. The nurses explained they didn't have the staff to be with her every moment. Although she was being monitored, they needed to know that she wouldn't hurt herself if she had a seizure or if she tried to get out of bed by herself.

I called Kristen's doctor, Denise Miller, who had become a friend, as well as Kristen's pediatrician. Denise was also upset about the restraints and ordered the hospital staff to remove them immediately. If Kristen wasn't safe when I couldn't be there, she said the hospital would have to hire a minder to sit with her. I faced the same guilt that tortured me so many times in the past, not knowing how I could possibly be in two places at once.

With the restraints removed, I wheeled Kristen to the playroom where we had fun coloring Easter eggs for the next hour. We even shared some with her nurses. When we finished, I tucked her back into bed and waited until the minder had arrived and she fell asleep. Then, I dashed to my car and got back to Kennebunk just in time. I ran to the bathroom, threw on some lipstick, pinched my cheeks, and was as ready as I could be for my first date in 20 years.

# CHAPTER 23

# "*Lady in Red*"

## Chris de Burgh

Kennebunkport, Maine
Portland, Maine, 1987 - 1988

When Hank arrived at my door with wine and flowers, he looked as handsome as I remembered him. On the way to Portland, "Lady in Red" played on the car radio, which seemed fitting considering the red dress I had chosen to wear. The evening at Hu Shang was fun. We had drinks at the bar, ate Szechuan shrimp and chicken, and danced for a while downstairs.

Hank was great company, we found that we had a lot to talk about, and I felt comfortable with him. That was especially good since I embarrassed myself by spilling my drink on the coat of the lady sitting next to us at the bar. When we left, we drove up Munjoy Hill and stopped at the top of Portland's Eastern Prom to watch the lights of the city glimmering over Casco Bay. I was smitten. I already admitted to loving this man at first sight. After our date, I even liked him. A lot.

Hank and I continued to date that spring, through the summer, and into the fall of 1987. He was a distance runner and an excellent tennis player. I was neither. Even though I took a semester of tennis at Russell Sage, I wasn't good at it. Being chosen as a center for the girls' basketball team at Bedford Junior High in Westport had been the height of my athletic career. Thankfully, Hank was a patient teacher, and we had fun hitting tennis balls together. Kristen sat courtside on a blanket in the shade with a basket of toys and a bottle of water, and I was beginning to remember how to relax.

Christmas Eve on Munjoy Hill was like nothing this English-Irish girl had ever experienced! Robert and Kristen came with me and were quickly swept up by Hank's huge family. They accepted and welcomed all of us. Hank's Italian mother, Elinor, had been one of 12 children. Some were born in Benevento, Italy and some were born in Portland after their parents arrived in the US. Robert got to know all of "the uncles" and "the brothers" quickly. Hank's mother showered Kristen with hugs. Elinor took her Catholic faith seriously and lived up to this Matthew 25:40 parable: "Truly, I say to you, as you did to one of the least of these my brothers, you did to me."

On Christmas Eve, "Ma" cooked the traditional meal of the seven fishes. Each of Hank's 10 brothers and sisters, as well as cousins, aunts, and uncles brought dishes to share. Plates of pasta were topped with homemade sauce, meatballs were filled with pine nuts, and braciole with raisins. Hank's sister roasted potatoes with peppers, onions, and Italian sausage. Huge loaves of crusty bread arrived, fresh from Micucci's, the nearby Italian market.

Dessert included homemade rum cake surrounded by huge platters of Italian cookies: neapolitans, wedding, lemon, and amaretto. There were also cannolis and pizzelles. The house was filled with so many people that the family sat at Ma's dining room table in shifts. Since Ma lived on the second floor of a triple decker built in the last century, I always wondered why the floor didn't collapse under the weight of such a huge family on Christmas Eve. Maybe love held it up.

Hank and I dated exclusively for a year. One cloudy early-spring day when Village Greetings was quiet, he asked if I'd like to have lunch with him at the local Chinese restaurant, Mei Le Wah. After our meal, the waiter brought the typical plate of fortune cookies, one each. Cracking mine open, I pulled out the thin paper fortune. It read: "I love you. Will you marry me?" I hesitated for a moment, wondering if this was real, I looked up. Hank was smiling at me with a questioning look. Of course, I said, "Yes!" I had been in love with Hank since he wandered into my store over a year ago.

After all I'd been through in the past few years, I could only sit there and cry as he placed the engagement ring on my finger. Hank was my perfect other half. He was easygoing, and I was a bit OCD. He was soft spoken. I talked a lot and could swear like a sailor. Hank got a task done quickly, while I was a slow and methodical perfectionist.

We had a lot in common, yet we balanced each other. Hank already accepted Robert and Kristen as if they were his own. That was not an easy commitment to make, especially with Kristen's medical and behavioral needs. I was getting to know his two grown children who, ironically, had similar first names to mine: Rob and Crissy. I was excited to get back to Village Greetings to proclaim our engagement to the world, starting with Charlotte and Lousie. I was still a little shocked: good things didn't usually happen to me.

August of 1988, a couple months before Hank and I exchanged vows, my youngest sister Joanne and her fiance Mark had a fairytale wedding in Kennebunkport. Joanne wore a dress from Priscilla of Boston—who, Mom never let us forget, designed Grace Kelly's wedding gown. The dress Joanne chose was not white but "blush;" it had a very slight pink cast. The dress was absolutely beautiful but Mom, still a little concerned that it was not pure white, was quick to inform us all that blush was close enough to white to still be virginal.

Mark was the boy next door. Everyone liked him; he was friendly, thoughtful, and easygoing. At about 5'10" with light brown hair and Irish eyes, he was a hard worker, non-judgemental, and always fun to be with. He often played the straight man to Joanne's over-the-topism, rolling his eyes and chuckling in a good-natured way. Mark was the kind of brother-in-law everyone wished they had. He was generous to a fault, and always the first to offer to help whenever there was a need.

The wedding was held at St. Anne's by the Sea, the Bush family chapel on the ocean in Kennebunkport. Joanne arrived with Dad in a horse-drawn carriage adorned with *blush* roses. After the ceremony, the carriage transported the newlyweds down Ocean Avenue and through the center of the 'Port to their reception venue, the Grist Mill Restaurant. The tablecloths and napkins were blush, as were the floral centerpieces at each table. Instead of a DJ, Joanne and Mark had the most popular dance band around: Straight Lace. They were sought after and hard to book, but for Joanne, anything was possible.

Early in her marriage to Mark, Joanne decided that she didn't want to have children. This left more time for their travels, a bigger decorating budget, and lots of free time for concerts and barhopping, which she and Mark both enjoyed. Joanne always liked nice things and was willing to pay for them. As a student, she walked to Boston's upscale Newbury Street to get her hair done and check out the local boutiques. After she established herself as a physical therapist in the Boston area, Joanne could afford more luxuries—a lot more luxuries than sisters one, two, and three, who had all had children, taught school, and been through divorces.

Joanne and Mark took many vacations to Mexico and the American Southwest, where they fell in love with desert colors, cacti, pottery, folk art, and its whimsy—even the rust. They built a home on a secluded wooded lot in a suburb of Boston called Londonderry, right over the state line in New Hampshire. Joanne converted their Londonderry home into a "casa hermosa" worthy of any high-end decor magazine that features home interiors in Arizona or New Mexico. She inherited Mom's artistic skill for interior decorating and had a budget Mom could have only wished for. Joanne's long-term goal was a home in Arizona where she could display her collections in their cultural context.

In October of that same year, Hank and I were married at St. Joseph's Catholic Church in Portland at noon on a rainy Saturday. Folk wisdom holds that rain on your wedding day is good luck, and for our marriage that has been true. I wore an ivory tea-length lace dress by Jessica McClintock. Hank wore a gray suit with a red tie as a nod to the red dress I wore on our first date.

*Lady in Red.*

Our wedding Mass was beautiful. We loved Father Steve, the white-haired Franciscan priest who married us. An upside to the devastation I felt when going through the annulment meant I could marry Hank in the church; an unanticipated happy consequence. My son Robert walked me down the aisle and did a reading from Corinthians 13, and Hank's son, also named Robert, was our best man.

Everyone in both of our families was there to celebrate, as well as friends from our Gourmet Group, the Epilepsy Foundation, and our respective pasts. I was especially pleased that Diana flew in from Baltimore to join us. Our wedding reception was hosted at DiMillo's Floating Restaurant in Portland, the legacy of another Italian family who immigrated to Munjoy Hill in the early 20th century. My heart was full when Kristen danced with Hank to "My Girl," which the band dedicated to her.

Father Steve and my Grampa Smith would have gotten along well, both full of Irish bluster and both welcoming any chance to be on stage. Who knew that Father Steve enjoyed a party as much as the next guy? He surprised us by walking up to the mic and singing "If" by Bread in a beautiful tenor voice:

*If a man could be two places at one time*
*I'd be with you*
*Tomorrow and today*
*Beside you all the way*
*If the world should stop revolving*
*Spinning slowly down to die*
*I'd spend the end with you*
*And when the world was through*
*Then one by one the stars would all go out*
*Then you and I would simply fly away*

It was as if everyone could just feel the intensity of our love and the second chance for happiness it offered both of us. Father Steve's song to us, unexpected as it was, meant the world to me.

I'll never forget our last dance. We were encircled by everyone we loved in a big musical group hug as we swayed to "Lady in Red." That moment on the boat was magical. It felt like a dream. As Frank L. Baum put it: "But it wasn't a dream. It was a place. And you and you and you and you were all there." And we simply flew away.

# CHAPTER 24

# "*Photographs and Memories*"

## Jim Croce

Portland, Maine
Jackson, New Hampshire, 1988 - 1990

In 1988, when Hank and I were newly married, we sold my little raised ranch on Woodside Drive in Kennebunk. I was not going to miss the wall-to-wall olive green shag carpet and harvest gold appliances. We purchased a contemporary waterfront condo, #109, at Chandler's Wharf in Portland. Hank grew up on Portland's Munjoy Hill and we both loved the city. Chandler's Wharf was literally built on an old wharf that extended out into Portland Harbor, providing amazing views from all sides.

After Dad retired, our parents joined us in Portland. They liked the harbor views from our condo so much that they purchased #310 just down the way. Dad loved spending hours cataloging the boats that came in and out of the harbor. Joanne and Mark still lived in New Hampshire but missed Maine and frequently came up to spend weekends with Mom and Dad. They loved the bar scene in Portland's Old Port and knew most of the bartenders in town by name.

One summer day, Kristen was home with me recuperating from oral surgery, and Nancy stopped by for the afternoon. We decided to enjoy two tall glasses of Tab, Nancy's signature drink, out on the deck. Nancy and I relaxed and watched the boats go by in the busy harbor.

Kristen was content watching episodes of her favorite shows, *Sesame Street* and *Mr. Rogers*, right inside in the living room. I kept an eye on her through the sliding glass doors, a necessity with her seizure disorder. At one point as we sat there talking, we saw Kristen walk to the inside of the sliding door and... What? She turned the lock!

I tried the door, but it didn't budge. We yelled through the double-paned glass, instructing Kristen on how to unlock the door. She didn't understand what she had just done, and it was upsetting her, which can bring on seizures. I convinced Kristen to go back to watching her shows. Nancy and I were stranded on a 6x12-foot deck hanging over Portland Harbor with no way off! Unfortunately, both of our cellphones were inside. If Kristen had a seizure, we couldn't get to her. We had to think of a way to get back inside.

Our condo was across the marina from DiMillo's Floating Restaurant, where we had had our wedding reception, and Nancy and I thought we might attract the attention of someone dining on the deck. But then what? They might see us, but they wouldn't be able to hear us. Just then, we saw the *Bay View Lady* sightseeing boat leaving the dock. Nancy and I both got the same idea: when the boat full of tourists slowly made its way by, we yelled down to the captain for help.

"Help! Help!" we hollered. We eventually got the attention of the captain and almost every other boater, tourist, diner, and shopper in the Old Port. Nancy and I screamed that we were locked out and asked the captain to call Dad, who had a key to our condo. We yelled his phone number and asked the captain to hurry. Aside from the fact that there were 50 or 60 tourists and one confused skipper looking up at us as if we were crazy women, this could work!

About 10 minutes later, we heard Dad unlocking the door. He wasn't happy. We could just make out his raised voice asking, "Kristen Underwood, what did you do?" Needless to say, Grampa wasn't angry, nor were we. It was impossible to be angry at Kristen's behaviors for long because most of them were not intentional; she just didn't know. Once Dad rescued us from the deck, we all took one look at Kristen, looking totally innocent, and burst out laughing. Nancy and I traded in our Tabs for gin and tonics. Grampa joined us.

Nancy met Aaron on a blind date. Aaron was not at all like her first husband Kit, who left her to raise their son on her own. Kit was a tough guy who hunted deer, had a CB radio, and drove big muddy trucks. Aaron was a soft-spoken banker of average height with dark brown hair and a nice smile. Nancy spent lots of time with Aaron over the next few years after their blind date, finding that they enjoyed many of the same things: Christmas, summer theater, being with friends, and going on road trips in rural Maine and New Hampshire. I was happy for her; she had been alone for a long time.

One winter, Hank and I decided to give downhill skiing a try. It was the early 1990s, and we were in our mid-40s. We signed up for a lesson at Black Mountain in Jackson, New Hampshire, with a ruggedly handsome instructor named Tom. He was about our age, with a great sense of humor and the patience of a saint. Once we got the hang of snowplowing and made it down the beginner hill a few times without falling, we were hooked. We thought, "Why should we sweat our way over the rugged cross-country trails when gravity will do the work for us?" From then on, we were downhill skiers.

Tom became a good friend, and we learned that, in addition to skiing, he was also a realtor. He even happened to have a new listing right on Black Mountain near his own home, steps from the trails. Of course, we had to see it! The ski house had a stone chimney and big deck overlooking the valley below. There were built-in benches in the entryway for removing ski boots and walls of pegs for hanging skis.

Up a few stairs there were more mountain views and a large open space that housed the kitchen, dining, and living areas, plus a huge stone fireplace. Down a few steps from the entry were three bedrooms, two furnished with multiple "This End Up" bunk beds for kids and guests. One sported an original Atari arcade game called *Gorf*, which we knew even the adult kids who visited would love. The price was right and before the month was out, the ski house was ours. Now, we were officially ready to start going upta camp!

Everyone was welcome at our ski house on Black Mountain, and it soon became a hub for family and friends who all brought wine or Bailey's and a dish or two to share. In the winter, we skied or rode down Black Mountain on our L.L. Bean toboggan or one of the two "suicide sleds" the previous owners had left for us. They were trim, fast, and equipped with full-size steering wheels.

After greasing the runners, Hank and his buddy, Mark, became experts at surviving ever-more-daring sled runs down the mountain. One particularly snowy winter, they made a DIY luge run from our second-floor deck to the woods below. They used our hose to coat it with water, which immediately froze, and rode the suicide sleds down it at lightning speeds, whooping and hollering with joy the whole way.

When they were finally worn out, Hank and Mark gathered by the fire to enjoy a bottle of their very own *Number 9* beer. Earlier that winter, they had decided to try their hand at brewing beer. Although they swore they followed the instructions, something went wrong and the beer never settled. It kept fermenting, kept brewing, kept seeping out of the bottle tops all winter. To drink a *Number 9*, you had to be fast, before the foam got you. That beer quenched thirsts and provided enough laughs to last until spring.

My sisters loved coming upta camp at Black Mountain, especially Nancy, who brought Aaron. Neither of them were skiers, but they loved all the trappings of the ski culture. They hung out with hot chocolates and watched skiers coast down the trails, checked out the shops in North Conway, met us for après ski, and sat around the fireplace telling stories back at the ski house.

One day, Aaron decided to try downhill skiing on the bunny slope, with me as his instructor. He made it about 10 or 15 feet before being gripped by a panic attack. He ripped off his skis and walked off the mountain. We named the trail he made from the mountain to Whitney

Hill Road "Aaron Pass." I even placed a wooden sign there memorializing the event. He treasured the aging paper Black Mountain ski pass that hung from the zipper on his jacket for the next few years. He joked that it made him feel like part of the "in crowd" on the mountain.

Nancy's son Ken loved to ski and was a frequent guest in the winter. My son Robert sometimes brought friends from Colby College with him for the weekend. In 1993, Kristen celebrated her 18th birthday with me and Hank in Jackson. We took her up on the Loon Mountain gondola and later visited the horses at the base. She loved petting the horses and feeding them carrots. That evening, we dressed up and went to the Christmas Farm Inn for a fancy birthday dinner. We wanted Kristen to feel special. I think she did. She had been through so much, including two jaw surgeries and frequent seizures, to become the beautiful 18-year-old young woman who accompanied us that special night. I was so proud of her.

One summer, my sister Andi and her three children flew in from Arizona to spend a few days with us in Jackson. Her youngest, Kaylin, was only five or six years old and loved to entertain us around the campfire with original stories. With her vivid imagination and enthusiastic style of delivery, we looked forward to hearing them around the campfire as she sat upon the official "Story Stump" Hank cut and carved for her. I still treasure the photograph I took at that moment.

Mom and Dad often found an excuse to take a ride to Jackson.

*Kaylin on the Story Stump, Jackson, NH*

They enjoyed the ski house and going antiquing in North Conway. We loved having them join us for potluck meals followed by campfires. It was good to see Mom finally relax in the outdoors—and to hear the infrequent sound of her laughter. Dad especially seemed to enjoy those campfire moments, sitting under the stars with his family all around him. I treasured those memories, grateful that the ski house brought our family together.

Years later, after we sold the ski house, we would still meet Robert with his wife and kids at Whitney's Inn to stay and ski. It's good to know that our grandchildren will have happy memories of Black Mountain and maybe, someday, bring their own children to the Mount Washington Valley to ski.

*Ski House, Jackson, NH.*

# CHAPTER 25

# *"Summer Place"*

## Andy Williams

Portland, Maine
Unity, Maine
Jackson, New Hampshire
1995

Hank and I loved walking from Chandler's Wharf to restaurants and shops in the historic Old Port or just sitting and watching the boats sail in and out of the marina below our deck. Eventually, as beautiful as it was, it felt as if Chandler's Wharf might be too small; we wondered if we had downsized too soon. Both of us missed having a yard and a garage with storage for things like bikes, skis, and canoes. Those were nonexistent at the condo. The three flights of stairs to get to her room in the loft were a challenge for Kristen when she came home and made it difficult for us to monitor her seizures at night, even with the use of a baby monitor.

At about that time, I drove through a new Portland neighborhood named Cottage Park on my way home from the grocery store. Often, I found myself driving through neighborhoods I hadn't seen before to look at the houses. I never knew when I'd see another one that would beg to be added to my collection. Cottage Park featured some of the most unusual residential architecture I'd seen. The homes were contemporary yet reminiscent of the shingle style used for generations in upscale cottages along the Maine coast. I called Hank from my car and begged him to come meet me. Research revealed that the builder/architect, Ric Weinschenk, was planning a new development of similar homes in Portland on land featuring distant views of Casco Bay.

We met with Ric for lunch and asked if he could design a friendly and welcoming shingle-style home for us. We wanted a big garage and lots of storage. He said that the words welcoming and friendly, as well as the way Hank and I described ourselves, reminded him of circles instead of stark angles. While we sipped our coffee, Ric proceeded to sketch the perfect home for us on his paper napkin.

Over the next few months, design details were finalized and construction began. When completed, our home at 65 Summer Place was so unique that it was featured on the cover of *Better Homes and Gardens*. I loved our house, especially its round library, where shelves of my favorite books alternated with windows that overlooked Casco Bay.

Under each window was a window seat sporting an upholstered cushion and coral throw pillows I'd sewn. The exterior of each window was framed by tall decorative grasses which made a brushing sound against the glass when the wind came off the ocean. Ric, who knew I loved sewing, included a craft room with a sink and a big built-in work table. Even in the summer, when our decks beckoned, I spent most of my time in that little craft room or library.

On June 29th of 1996, the day of our Mom and Dad's 50th wedding anniversary, Nancy and Aaron married in the gazebo at Summer Place. I was Nancy's matron of honor and Hank stood up for Aaron. Nancy and I took what was a fashion risk for us and wore big flowered summer hats ala Kentucky Derby. Making the day more memorable, Dad's Aunt Eunice, the last surviving Parker sister, came to Nancy's wedding. It was a glorious day!

Not long after Hank and I moved in, Nancy and Aaron had Ric build them a house next door. It was great to have not just my sister, but my best friend, living next door. Being so close meant we spent even more time together. We had fun helping each other decorate our new homes;

Nancy's in blues and yellows and mine in golds and corals. We also found comfort in venting to each other about teaching, family, and politics, working on our dollhouses, and watching the Saturday night decorating shows on HGTV. I spent innumerable hours sitting with Nancy in the 1950s-style booth that Ric built in her kitchen. We curled up there and talked for hours over cans of Tab. During difficult times, when I was hanging by an emotional thread, those talks kept me sane.

*Christmas Tree Hunt – Aaron, Nancy, Hank, & Cheryl.*

In our warmest L.L. Bean outdoor gear, Hank and I joined Nancy and Aaron each December, heading up Route 1 to Waldoboro to cut our Christmas trees. Most years our grandsons, Robert and Brian, joined us as well. The tree field was on a working farm owned by Scott, with a big barn housing horses, cows, and chickens. Scott's multi-generational family lived in the white Cape next to the barn and all of them were involved at Christmas. The women made wreaths while the men took care of the Christmas trees.

After turning off Route 1 and parking at the farm, we trudged along a dirt track down the long hill to the pasture; acres of Christmas trees spread out before us. Once we finally found the perfect tree, Hank cooked up a whole ceremony to accompany the cutting of it. We'd sing "O Christmas Tree" while taking turns with the bow-cut saw. When the tree began to fall, tradition dictated that we yell, "TIMBER!" Then Scott drove up in his hay wagon to transport the trees back up to the house. We jumped into the wagon too and sang Christmas carols as we chugged up the hill, our cold noses drinking in the festive smell of balsam—the ever-familiar scent of our childhood holiday season.

Getting the trees home was a challenge. With only seven-foot ceilings, Nancy didn't look for the tallest tree; she searched for the fullest tree she could find. Once our normal-sized tree and Nancy's monster tree were tied to the top of our 4Runner, branches of balsam cascaded down on all sides. This required Hank to steer by, peering through notches in a couple of well-placed boughs. We chuckled at the puzzled stares we received when we parked at Moody's Diner for our annual suppa' on the way home. Other diners surely wondered how we even got in and out of the vehicle. Hank's tree hunt was not for the faint of heart!

Nancy loved her mammoth trees, which she adorned with thousands of tiny white lights. If it weren't for the foliage that surrounded her little house, the glare from her Christmas trees blazing through the living room windows could probably be seen from as far away as Boston.

During the ice storm of 1998, both of our driveways were so slippery that walking to each other's houses proved impossible. There was no school, a welcome surprise for teachers and students alike, and I tried to shuffle over the ice to Nancy's to spend the day. It was so slippery that after just a few feet, I could go no farther without the certainty of breaking a limb. Thankfully, I got a brilliant idea: I'd drive over! I called Nancy to suggest that she open the garage door before I slipped into my trusty Subaru Forester. Then I successfully drove the 75 feet or so between our two garages without having to step a foot on the ice. Brilliant!

I made many friends among the faculty while I was teaching special education at Gorham High School in the 90s. The closest one, Sandra, became one of my very best friends. A few years older than me, Sandy had spent 39 years teaching Biology and AP Biology at GHS. She was already a legend since almost everyone in the small town of Gorham had studied under her at one time or another.

Sandy dressed her five-foot-tall figure well and always looked professional. While some might describe her shape as matronly, her energy and sense of style were anything but. That woman performed wardrobe magic with scarves! Sandy loved adventures, knew how to do any craft project I could conjure up, and was one of the most intelligent women I'd ever met. We became almost inseparable—sisters by choice.

Sandy's family, Mainers through and through, went "upta camp" all the time. In fact, they had more than one camp. Her husband had a camp or two, as did her grown son. They built the camps themselves in the woods of central Maine. In the fall, they used them to hunt deer and moose.

One weekend, Sandy and I had the opportunity to stay at her sister Jolene's camp on Unity Pond in Unity, Maine. Hidden from the dirt road by thick pines, it sat on a rock ledge right next to the lake. The small camp had been part of a church campground there early in the 20th century. The church camp concept originated during the 19th century, most notably through the Protestant Camp Meeting movement. This allowed people from sparsely populated areas like Unity to gather for preaching, prayer, and community, often camping out for several days at a time.

I loved Jolene's camp! Sandy and I talked, canoed, drank wine, and sat by the lake watching the red and orange sunsets. She showed me the Field of Dreams, Unity Pottery, Unity Theatre, the antique railroad station, and the campus of Unity College. We snacked on Indian samosas at the Saturday Farmer's Market and then enjoyed dinner at the Homestead, the only restaurant in town. I fell in love with Unity and couldn't wait to bring Hank back to Lake Winnecook, the official name of Unity Pond.

Hank fell in love with Unity too, so we decided to buy a camp on the Burnham side of the lake. We had sold our Jackson ski house and were anxious to start going upta camp again. Our new camp would be more of a summer camp than Jackson, with the lake and a little beach at our door. The property included four or five other camps along the lake, and a little clubhouse. Our Unity camp was located next to a little 9-hole golf course owned and maintained by the Reynolds family, who had lived on that land for generations. "Brother" and Connie Reynolds lived in the white Victorian home with their extended family right next door.

In addition to a small kitchen and two baths, our camp had big picture windows looking out over the lake, a huge stone fireplace, two bedrooms downstairs, and a quaint little loft bedroom above. With a brass bed! There was a deck on which to enjoy summer afternoons and a dock for fishing where we could tie up our canoe. As we lay in bed at night, we listened to the cries of the loons who nested in the reeds along the edge of the pond. They made some of the most beautiful and haunting sounds in nature. Camp Unity Pond was perfect, and we enjoyed as much time there as we could in the late 90s and early 2000s.

We were often joined at Unity by our young grandsons, Robert and Brian. They liked to make homemade donuts with Hank and walk up to the big house on Sunday mornings to bring some to "Brother" and Connie Reynolds. They learned to fish, swim, canoe, and golf there. We brought Kristen to camp too, and we converted our huge walk-in closet into a cozy little bedroom for her. This way she could sleep where we could hear her if she had a seizure.

In 2001, Andi's teenage daughter Keri spent the summer with us. She spent halcyon days eating cherry vanilla ice cream, her favorite. She helped me fold dozens of paper cranes for Robert and his Japanese fiance's upcoming American wedding, at which she was excited to be the maid of honor. I wrote a lengthy travel guide to the area, accompanied by color-coded maps, of course, for any visitors who came when we weren't there. Mom, Dad, Uncle Ed, and his wife Barbara drove up and enjoyed the camp. It made me happy to picture them enjoying that quiet time at the lake together, listening to the loons.

After a few years, we reluctantly decided to sell the camp. It needed a new septic system, and we didn't want to invest the money. Plus, we got tired of commuting. We quickly regretted our decision, especially whenever we drove through the area. We wished we had kept that camp.

When we spotted a small teardrop trailer right across the street from Kristen's group home with a "For Sale" sign on it, we decided to purchase it. It had been a couple of years, and we really missed camping. The little camper was my favorite color, orange crush, and it was the perfect size for the two of us. It had a double bed which folded up to make a settee, and a dinette during the day in its tiny kitchenette. We could still go to Jackson or Unity or wherever else we wanted, but now we would bring our camper with us.

Our grandsons, Robert and Brian, couldn't wait to join us on our camper adventures. They loved setting up their tent and sleeping bags just outside of our camper. It was close enough that they felt safe, but far enough away that they could stay up late thinking we wouldn't hear them. They especially liked our trips to Lost River Campground in North Woodstock, New Hampshire.

One day as we sat outside the camper eating lunch, there were suddenly frantic shouts warning us of a nearby "BEAR!" Scared, we hustled the boys into the camper and waited. We heard the bear rustling around our campsite. After he left, we saw that the bear had gotten into our big blue cooler, scattering the food and leaving deep teeth marks in its side. As we tucked our grandsons into their sleeping bags that night, Robert looked up and said, "Nanny, Grampy, this was the *best* day of my life!" We've kept that cooler as a reminder of our adventure with the black bear, but especially as a souvenir of "the best day" of little Robert's life.

Not long after our camper purchase, Joanne and Mark purchased their own camper, and we planned to go upta camp together. We booked adjoining sites on Horse Island in Raymond, New Hampshire. As the name implied, the island was surrounded by water and shaped like a horse. Horse Island was our favorite part of Pawtuckaway State Park because each wooded site had its own little beach on the lake.

Joanne liked glamping, decorating every inch of her campsite in addition to preparing exotic cocktails and elegant meals over the campfire. Long after Hank and I climbed into our sleeping bags at night, we could still hear Joanne setting up flamingos, fake palm trees, strings of lights, lanterns, sitting areas, and cooking paraphernalia around her campsite. She loved making the site homey, and it could last until the wee hours of the morning where you'd spot her with a cocktail in one hand, hammer in the other.

One summer I invited our Weight Watchers leader and dear friend Bernadette to visit us at Pawtuckaway for the day. We planned to take her on a boat ride, cook out, and just enjoy the afternoon outdoors. She was a thin woman (lost almost 100 pounds!), a little older than me, with a huge beehive of her signature stark white hair. She was also adventurous and had a great sense of humor. When Bernadette arrived at the campsite that morning, we were all helping Joanne inflate the blow-up two-man, or more accurately, two-*woman*, boat she had recently purchased at LL Bean. This was to be its maiden voyage. The whole time, during the direction reading, air pumping, and initial launch, Joanne's special (read: strong) cocktails were being served to campers and would-be sailors alike.

There are a few givens about camping with Joanne and Mark:

1. You'll never get cold; Mark has a campfire going from dawn to dusk;

2. You'll never go hungry; they bring tons of food with them;

3. You may need to crawl back to your campsite. Joanne fills her red Solo cups to the brim with strong camp cocktails.

They might look ladylike and tropical, but they really pack a punch. I seemed to forget that part every time we camped with them. And I neglected to warn poor 100-pounds-soaking-wet Bernadette before she joined us.

As the afternoon wore on and everyone had had a turn in the "SS Joanne," our hosts refilled our drinks and we sat around the campfire for cocktail hour. Which turned into two hours. I realized that Bernadette hadn't talked for a while. I looked over and noticed that she was slumped over in her camp chair, sound asleep. I got up to check on her and, when I couldn't rouse her, got worried. Figuring that a physical therapist was about as close to a doctor as we were going to get out here in the woods, I called Joanne to make sure Bernadette was okay. Joanne checked her breathing and pulse, but she couldn't wake Mary up either. Now I was getting scared.

The year before this fateful day, Hank and I traded in our little teardrop camper for a somewhat larger RV, a 17-foot Casita with a dinette that converted into a third bed. We enlisted the guys to help carry Bernadette, still in her lawn chair, over to our site. Thank goodness she had lost all that weight! As they struggled to carry her and the chair, I started crying, "Oh my god, we've killed my Weight Watchers leader!" It came out as a weird combination of laughter and tears and by now, Joanne had joined in. After good-naturedly rolling their eyes a few times, our husbands calmed us down and helped us get Bernadette into our camper and onto the little twin bed. We got a pillow, raised her head, removed her shoes, and covered her with a light blanket. Joanne checked again; she was still breathing. She had a pulse. I sat by her side for a while until I was sure she was okay, and then returned to the group, accepting another gin and tonic from Joanne to calm my nerves. And Bernadette? We never heard a peep out of her until she woke up in our camper the next morning, no worse for the wear, but wondering where the hell she was.

Whether it was a ski house, lake cottage, tent, or teardrop camper, "upta camp" was a chance to be outdoors with the people we loved. We told stories on our Story Stump by the warmth of a campfire. Some of us flew down icy slopes on an old sled with our best buddies. We heard the rain pound the roof, snug under our quilts. It was the perfect place to listen to the mournful sound of loons, forget the everyday, and just breathe, read, and rest. Or, as John Muir said: "To go into the woods, to lose my mind, and find my soul."

*Camping at Searsport Shores.*

# CHAPTER 26

# "*Goodbye Earl*"

## The Dixie Chicks

### Phoenix, Arizona, 2001

Over the years and through the births of three children, Tim's abuse of my sister Andi increased. Not only did he move Andi about as far from Maine as you could get–Phoenix–but we were all kept in the dark about what was happening. Andi learned our mom's lesson well. "Never talk about what goes on in this house to anyone outside of this house."

I was invited to speak about epilepsy at a conference for school nurses in Las Vegas and Hank came with me. We planned our itinerary on Southwest to include a stopover in Phoenix on the way home. I couldn't wait to tell Andi. When I did, her e-mailed response was totally unexpected: she might be able to meet us at a restaurant for lunch but we couldn't visit her at their house.

What? We weren't welcome at her house? We couldn't see the kids? I was hurt and angry, selfishly taking it as a personal rejection at first. As I thought about it more, I realized that this was totally out of character for Andi. She had been begging us to visit her. There had to be something she wasn't telling us. She finally admitted that Tim didn't want us there and she was afraid to defy him. Her own sister, having flown 2000 miles to see her, wasn't allowed to visit? Really? That's when Nancy and I realized how bad Tim's emotional abuse of Andi had gotten.

After years of ongoing abuse, Andi finally divorced Tim. We were all so relieved! Until, less than a year later, Andi and Tim flew to Florida and secretly married. Again. Andi told us she was sure Tim had changed. He'd promised her that he had.

Things only got worse. By 2001, Tim knew that Andi was unhappy and was prepared to do whatever it took to keep her with him. He worked from home so he was able to supervise Andi's every waking moment. He obsessively planned the menus for the family for the week; there could be no deviation. He convinced Andi that she wasn't capable of even the simplest household tasks. She didn't dare boil an egg without his permission. He even insisted on choosing the children's clothes, including his daughters.

Tim intimidated our parents from afar and threatened Nancy and me for supporting Andi. His harassment of Mom and Dad included phone calls in the middle of the night, during which he would breathe and hang up. He sent Andi roses with no card attached. When she called the florist to ask who sent them, he answered, "Fred Smith"—our father's name. Tim mailed a package of stinking raw meat, ala *The Godfather*, to our now-grown sister Joanne and her husband in New Hampshire. He was escalating. Even though he was in Arizona, we were absolutely terrified of him. We didn't know what he might do next.

Life became hell. Nancy and I were worried about Andi's safety but also about how this stress was affecting our parents, who were in their 80s. Mom had insomnia now, frantic about the hang-up phone calls in the middle of the night. This was in the early 2000s and we didn't have caller ID yet; there was no way to identify or block the calls. Andi's lawyer in Phoenix received threatening calls as well. In one, Tim threatened to throw him out of the 10th floor window of his downtown office building. These threats were reported to the police but, because Tim had not actually injured anyone, there was little they could do. We were kept in a permanent state of distress. Our everyday lives were affected now; it was difficult to concentrate at work. Most evenings, I found myself with Nancy, in her kitchen booth, reviewing that day's torment and asking ourselves, "What can we do?"

Andi's oldest daughter Keri was already living with Hank and me in Maine. Tim had begun to abuse her as well and Andi begged us to take her. She flew to Maine and moved into our downstairs guest room. With Andi's support, we enrolled her in the local Catholic girls' high school, Catharine McCauley, as well as Karate classes twice a week. She loved McCauley, and especially its uniform, a red wool plaid skirt, white blouse, and grey tights. Keri was and is a very smart young woman, and school studies came easily to her. She made friends, got a part-time job, and was thriving in Maine. We came to love her as a daughter.

And then 9/11 happened. I was with my homeroom students at South Portland High School that Tuesday morning when another teacher ran in to say that a plane had crashed into the World Trade Center. Everyone was upset and confused, but my job was to keep my sophomore students calm. In the meantime, my secretary was freaking out and left, insisting that she "wanted to die at home." Talk about modeling calm behavior for our students! Soon after, I received a message to call the Sister Superior at Catharine McCauley ASAP. Keri wanted to come home. She was worried about her "brother" (cousin, actually)—my son Robert, who worked in lower Manhattan. I emailed Robert but got no answer until late that afternoon. He was okay. He'd been on the subway with no cell reception when the planes hit. His wife of three months, who recently arrived from Japan to join him, watched the towers fall from the roof of their Brooklyn apartment building. Welcome to America!

Once the students at SPHS were dismissed, I rushed to McCauley to pick up Keri, who was a wreck. We sat on my bed for the rest of the afternoon watching the coverage, occasionally hugging or crying. 9/11 was a horrific day for all Americans; for our fragile family, it was just one more shock at a time when we were already on edge.

On a hot early-fall Sunday afternoon, five days after 9/11, I received a strange call from Andi's son Kieran. It was strange because he had never called me before, and even stranger because for a teenage boy, he sounded as if he'd been crying. He said he was worried about his mother. His Dad threw her phone in the pool so that she couldn't call for help. And once again, Tim had a gun.

I called Nancy and asked her to run over. Together we called the Portland police, who told us to call the Phoenix police. We called the Phoenix police, who told us to call the Scottsdale police. We called the Scottsdale police, who told us to call the Portland Police. I was so frustrated. I was supposed to protect Andi; she could be dead. I called Kieran back and he said his mother had gotten away. She was okay for now. Wisely, Andi had grabbed her youngest daughter Kaylin, and taken her with her. I worried about Kieran. If Tim found out that Kieran had called me, would he hurt him?

In the meantime, Nancy and I called lawyer friends, advocates for battered women, even the Phoenix Chief of Police. Because we were calling from Maine about an abuse that might or might not be occurring in Arizona, we got sympathy, but no solid help. The next morning, fearing that Andi was in imminent danger, we grabbed a Southwest flight to Phoenix. Andi was relieved to see us. We asked her to take us directly to the Phoenix Police building downtown. Nancy and I took the elevator to the top floor where we asked to see the Chief. We said it was urgent. Needless to say, he was unavailable. "That's okay" we said, "We'll wait." And we did; we were determined to wait as long as we had to, all night if necessary. As much as we might argue among ourselves, don't even think of messing with one of our sisters.

When we eventually met with the Chief, he acted swiftly. He walked us down a few floors to the Phoenix Police Department's "High Lethality Unit" and introduced us to the two officers assigned exclusively to Andi's case, Mary Freund and Rosie Mendoza. That's when everything changed. Mary and Rosie investigated the calls to my parents, the flowers sent by "Dad," the gun, and the threats against Andi and her attorney. They moved Andi and Kaylin to a hotel and registered them under an assumed name. They gave Andi 24-hour protection. I'm pretty sure they saved her life.

Thanks to Mary and Rosie, Tim was charged with domestic violence and convicted of threatening Andi with a gun. He was sentenced to four years in prison. Their children began to heal, and in 2002 with Tim safely behind bars, Andi and her youngest daughter Kaylin finally moved to Maine. She made it! Goodbye Tim!

Nancy and I helped Andi and Kaylin settle into a cute two-bedroom apartment in nearby Yarmouth. Andi had no furniture; she and Kaylin had left with only the clothes on their backs. No problem; the "Stunning Smith sisters" came together to remedy that situation: we hunted Craigslist and yard sales, we painted, wall-papered, and sewed, we shared what we had extras of, like kitchen items and linens. To make Andi happy when she woke each morning, we stenciled her favorites, blue hyacinths, on her bedroom walls.

As much as we disagreed on politics and other issues, as much as we occasionally bugged each other about little things, my sisters and I always seemed to come together when one of us was in trouble. Through all of our moves, disappointments, and losses, we had become a pretty resilient bunch. That proved to be a good thing because what we didn't know was that our biggest challenge, our family's worst nightmare, still lay ahead.

# CHAPTER 27

# *"The Way We Were"*

## Barbara Streisand

Falmouth, Maine, 2002 - 2012

There are few things more tedious than sitting in a doctor's waiting room, watching the clock until it's your turn to be seen. I felt a bit anxious, like Dorothy waiting to see the Wizard. While I waited to be called for my annual eye exam, I picked up a real estate magazine from the coffee table. Flip, flip, flip, STOP! There it was! On the bottom of page eight was my dream house! Like the Goodwill commercial in which the little black dress glows from the back of the box truck, this house emitted an aura from the printed page. Now I didn't want the eye doctor to be on time. I wanted to read about the house.

Another house had taken hold of me, and like the most obsessive collector, I couldn't turn the page. I waited until no one was looking, ripped the page from the magazine, and slipped it into my purse. We'd only lived next to Nancy and Aaron for six or seven years, and even to me it made no sense to move again. I loved Summer Place and Nancy's proximity, but the ad for the historic farmhouse was pulling me in another direction.

As much as I hated moving as a kid, here I was thinking about doing it again. The psychiatrist who helped me through my divorce might have called it repetition compulsion. Dr. Collins might have explained that I had the tendency to repeat a traumatic event or its circumstances and the drive to repeat formative early life experiences, for good or ill. Basically, I may have been reenacting past traumas, like the three times I moved in high school, as a way to master them.

Or, maybe I should cut the psycho-babble and listen to Occam's razor: "When faced with competing explanations for the same phenomenon, the simplest is likely the correct one." In that case, my residential wanderlust might be attributed to the fact that, like my mother and sister Joanne, I loved to decorate houses. When I was done with one, I couldn't wait to get started on another.

I was getting ahead of myself. We hadn't even seen the farmhouse yet. When I got home from the eye doctor, I couldn't wait to show Hank the ad for Winn Farm. He was curious about it as well and agreed that we should take a look. It looked palatial in the photo, but some research showed that it had been on the market for a while, which concerned us. What kinds of problems might hide in a home that had been built almost 200 years ago?

I called Pam, a friend and realtor I met at Gorham High School. Her son Joshua was in my program for students with special needs. He was one of my favorite students and Pam was one of my favorite parents. She was a kind, empathetic woman who I loved for her sense of humor and remarkable strength. Pam persevered through the ups and downs of type I diabetes for much of her life while raising a son with special needs as a single parent.

Pam arranged for us to visit Winn Farm for a showing. When I walked up to the front door, I felt as if I was approaching the front of a time-worn antebellum mansion. The large Federal-style home was built in 1830. Its exterior walls were constructed of locally-molded bricks, three courses thick. As I rapped on the front door with the aged-brass knocker, I felt a bit like Scarlet O'Hara off to visit Melanie in *Gone with the Wind.*

Pam welcomed us into a spacious family room with a brick fireplace and a spiral staircase leading to the second floor. This part of the home had been an addition to the rectangular Federal original. A second foyer with a much grander stairway was just inside massive double exterior doors that marked the old front of the house. Guests rode over a wooden bridge that spanned a small stream when they arrived from Winn Road in the 19th and early 20th centuries. In the 1970s, a new driveway was added while the old dirt drive was sodded over, and the bridge was left to rot. Only a few old beams from the bridge remained, decaying at the bottom of the stream.

Behind a door on the second floor, there was a hidden staircase that led to a slant-roofed third floor. Half of the third floor was finished with rows of cupboards and shelves under its eaves, while the other half of the third floor was attic space. In there you could see the age of the house by looking at the huge old hand-hewn wooden beams that supported it. I imagined Nancy Drew would have loved that little stairway and secret attic room, and she could have found a mystery or two to solve at Winn Farm. If my sisters and I grew up there, we would have had a secret clubhouse, assuming we could agree on who to invite to join such an exclusive sorority.

Our home at Summer Place sold quickly, and our offer on Winn Farm was accepted in June of 2002. We enjoyed seven years at Summer Palace, but it was time to move on. Since Winn Farm wasn't far, I left with a promise to Nancy that we would see each other just as much as we always did. That was a promise I kept.

The old Winn Farm kitchen was a huge job to update. Thankfully, it was made a little easier with three out of the four Stunning Smith Sisters working together. Having learned DIY skills from our parents, we painted the dark kitchen cabinets white and installed a wooden floor to replace the 70s linoleum. Andi and Nancy each signed the inside of one of the cabinet doors they painted. Nancy's was my favorite. She painted the words "Life is better with Tab" under the bright pink can of Tab she'd painted. I chuckled every time I opened that cupboard.

My favorite room at Winn Farm was my craft room under the eaves on the third floor. I was too humble to call it a studio because I didn't see myself as an artist, just a creative tinkerer. I went up to the craft room to be alone, think, and read. It was my place. Up there, I imagined myself as a real artist, an aspiring Mary Engelbreit perhaps. Although I looked more like her alter ego, Ann Estelle—chubby, with blond hair and glasses. I painted bold flowers, round children, and Scotty dogs in bright primary colors. Or maybe I was a moody Van Gogh wannabe washing gray and blue acrylics with streaks of yellow.

I sewed up there as well, not always sure what I was going to make until the fabric found its noisy way through my machine. I've transformed placemats into pillows, dish towels into curtains, curtains into coverlets, and coverlets into capes. Grammy Smith taught me to knit when I was young, but I just can't seem to get the finer points. Maybe it's because I'm left-handed? A fine enough excuse! To date, I have only completed two knitting projects. One was a very long scarf—think yards, not inches or feet, because I didn't know how to cast off. The other was a basket of bright pink "pussy hats" for the 2017 Women's March.

Sometimes I just sat quietly in the craft room and sorted buttons into mason jars by color or shape. I had thousands of old buttons from my mother and grandmother, who both lived through the depression and frugally removed buttons from worn or outgrown clothes to reuse. Many of the buttons had a memory attached. I held them and remembered my First Communion dress, my polka-dotted dance recital costume, Dad's army uniform, and the dress Mom wore on her honeymoon.

Inspired by Rob's wedding in Japan, when I tired of sorting buttons, I folded origami paper into cranes, kites, or flowers. When my sister Nancy or my creative teacher friend Sandy came over, we'd often sit across from each other at the craft table, not make much, but talk for hours. Other times, I just sat up there alone and made lists: things to do, things to make, things to never *ever* do again. The craft room was a place where things often started out as one thing and left as something else. Even me.

The real selling point of Winn Farm was the exterior: the lawns, woods, and landscaping were lush. Hank added apple and peach trees, which bore bountiful amounts of fruit. Who knew that peaches could thrive in Maine? We also grew a vegetable garden with squash, corn, lettuce, tomatoes, cucumbers, peas, carrots, beets, eggplant, and pumpkins. Hank added a garden shed with window boxes bursting with bright red geraniums in the summer. He created a pergola out of old fence posts and planted grape bushes to grow over the top, creating a shady little spot for a bistro table and two chairs. But the pièce de resistance was what we called the "Wizard's Forest."

We didn't set out to create a Wizard's Forest, but it evolved as we explored the stream and woods at the back of our property. We had worn a path around the perimeter of the woods to the stream, which we spent a weekend covering with wood chips. For a housewarming gift, friends gave us two tree wizards, clay faces meant to hang on a tree trunk–one that smiled and one that scowled at passersby. We hung them along the paths on two of the oldest trees in our magical little forest, and since that day it became known as the Wizard's Forest.

Once we came up with the wizard concept, we went a little crazy adding elements to our forest to compliment the medieval theme. We added a secluded grotto, complete with a cement statue of Saint Francis. A sandy area on the side of the stream became Brian's Beach, named after one of our grandsons. A wooden bench was christened Robert's Rest, after our oldest grandson. Hank built a walking bridge over the stream, which became the Fishing Hole, for visits from our newest grandson.

The coup de gràs was when our carpenter friend Gino built a rustic playhouse for the boys, which we named the Hobbit House. And I helped them build a treehouse, which amazingly, actually held them! We loved spending time in our enchanted forest raking, planting wildflowers, painting signs and rocks, and coming up with new ideas to make it even more fun for our grandkids. As kids at heart, the forest was great fun for Hank and I too.

*Wizard's Forest.*

The Wizard's Forest was the perfect place to celebrate Halloween. Grandsons Robert and Brian helped us get ready for their parents and the trick-or-treaters. We added little orange and black lights along the trails. Then we hid a battery-operated sound machine guaranteed to generate frightening wails and earth-shattering screams all evening. We simulated graves with mounded dirt and placed faux gravestones on them. Old white sheets hung high up in the trees so they danced in the breeze like ghostly apparitions. Robert and Brian chose hiding spots from whence they would spring out in scary costumes to startle unsuspecting visitors wandering along the paths.

The scariest forest creature of all at Halloween was Nancy, who transformed herself into a witch, complete with a smoking cauldron of dry ice she stirred with a gnarled stick. She painted her face green and wore a long gray wig under her black pointed witch's hat. Her ragged black robes were accessorized with black gloves adorned with skeletal fingers that glowed in the dark. Nancy sat quietly in Saint Francis' nook until a child approached. Then she stepped on a hidden switch that turned on an eerie green spotlight which would unexpectedly proclaim her presence. Unsuspecting kids who survived the shock were treated with candy from Nancy, who was able to magically transition from bad witch to good witch before their very eyes. Tales of the Wizard's Forest traveled through Falmouth by word of mouth, and the second Halloween brought even more visitors than the first.

One of my favorite Winn Farm memories was in the fall of 2003, when we hosted 24 guests for Thanksgiving dinner. In order to accommodate everyone, we swapped out our dining room with our larger living room. The room still had its original fireplace, which added warmth and a woodsy fragrance to the occasion. Small pumpkins, knobby gourds, and Indian corn were interspersed with tea light candles down the middle of the now expansive dining table. For favors, each place held a single amaryllis bulb in a little glass bud vase filled with small white rocks. We hoped it would produce a sweet, vanilla-scented bloom during the Christmas season ahead.

It was a mild day for Thanksgiving in Maine, and Hank held court in the backyard where he delighted his mostly-male audience by cooking a turkey on the rotisserie. I roasted a second even larger one in the kitchen's big lower oven while warming a spiral sliced ham in the smaller upper oven. Favorite dishes of many of those in attendance filled the dining room table, including winter squash, Mom's famous baby onions, peas, turnips (Nancy's favorite!), green bean casserole, mashed potatoes, sweet potatoes, bread stuffing, pickles, olives, celery, and cranberry sauce. Both Hank and Nancy loved to bake, so the kitchen island was laden with tempting confections including pumpkin, pecan, apple, and mincemeat pies. Nancy baked her famous Captain's Dinner Rolls, named after those featured at the little restaurant in Cape Porpoise by the same name where she had worked, and their aroma lured us toward the vintage hickory basket that held them.

Even more important than the food were the people. We had so many people who were special to us sharing the holiday at the same place and time. My sisters and their significant others, Mom, Dad, our children, and even some of Robert's Kennebunk school friends all joined us. The highlight of every holiday dinner at our house was Kristen saying Grace before the meal. On this Thanksgiving Day and as always, she didn't disappoint. Kristen laid her forehead down on the table and prayed. "God is great. God is good. Let us thank him for our food. Amen."

Although Kristen struggled with articulation—we all smiled when God was invariably pronounced "Tom"—her intonation gave meaning to her words. In those few moments, my heart expanded to twice its normal size. I was so proud of Kristen, how she fought through so much pain, seizures, and surgeries. Yet she still remained at the heart of our family, spreading pure joy wherever she went. In fact, on this particular Thanksgiving, she was also in a wheelchair due to a broken ankle. Hearing her innocent voice leading us in this simple prayer always left me with a bittersweet tear in my eye.

As the day wound down, darkness was already upon us. Kristen was over-tired, making her more liable to have a seizure. I was tired too from prepping, cooking, and entertaining 24 dinner guests, while seeing to Kristen's personal and medication needs. I announced I would be leaving for a few minutes to prepare the borrowed wheelchair van and take Kristen home. But I asked everyone to please stay and continue to enjoy the holiday until I got back.

It had rained while we were inside, and as I rushed to undo the van's wheelchair ramp, I slid and landed flat on my back in the driveway. There I was, at the end of a beautiful day, splayed out on the pavement in the dark, looking up at the late-autumn moon, hurt and crying. I stayed there for a while, letting all of the day's emotions spill out while no one was looking. I was simply overwhelmed. Being the parent of a child with significant disabilities was like that sometimes.

I'd been gone awhile, and who was the one to come check on me? Nancy, of course. She saw me lying there and just knew. I didn't need to tell her why I was crying. She sat quietly with me for a few minutes and then, for no reason at all, we started laughing. Hysterically. There we were, two grown women dressed in our holiday finest, lying in the darkness on my wet driveway, while 22 guests waited inside. As strong women in difficult, often unexpected, and sometimes terrible situations, what did we do? We LAUGHED, of course! Then, we wiped ourselves off and carried on. Before long, we had Kristen safely belted into the van and on her way. Thankfully, no one inside was any the wiser on that long-ago starry Thanksgiving night.

Sometimes I think the healing power of laughter is underrated. As is the power of a sister who accepts you as you are, warts and all.

# CHAPTER 28

# *"Honeycomb"*

## Jimmie Rodgers

### Maine(ish), 2000s

The Four Stunning Smith Sisters had finally made it to Maine—Well, sort of. Andi came and went while Joanne made it to nearby Londonderry, New Hampshire; she was close enough to visit Mom and Dad at Chandler's Wharf often. Once I made it, wild horses could not drag me away—although, the number of homes I had gone through since arriving was climbing. Nancy seemed to agree that Maine was where she wanted to be. We no longer lived next door to one another, but we still enjoyed a lot of sisterly bonding time. Whether we were in her Summer Place kitchen booth with Tabs or on an outing with Kristen, our sisterhood seemed stronger than ever. However, the bond across all Four Stunning Smith Sisters ebbed and flowed—sometimes more ebb than flow.

We were grownups now—weren't we? As we began 2004, Joanne would be turning 43, Nancy would be turning 52, Andi would be turning 54, and I would be turning 57. Okay, we were definitely grownups. Didn't they say that as siblings get older, their bonds deepen? Unfortunately, that wasn't always the case with us. We didn't resemble Grammy's Smith's happy Parker Sisters, as I hoped we would so long ago. Sometimes it was small petty things that caused frustration, sometimes it was deeper wounds that festered over time. Mom seemed to know just the buttons to push for some. She rarely spoke of her own two sisters, but I had to wonder if her family had a similar dynamic to ours.

Being the oldest, I wondered if my younger sisters ever resented me. I had my own room when they had to share. I got an English bike while they still had Huffys. I had the first bra, the first boyfriend, and unfortunately, the first heartbreak. However, I was never our parents' favorite like Andi, and later, Joanne. As it turned out, Joanne's age gap was what created the biggest divide in our sisterhood.

Nancy, Andi, and I were early Boomers. Although Joanne technically qualified as a Boomer, she was right on the cusp and grew up more like Gen X. While Nancy, Andi, and I wore dresses to school, Joanne wore bell bottom jeans. We listened to Johnny Mathis and the Beatles while Joanne liked Huey Lewis and the News. When lucky enough to have a car, we drove used VW Beetles; Joanne had a Camaro. We were sisters by blood, but we didn't have many shared childhood memories.

*Magic Dick with Joanne.*

Joanne attended Northeastern University in Boston for five years, graduating with a master's degree in physical therapy. She loved Boston, especially because all the big-name rock bands of her generation played concerts there. She shared stories of sneaking backstage to get guitar picks from members of her favorite groups—which she wore around her neck—before having band members back to her apartment. The most famous of these was Magic Dick, the harmonica player from the J. Geils Band.

Hank and I still laugh about when we went to a concert at Foxwoods and Joanne introduced us to Magic Dick backstage. My ever-polite husband, never the cool groupie type, put out his hand and said the line now famous in the mythology of the Stunning Smith Sisters: "Nice to meet you, Mr. Dick." Needless to say, there was a moment of *Did Hank just say that?* silence before we were all able to pull ourselves back together.

Long after college, Joanne was still a proud groupie, flying around the country to see and get selfies with Huey Lewis and her favorite band member, guitarist Stef Burns. Joanne lists "going to rock concerts" as a hobby on her Facebook profile. Imagine how Boomer-boring I felt by comparison; my profile listed reading, writing, crafts, and sewing. Same family, different generations!

Were sisters one, two, and three a little jealous of Joanne? Sure. But with Andi living in Arizona, only Nancy and I experienced much of it firsthand. Surprisingly, the hardest part for Nancy and me was not what Joanne had or did, but how Mom spun it. No matter what Nancy and I did, it never seemed as good as whatever Joanne accomplished.

Since Mom and Dad lived close to Londonderry, they spent a good deal of time at Joanne and Mark's home. On both phone calls and visits, Mom would wax poetic about how pretty and thin Joanne was looking, her "posh" new outfits, the antique cabinet she had just had shipped from Tucson or Taos, her latest Newbury Street haircut, or her recent trip to Turks and Caicos. Even her countertops!

In Mom's eyes, if Joanne was quartz, Nancy and I were Formica; we could never be as good, no matter what we did. That was difficult. We reminded ourselves that Mom grew up the child of immigrant parents, self-conscious of how little they had. While we tried to cut her some slack, it seemed like she lived vicariously through Joanne. We understood the psychology of it, but it still hurt.

True to form, Nancy had a theory about all of this: the Theory of the Queens and the Drones. Although Darwin or Einstein may not have been impressed, Nancy's theory was brilliant in describing the four sisters' roles in our family. Nancy hypothesized that, like in every bee hive, there had to be both queens and drones in every family to ensure the smooth workings of the unit.

The queens were the special ones. They were raised on royal jelly—smoked baby clams, anyone?—from the moment they hatched. A queen was identified by her long, narrow abdomen, or the "thin sisters," as Mom would have said. Drones had a rounded abdomen, which Mom likely would have said fit Nancy and me. In a family, as in a hive, the drones were the worker bees that carried out the majority of tasks necessary for the hive to function. Our family consisted of two queens and two drones. Joanne and Andi were the queens, while Nancy and I were the drones.

Whenever there was a family event that involved cooking, like Thanksgiving or Christmas, it was left to the drones to plan, host, and cook. We had to pick up the slack since Andi "doesn't cook" and Joanne was "too busy to cook" because she had a "man's job," according to Mom. Why didn't we just say no? Maybe we both secretly hoped that if we worked hard enough and made everything nice enough, Mom might eventually promote one of us to queen status.

All of the planning and cooking was a job in and of itself, but to make matters worse, Mom wouldn't RSVP for any event until she was sure Joanne was coming. With Joanne so busy with her man's job as a physical therapist, we never knew her plans until a few days before. That left Nancy and I unsure if we were setting the table and preparing food for four people or 10. We didn't know whether to make turkey or chicken, roast beef or meatloaf. It was almost impossible to get a straight answer.

It seemed as if the rest of the family would follow suit—what Joanne did, Mom did, and what Mom did, Dad and Mark would do. It was crazy-making. To be fair, Joanne likely never realized how her holiday indecision impacted Nancy and me. In her mind, she probably did not want to inconvenience anyone by having us plan on her being there, only having to cancel at the last minute. But Joanne's RSVP was the catalyst for everyone else's, and that did put a lot of stress on Nancy and I—year after year. We both had demanding full-time careers as well, even though teaching school was not Mom's idea of a "man's job." Resentment often resulted.

To be fair, Joanne never bragged about being the queen; it was Mom who perpetrated that royal mythology. Sadly, it created a wedge between us that Joanne didn't deserve. Maybe we were all just clamoring for a little piece of the limited love Mom was emotionally able to give. I knew that Mom loved us, but since she felt so little love in her own hardscrabble childhood, she often didn't know how to show it to us.

# CHAPTER 29

# *"Fix You"*

## Coldplay

### Portland, Maine, 2005

At 7:30 a.m. on May 23rd, 2005, my sister Nancy was admitted to Maine Medical Center for a routine laparoscopic hysterectomy. She was 52 and was experiencing irregular bleeding, intense fatigue, and abdominal bloating. When she arrived at school one morning in December of 2004, she sat in her car crying. She was in so much pain she didn't think she could make it up the stairs to her second-floor classroom.

A trip to the emergency room resulted in transfusions. She was so anemic that not enough blood was reaching her heart—a variety of tests did not identify the cause. Nancy was given an anti-depressant and told to rest. By spring, she was not feeling any better. Further tests were done before she and her gynecologist agreed that doing a hysterectomy may offer her some relief. The routine laparoscopic surgery was estimated to take one to three hours. It was almost noon. We waited.

At 3:00 p.m. Nancy was still in surgery. We were told that there were some complications and that the surgical team had to call in a specialist. They would leave Nancy under light anesthesia in the operating room until he got there. We were assured that she wasn't in any danger, but we could sense from what was not said that the complications weren't good. Nancy and I were not close as kids, but in late middle age, we became inseparable. We were the closest of the four sisters and seemed to share some kind of genetic ESP—always able to sense

when the other needed us. As I realized we were going to have a long afternoon, I opened my purse and retrieved an Ativan to slip under my tongue.

We were still waiting at 5:00 p.m. This felt crazy. I was beside myself, and Nancy's husband and son, Aaron and Ken, were not far behind. The specialist, Dr. Hector M. Tarraza, was a noted gynecological surgeon and an honors graduate of Harvard Medical School with 30 years of experience. Nancy was in surgery with him. We were assured that he was the best; we shouldn't worry. Easier said than done.

At 7:00 p.m. we were still at Maine Medical Center waiting for Nancy to come out of surgery. Aaron was encouraging me to go home and promised to call as soon as he knew anything. I wanted to stay longer, but having taught school all day without a lunch break, I was exhausted. Ambivalent about leaving, I finally agreed to head home and wait for Aaron's call.

My phone rang at 9:00 p.m. It wasn't Aaron; it was Nancy. She woke up in a darkened room on the surgical floor. Dr. Hector Terraza, the specialist surgeon, had stopped by to talk with her. He quietly explained that earlier in the day, her gynecologist saw that her belly was full of cancer and stopped the surgery. Her gynecologist decided to wait for Dr. Terraza, the head of the department of gynecological oncology at Maine Medical Center, to perform what would now be open surgery. The goal now was to remove her ovaries and debulk her, removing any cancer cells visible to the naked eye or under the microscope. Dr. Terraza said he had gotten as much of the cancer as he could, but that if even one cell was left, it could spread. His diagnosis: stage IIIC ovarian cancer.

Nancy, never one to be at a loss for words, asked the doctor, *"Cancer,* cancer?" Dr Terraza nodded. Nancy then asked, "Like lose your hair and die cancer?" After a moment, Dr. Terraza nodded again.

*Nancy with therapy dog at Maine Medical Center.*

Nancy spent five days at Maine Medical Center following her diagnosis of ovarian cancer in 2005; she began chemotherapy shortly after her discharge. We had not yet found a way to fit this news into the mosaic of our lives. On the morning of her first infusion, I wasn't surprised to see Mom and Dad. As always, they came through when one of their daughters was in trouble. As I saw them sitting there, quietly waiting on a bench together, tears came to my eyes; especially that Dad made the effort in spite of his worsening Parkinson's disease. None of us knew what to expect, but we had each chosen to be there.

Nancy arrived carrying a big canvas L.L. Bean bag covered in colored Sharpie with messages of love and encouragement from her friends. The handles and trim on the bag were teal, the color for ovarian cancer awareness. Teal was not nearly as well known as pink for breast cancer, but to us now, equally important. Every October when everything in the stores turned pink, Nancy would quip, "I wonder if I got the wrong cancer?" No cancer is the right cancer, but we were happy to wear both teal and pink for Nancy and Mom, who had developed breast cancer. Mom's cancer was at an early stage. Since she was in her 80s, her oncologist believed that it could be monitored rather than treated with chemotherapy or radiation.

At the Infusion Center in Scarborough, Nancy was welcomed by the care team and seated in a big blue chair in her own curtained cubicle. The contents of her bag featured her signature drink of Tab, her favorite candies of Swedish Fish and Reese's, a book, and a pillow. Once the infusion began, Mom and Dad hugged Nancy and headed home, while Aaron and I stayed. We never read the books we brought with us. Instead, we gabbed throughout the procedure. Nancy said the infusion didn't hurt, but she was warned that she would likely feel worse in a day or two.

Indeed, a couple of days later, in addition to the nausea from chemo, Nancy felt what she described as heartburn. However, when she was rushed back to Maine Medical Center by ambulance Memorial Day weekend, we found out that she had actually experienced a heart attack. Yet another surgery for Nancy, this time to place three stents in blocked arteries feeding her heart. Upon her return home, she only had days before she was scheduled for chemo again. My heart was breaking for her. She was so sick.

That summer, Nancy's hair was beginning to fall out in chunks. We laughed about it together, obviously a reptilian-brain coping mechanism. Next, her eyebrows and eyelashes disappeared. Suddenly, this wasn't funny anymore. As Nancy discovered each horrible side effect, the unshakable reality came to the forefront. This was actually happening. Nancy—our strong, crazy Stunning Smith Sister—my best friend, our family's glue, had CANCER.

Nancy decided she would rather lose all her hair at once than watch it fall out a little at a time. Lately, we looked for any small reason to celebrate joy in this horrible mess, and I decided to plan a surprise

"Hat Party" for Nancy. Everyone was asked to bring a hat for Nancy—the sillier the better. Since I knew elementary school teachers, I was sure there would be some creative offerings, and her friends didn't disappoint.

Out on the patio at Winn Farm, we toasted Nancy with champagne as her hairdresser Pam shaved her head. Then, over summer cocktails, we watched her model the hilarious assortment of headwear gifts. There were baseball caps, cowboy hats, flowered bonnets, scarves, and sun hats. Some hats had sayings like "Cancer Sucks," "Fuck Cancer," "My Oncologist Does My Hair," and "Bald is the New Black." As Nancy tried on each hat, it was great to hear her laughing. It had been quite some time without it, which is odd when it was so much a part of her—always laughing and joking.

As the badass she was, Nancy didn't intend to rely on hats alone to cope with her hair loss. She made a wig fitting appointment, and I drove her for moral support. Nancy tried on every kind of wig imaginable: short, long, upswept, brown, black, blond, afro, and even dreadlocks. The worse they looked, the more we laughed. When we finally settled down, Nancy chose a mid-length blond wig. She said that she'd always wanted to be a blonde, so why not now? Indeed, Nancy was the only Smith sister with brown hair; the rest of us had been blond from birth. It was her turn.

Nancy only wore her wig for special occasions, preferring a scarf or baseball hat for everyday activities like school. She used her cancer as an opportunity to teach her fourth grade students about the disease and how they could support people with cancer. Nancy was not ashamed of her baldness; she was proud of it. She wanted her students to understand that people with disabilities, whether epilepsy like Kristen, or cancer like her, had the same needs and feelings as everyone else.

Nancy's hair loss led to a new side business for me, albeit a non-profit one. I began sewing chemo scarves for cancer patients. I designed a casual cotton reversible scarf that could be tied in a number of different ways. Nancy was my fit model. Once I perfected the design, I raced home from school each day to make scarves.

I sewed and sewed and sewed. I named my new endeavor "My Sister's Scarves" and ordered little tags to sew inside each scarf.

Nancy soon had a scarf for every mood, in every color, for every day of the week, every outfit, every Boston sports team, and especially every holiday. The scarf project helped me deal with the anxiety I felt and temporarily quieted my fear of losing Nancy. While I sewed, I had to think about bobbins, thread color, seam allowances, and stitch length. I could not think about cancer. Or death.

*Nancy models her*
*New England Patriots scarf.*

# CHAPTER 30

# *"Wind Beneath My Wings"*

## **Bette Midler**

Portland, Maine, 2005-2009

Everyone wanted frequent updates on how Nancy was doing. Eventually, we were overwhelmed with returning individual phone calls, thoughtful as they were. So we decided to start a blog. We used the book *Blogging for Bliss* by Tina Fey to learn how to get our blog up and running. We named our blog *It's Always Something*, as a nod to Gilda Radner, who used the phrase to describe her own battle with ovarian cancer. Both Nancy and I were contributors, each writing posts, which you can still read here: *cheryllawsonsblog.blogspot.com*. The blog was informative, but we also wanted to write about some good things–things not about cancer–so we also shared a few of our many crazy misadventures on the blog as well.

One story we didn't share on the blog was about some books I brought Nancy to read while she was in the hospital. When I arrived, Nancy was still a little groggy from the anesthesia a few hours earlier. She had had a port surgically placed in her chest for chemo delivery so she could avoid repeated needle pokes. Once she was fully awake, Nancy had a funny story to share. At 3:00 a.m., a lab tech came in to draw some blood and noticed the three books on her bedside table. He asked, "Who brought you these?" and she replied, "My sister." He said something like, "Hmmm... Interesting choices."

Laughing, Nancy showed me the titles I had unwittingly chosen for her: *Terminal*, *Likely to Die*, and *The Dark Road Home*. Fine selections for some light reading in the Gibson Cancer Unit at Maine Medical

Center! Of course, my innocent but stupid choices threw us into more unbridled fits of laughter.

Nancy eventually settled into a pattern of chemo with carboplatin/taxol every three weeks and continued to teach as best she could. Then she opted to do a 12-month regimen of maintenance chemo with taxol only. During maintenance, she had more energy and became active with the Maine branch of the American Cancer Society. Nancy attended survivor's discussion groups and the "Look Good, Feel Better" program. They taught her how to use makeup to offset some effects of chemotherapy, including drawing on new eyebrows.

In June of 2006, Nancy, Hank, and I attended the Falmouth Relay for Life, sponsored by the American Cancer Society, just to see what it was all about. We met wonderful people there and were inspired to become involved. We wore our Relay t-shirts with pride and had tears in our eyes watching Nancy walk the Survivor's Lap. After she walked the luminaria-lined track with other cancer survivors that night, Nancy was excited to form her own team for the 2007 Relay. She named her team "Tufts Teal Warriors" and we looked forward to returning next year.

After a failed attempt to sleep on the rough ground at our first Relay for Life, Hank and I decided to bring our little camper the second year so that Nancy and I could get a couple comfortable hours of sleep. Hank parked it with a few other campers on the side of the road that circumvented the Windham High School track. He walked with us through the evening, helped light our luminaria, and stayed for the program, Survivor Lap, and fireworks.

Activities throughout Saturday included music, games, and food every hour through the night to encourage teams to keep walking. Every lap increased the amount donated through pledges. Sunday was the last day, and the Cancer Society provided breakfast Sunday at

7:00 a.m. followed by the closing ceremony. Then the teams dismantled their campsites and decorations, leaving the track area clean for the high school to use Monday morning.

Around midnight on Saturday night, Hank headed home. He promised to return Sunday morning and help us pack up our site, hitch the camper, and drive it home. After a few more laps, Nancy and I closed the black-out shades and curled up under the quilts in the camper. We slept so well that when we woke up, our cellphones said... 11:00 a.m.?

What? We missed breakfast? We missed the Cancer Society's closing ceremony? We missed saying our goodbyes? No, no, no! We felt stupid and hoped no one would notice our tardiness as we slowly opened the camper door and crept out. As we looked around, we saw not a single soul nor heard a single sound.

The track was empty, the street was empty, the field was empty—except one slightly lopsided campsite decorated in teal. Even the porta-potties were gone. We felt like fools! Nancy and I looked at each other. We looked around the track area again. And then we burst out laughing, like we might never stop!

Later that year, Nancy needed another surgery to remove additional cancer from her abdomen. She was in her favorite spot on the blue striped living room couch where she recuperated with her cat, Nala. Propped up with pillows, she could watch both Casco Bay outside her window and *Judge Judy* on TV. I stopped by after school at around 3:30 p.m. to keep her company until Aaron got home.

We shared a few cans of Tab and I offered to make her a snack, but she didn't want anything. Nancy had little appetite during her cancer treatment and had lost a great deal of weight. Mom was worried, urging her to eat, but that just ended up frustrating Mom and annoying Nancy. So when she said no, I didn't push.

Nancy told me she was expecting a delivery, and I told her I'd stay until it arrived just in case she couldn't make it to the door. Her latest surgical incision wasn't healing properly and Nancy's doctor ordered her a wound vac. Nancy's nurse assured her it was a small device she could wear beneath her clothing. Apparently it came with "a convenient carrying case" that would "allow discreet delivery of therapy," according to the pamphlet the nurse gave Nancy.

The doorbell rang just before *Judge Judy* was about to announce who the real father of the baby in question was. Nancy muted the TV while I ran to answer the door. As I opened it, I yelled something to the effect of "Holy shit, Nancy! It's a major award!" (Thanks to the movie *The Christmas Story*, we had conferred upon one another more than one "major award" over the years.) At the door was a delivery man with a dolly holding a box the size of a small refrigerator. The wound vac? He managed to hoist the box up the half flight of stairs to Nancy's living room, had her sign the receipt, and scurried out.

We looked at each other, looked at the box. This was the wound vac? We looked at each other again, and then burst into convulsions of laughter. Every time we looked over at the box, we started up again. Our laughter was punctuated with, "What the hell is that?" Occasionally, there were some more "Holy shit"s and finally, "What am I supposed to do with that fuckin' thing?" asked Nancy. "If the wound vac is this big, how big is the 'discreet convenient carrying case'?" I snorted.

Even though Nancy had been feeling better, and we all prayed for another remission, cancer wasn't done with her. She had to start a new round of chemo in 2008. This time it was a Carbo/Gemzar cocktail with periodic blood transfusions to combat her anemia.

Nancy did her best to keep teaching through the 2008-2009 school year, taking one week out of every three off to recuperate from chemotherapy. In addition to cancer, Nancy also battled anemia and dehydration most of the fall. Then she developed pneumonia in early December. She had every right to just give up but, being Nancy, she didn't.

In December of 2008, Nancy wrote on our blog. "At the top of my Christmas list this year is only one thing from Santa—a cure—or at least a good long remission, not just for me but for all the others on this journey as well." She mentioned that one thing that kept her going in 2008 was her students. Nancy shared this letter she received from a mother:

*Nancy,*
*I have an angel of a daughter fast asleep with you in her heart.*
*She misses you and longs to see you. UGH!!! I feel so stupid.*
*You have cancer. A cancer that left and was never supposed to return.*
*Tonight, as we drove home from an open house Elise said,*
*"I just wanted a hug from Mrs. Tufts." Elsie went to bed holding you*
*in white healing light and I am doing the same. Be well!*

In January of 2009, Nancy's oncologist Dr. Small said the magic words: "Nancy, you're in remission." If prayers could work, I guess all of ours, Elise's included, did. The nasty chemo of the previous fall had done its job. Nancy was going to make it!

While Nancy was in remission, cancer had still taken its toll. Try as she might, Nancy's body needed to slow down to rest and regain her strength, made difficult by the 45 minutes she drove to and from school. Sadly, she knew it was time to retire from teaching. Except Nancy wasn't just a teacher, Nancy was the BEST teacher.

Every August, she arrived early to organize and decorate her classroom for the first day. Nancy also had costumes for every holiday, school occasion, or book being read. She was a pumpkin or witch at Halloween, an elf or a reindeer at Christmas, and a bunny at Easter. The kids loved how she went above and beyond almost as much as they loved her.

If she couldn't give her students 100 percent, she said she didn't want to continue. Nancy felt they deserved more. So in June of 2009, after 34 years at Wells Elementary School, she reluctantly retired. I wondered if they knew how lucky they were to have her—to have Nancy as their teacher and to know her as a person, to have experienced her strength, and to have heard her infectious laughter.

I planned a huge surprise retirement party for Nancy at Winn Farm. Everyone from her past and present was invited: teachers old and new, family young and old, and all of her high school and college friends. Nancy cut a big sheet cake frosted with the image of a hot pink can of Tab and got to spend time with people she hadn't seen in years. The biggest surprise was when Aaron drove up with a surprise for Nancy: a brand-new silver VW convertible with red trim and a license plate reading "Endless Summer."

We each wished that for Nancy: an endless and healthy Maine summer—this year and hopefully, for many more.

*Nancy - Relay for Life.*

# CHAPTER 31

# *"On the Road Again"*

## Willie Nelson

New York State
Searsport, Maine
Newington, Westport
Guilford, Connecticut &
Raymond, New Hampshire
2006 - 2009

In the spring of 2006, I made a proposal to Nancy: I suggested we go on a road trip together that summer, and maybe future summers if the first one was a success. I felt the need to hold her close to me but also to look ahead, to believe there would be a future for our sisterhood.

Our first road trip was an ambitious one. In the late summer of 2006, with Nancy in remission, we headed for New York State. I had stumbled upon an article in the *New York Times* entitled "On Route 20, Where the Past Is Present." The article enchanted me. I sprinted over to Nancy's house and darted up the stairs, screen door slamming behind me. "I know where we should go on our first road trip!" Knowing that Nancy also loved history and old abandoned buildings, I shared the article with her. It explained that:

*When the New York State Thruway was built in the 1950s, to the north of the old highway and roughly parallel, progress along Route 20 skidded to a halt. To historians, the road is like a highway set in aspic, with vignettes of architecture, some of which may not be around next year. The 290-mile route is lined with antiques shops, bed-and-breakfasts and signposts to nearby gardens, caverns and spectacular water-falls. Lakes lap the sides of the road in towns with evocative*

*names—Geneva, Cazenovia, Skaneateles. Route 20 developed
with the automobile. The road represents the architecture of
travel: early gas stations, tourist cabins and burger chains
that pre-date McDonald's—so much is virtually unchanged.*

We were both excited and spent the next few hours drinking Tabs in the little booth in her kitchen while we perused maps and made our plans.

And what a trip it was! We visited historic Skaneateles, enjoyed wine tastings, combed through the ruins of abandoned buildings from another age, and sat in Mark Twain's chair at Elmira College. We visited a Civil War cemetery in which the Confederate soldiers were buried facing south and the Union soldiers were buried facing north. We crept through the ruins of what was once a fine hotel in Saratoga Springs, imagining it populated by guests and staff similar to those in one of our favorite movies, *Somewhere in Time*. We counted hundreds of black and white cows on low hills as we passed farm after farm. To complement the theme of our trip, we purposely stayed in little 50s-era motels along the way. It was our very own magical mystery trip.

Our first "Sisters Road Trip" was such a success that we decided to do it again in the summer of 2007. Nancy was feeling pretty well after six more rounds of chemo, so we decided to make this a camping trip. I was sure that I could drive, pulling our little camper; I wasn't so sure of my expertise in hitching and unhitching, but we were confident we'd figure it out. Now we just needed a destination. Again, over Tabs in Nancy's kitchen, we used her laptop to look up campgrounds in coastal Maine. We didn't want to go too far in case Nancy needed medical care during our trip. Many of the campgrounds looked good, but being Smiths, we seemed to be genetically programmed to choose the one that offered homemade donuts every morning: Searsport Shores.

Since orange is my favorite color, Hank and I had ordered our basic white camper with "orange crush" detailing. I went to work at my ironing board, stenciling orange t-shirts for Nancy and me to wear on our trip. The shirts bore slogans like "Searsport or Bust!," "Orange is the New Black," and "Tabbin' 2007." Searsport was about a two-hour ride up Maine's scenic coastal Route 1 and, with no problems pulling the trailer, we arrived at the campground mid-afternoon. As we pulled up to the office, we were surrounded by campers and campground staff, many with cameras admiring "the first orange camper and the first orange campers" to visit Searsport Shores. I still treasure that photo.

With a little help from other campers, Nancy and I eventually settled into site #22. As we sat around our first campfire, Nancy opened a big plastic barrel of puffy cheese balls, a cellophane package of wooden skewers, and challenged me to her favorite camp contest: She who could get the most cheese balls onto the skewer with one "stab" won. I think Nancy held the record at six, but that's probably because she'd had so much practice!

After a long ride and way too many cheese balls, we tucked into the little bed in the camper for the night, pulling the quilts over us. We were way too tired for ghost stories. (Do middle-aged women still admit to telling ghost stories?) Camper windows open, we slept deeply in the sea air and woke to a sunlit Maine morning, Penobscot Bay glimmering in the early light.

Nancy prepared a big breakfast for us over the Coleman stove: eggs, bacon, home fries, and toast. Unfortunately, because of the way we'd parked our camper, our picnic table was only a few feet from the huge RV next door on site 21. I set the table with a bright tablecloth, paper plates, and a mason jar full of wildflowers. Our first meal at camp!

We had just picked up our forks when the sound of a motor got louder and closer. Sure enough, a bright yellow wagon with a hose and tank on the back managed to squeeze into the small space between our picnic table and the RV next door. A young man got out, fiddled with something on the outside of the RV not four feet from where we sat, attached the hose, and the sound of the motor was amplified by a deep sucking sound. The sucking sound was accompanied by an odor we identified immediately: sewage. It seems that the little yellow cart goes by the euphemism of "The Honey Wagon" for good reason. Suddenly aware of how much we had to learn as nouveau campers, Nancy and I grabbed our food and ran for the camper. Even with the windows closed and the A.C. on, neither of us ate much of our breakfast that morning. Another camping lesson learned: don't place your picnic table next to another camper's black water tank!

Before we left Searsport on the third day, Nancy and I painted an ocean-worn round rock with our names and the year we were there, 2007. We placed it under a little pine tree at the back of our site where, all these years later, it still resides. The tree has grown, but our marker stakes our place there for eternity.

For our road trip in August of 2008, Nancy had the idea of visiting each of the many houses and towns we'd grown up in, from Connecticut to New York to Maine. They say you "can't go back again," but we were determined to try. One last time.

This trip was full of ghosts of family and friends with whom we shared special moments in these homes but who were no longer with us. There was a sadness when places looked so different from how we had remembered them. In Westport, our old house was still there, but Barkington's barn, where we had spent hours exploring and playing as kids, was gone. The Newington house that Daddy and Grampa Smith built was still there, well cared for and painted red now instead of brown. The young maple tree we planted in front of the Guilford house now almost obscured it from view. Had that much time gone by? Our last stop was Vestal, where the road we used to walk or bike to school was now four lanes, lined with TJ Maxx, Applebee's, and Home Depot. Sadly, it looked like every other road, USA.

In August of 2009, Nancy and I took what I didn't know would be our last Sisters Road Trip together. We reserved a wooded lakefront campsite on Horse Island at Pawtuckaway State Park in Raymond, New Hampshire. You approach it from a long winding park road through acres of marsh grass leading to a weathered wooden bridge. We'd learned a lot about camping since we pulled the camper to Searsport Shores in 2007, but Pawtuckaway presented new challenges: it was more remote and there were no utilities.

Hank was a godsend. Knowing how much it meant to me to take Nancy camping, he followed us on the 90-minute drive to the campground, helped us set up, and showed us how to use the generator. Because our site had a little beach, we brought the canoe with us as well, tied to the roof of the Toyota. Hank helped us get it down and tied it to a birch tree that bent over the lake. Just happy to be there, Nancy and I never gave a thought as to how we'd get it back on top of the Toyota for the trip home.

*On the Road Again.*

Nancy and I both loved to read, and our days at Pawtuckaway soon fell into a comfortable pattern: we'd sit in our gravity chairs with coffee (Tab for Nancy, of course!) and a book all morning, feeding puffy orange cheese balls to the ducks who waddled up to our chairs. After a quick lunch, we'd check our map and head out on an afternoon adventure. The area was rural and there were plenty of pre-Revolutionary towns, historic markers, and cemeteries to visit. We both liked to walk through New England's oldest cemeteries, read the stones, and imagine what that person's life was like 200 or 300 years ago. If there was a settlement of old homes nearby, we'd wonder which were theirs and marvel at how they'd survived the area's frigid winters. Pawtuckaway was also near New Hampshire's Rt. 3, which was known as "Antique Alley" for its miles of vintage shops, perfect for browsing. The Robert Frost house wasn't far, nor were the acres of apple orchards the area was known for. Our lazy afternoon adventures took us to all of them.

Every day we went canoeing. Our first trip was lovely; we paddled around the whole island, pausing to watch a mother duck followed by her obedient ducklings, turtles sunning themselves on rocks, and clusters of pink and yellow waterlilies. The late summer air was warm and the rhythmic thump-splash of the oars hitting the water lulled us into torpidity. When we returned to our little beach, I told Nancy to stay where she was, on the wicker seat in the back of the boat, while I pulled the canoe up onto the shore. I got out, took a deep breath, and gave the canoe a vigorous tug. Up onto the shore it flew, like an Olympic luge, throwing Nancy backward off her seat, legs splayed and Tab splashing onto her shirt. When the canoe finally stopped, she was a human tortoise, stuck on its back. There was my sister, beached. We were laughing so hard that it took a few minutes for me to find the strength to pull her out.

I'll never forget our road trips together. They were the perfect sisterly adventures, the little moments of calm in an enormous storm.

# CHAPTER 32

## "Sounds of Silence"

### Simon & Garfunkel

Portland, Maine, 2009

In 2009, I watched a TV interview with David Axelrod, senior advisor to President Obama. He spoke about his daughter's epilepsy and their family's struggles. I turned up the volume and tears filled my eyes as Mr. Axelrod told Lauren's story. I realized it was exactly the same as Kristen's story: same age of onset, same medication trials, same search for a cause, same horror for her parents. Mr. Axelrod shared that, "This [epilepsy] is like terrorism of the brain. You don't know when it's going to strike, where you're going to be."

I decided to write to Mr. Axelrod, saying that I understood his family's pain. My hands were literally shaking as I tried to hit the keys on my computer. I knew what I wanted to say, but putting it into words was so emotional for me that I found controlling my fingers almost impossible. After many failed attempts, I completed my letter, carefully folded it, and enclosed a photo of my daughter, Kristen—who I thought bore an uncanny resemblance to his daughter, Lauren.

*Dear Mr. Axelrod:*

*Since the day that I heard Lauren's story, I knew that I needed to write this letter. I hope that you will take a moment to read it... because your family's story is our story.*

*A cause was never found for Kristen's seizures and she has since been diagnosed with an epilepsy spectrum disorder called Lennox-Gastaut syndrome. Like Lauren, epilepsy is not benign or treatable for Kristen.*

*Thank you for speaking up about epilepsy, thank you for sharing Lauren's story, and thank you for helping to bring us a President with both wisdom and a good heart, who I know will help to make life better for our children. This has been an emotional letter to write... sometimes, as I'm sure you know, it is easier to stuff the emotions that telling our stories bring up.*

*Best wishes to you, to your family, especially Lauren, and to President Obama.*

*Sincerely,*
*Cheryl Lawson*

Two weeks later, I opened our mailbox to find a crisp white envelope with a simple return address: "The White House, Washington, D.C., 20502" and the initials "D.A." I hadn't expected Mr. Axelrod to write back, if he even read my letter at all. His handwritten note convinced me that we had indeed been through the same nightmare with our daughters:

*6-24-09*

*Dear Cheryl,*

*Thanks for your moving letter, encouragement and support.*

*Like Lauren, Kristen has a wonderful smile.*

*Nothing can retrieve what has been lost. But it is comforting to know others who have walked this horrific road.*

*Our hope is to make more advances, so others won't have to follow.*

*Best to you and Kristen,*
*Dave*

Mr. Axelrod's use of the word "horrific" really got to me; it made me even more sure that his family had shared similar experiences to ours, that Lauren did indeed share the same epilepsy syndrome as Kristen.

I joined the Epilepsy Foundation Board to give back, to find ways to help other parents dealing with childhood epilepsy—like Mr. Axelrod and so many others. After serving 12 years, I received so much more than I gave. So many special people came into my life, becoming great friends, like Diana and Jeanne. I even met many professionals who gave Kristen access to the latest research and some of America's best neurologists.

I was rewarded with experiences I never could have imagined– like traveling around the country. Some of my fondest memories are being welcomed by two Presidents in the oval office–Ronald Reagan and George H. W. Bush, a fellow Kennebunk resident who greeted me with, "Hi, neighbor." Diana and I even met with a young senator named Joe Biden.

Feeling a little better in the fall of 2009, Nancy offered to drive Mom to her annual breast cancer follow-up appointment. Although in remission, Nancy wore one of "My Sister's Scarves" at the appointment. After Dr. Miesfeldt introduced herself, she looked at Nancy and gently asked if she had cancer.

"Yes," Nancy answered. "Ovarian."

Dr. Miesfeldt looked concerned. She explained to Mom and Nancy that breast and ovarian cancer are related and sometimes passed down genetically. Since Dr. Miesfeldt had just identified two first-degree relatives with these cancers, Mom and Nancy, she recommended that the rest of us have genetic testing immediately. Which we did.

Mom and the Four Stunning Smith Sisters arrived at the MMC Cancer Center on the morning of November 2nd, about a week after that appointment. We were scheduled for a blood draw and our first session of required genetic counseling. Our blood was tested to see if any of us carried either the BRCA1 or BRCA2 genes that were known to cause breast and ovarian cancer. If positive, we would be diagnosed with hereditary breast and ovarian cancer syndrome.

The first counseling session on November 2nd dealt with understanding how cancer can be passed down genetically. Andi, Nancy, Joanne, and I had studied biology in college since the discovery of DNA. While much of this was not new to us, it was very helpful for

Mom. We were informed that the odds of us having one of the BRCA genes were 50 percent, and discussed the potential emotional toll of the results of the test.

They suggested that we should each think about how we would feel in the face of a variety of possible outcomes: If I was negative and my sisters were positive? If I was positive and my sisters were negative? We discussed survivor guilt. We were like figures on a mobile, connected with strings. The results for each of us, whether good or bad, were going to impact the others. We left that session with a lot to think and worry about... and then we waited.

The wait was excruciating. I struggled to focus at work. I was consumed and anxious over the possibilities each of us faced. I considered the fact that the BRCA genes were passed down through the female line, and I already had a daughter who was medically fragile. If I tested positive, I could have passed the BRCA gene down to her. If that were the case, how could she ever deal with that—how could I? The thought was terrifying, and the waiting was making me sick. A tiny gene mutation was doing its best to try and kill us all. I honestly didn't know how much more stress I could take.

We got our results on November 9th. Uncharacteristically quiet, we sat together in the waiting room until we were each called into a little office. An oncologist and a genetic counselor shared the task of giving us our results. My body shook as I walked into the office for my turn, as I'm sure my sisters did when it was their turn. Hank held my hand, which helped. Aaron was there for Nancy. Andi and Joanne were alone.

We had talked amongst ourselves, and we were pretty sure that both Mom and Nancy would test positive, as they already had cancer. Both of them did test positive for BRCA2, mutation 5578delAA, which originated in England. The counselors surmised that the gene probably came over on the boat from Liverpool with Mom's mother, Grammy Boocock. She died of what they called stomach cancer back in the day. The oncologist explained that when Grammy was young, people often used the euphemism "stomach cancer" for gynecological cancers, suggesting that Grammy may have had ovarian cancer as well.

Joanne and I tested negative. I was relieved beyond measure for Kristen.

When Andi walked out with her results, I held back tears. Her expression alone revealed that she tested positive. Andi had to be thinking of how she'd tell her two adult daughters, who might also be carriers. The genetic counselor advised we notify all the other females on Mom's side of our family, urging them to get tested. Mom and Nancy saved some lives that day. Those who tested positive were monitored closely, and some received treatment.

Since Andi tested positive for BRCA2, her risk of getting breast or ovarian cancer was extremely high. Later that year, Andi courageously opted for a preventative mastectomy and oophorectomy, removal of the ovaries. A friend from work drove her to the hospital; no one in our family was told.

When Nancy and I heard about the surgery a day later, we were shocked. We were proud of Andi for being so brave and relieved that she had made it through such extensive surgery. Yet, we felt disappointed that she hadn't allowed us to be there to support her. It hurt being shut out, but that was Andi—how she did things. We had gotten used to being on the outside of some of her biggest life events.

As before with her elopements, Andi often kept things secret until the deed was done. It happened again when she married Dave. Dave was a fair-haired, attractive former high school athlete from central Maine who was fun to be with, honest, and caring. We all liked him and were happy for Andi. They were married at Chandler's Wharf, overlooking Portland's Casco Bay. The officiant was a coworker of Andi's who was also a Justice of the Peace. Mom was the witness and only guest, and once again, Nancy and I didn't find out until the wedding was over. That one really hurt.

While we never understood Andi's need for secrecy, we took it less personally the more we understood it was just how she operated. Over the years, she got good at compartmentalizing all of the moving pieces of her life. It was as if she could close them off at will. Maybe that was a strategy that helped her survive her years with Tim. We just wished Andi wouldn't shut the door so completely. We wanted to be there for our sister.

# CHAPTER 33

# *"The First of May"*

## Bee Gees

### Portland, Maine, 2005 - 2010

Over the years since we left the Board, the Epiladies continued to stay in touch, visiting each other when we could and texting when we couldn't.

Jeanne Cahill, a dear friend since our work together for the Epilepsy Foundation of America, was an inspiration to me. She was one of many people who kept my hope and laughter alive, through Kristen's epilepsy and Nancy's cancer. Women of all ages throughout history kept coming out swinging against all odds—in education, politics, and health related battles. They did it; Jeanne did it. They conquered whatever was put before them. So could Nancy!

In spite of her father's disapproval, Jeanne entered Berry College in Rome, Georgia, as a freshman work student in 1949. She paid for two years there before leaving to work for newly elected sheriff Al Cahill, who she later married. Six decades later, never one to lose sight of a goal, Jeanne re-enrolled at Berry College. An English major, she graduated as Berry's oldest Valedictorian at age 76 in 2005!

In the Spring of 2009, we drove to Baltimore to visit another Epilady, Diana Pillas. We were surprised to see her wearing a headscarf. She wanted to tell us in person that she was being treated for advanced breast cancer, admitting that medical people are often the worst patients. Even though she worked at Johns Hopkins Hospital, she waited too long before having the lump on her breast checked. Diana was too busy helping others to help herself. I had never met another like her, before nor since.

On February 6th, 2010 at the age of 69, Diana Pillas, an amazing human, friend, chosen sister, and fellow Epilady, passed away. This loss deeply affected me. I hate cancer.

It was 2010, and after a long remission, Nancy's cancer came back. Now we were all back at Maine Medical Center. This time, the cancer was angrier than ever, bringing with it crippling anemia and dehydration. Nancy was in and out of the Gibson Cancer Unit through the rest of the summer and into fall–the leaves were turning and the days were getting cooler.

Nancy needed frequent transfusions and IV saline drips now. One of us was with her most of the time. We brought Mom in to see her, which was difficult to watch. Mom looked down at her sick baby, held her hand, wiped her brow with a cool cloth, and demonstrated strength I honestly never knew she had. I felt proud of Mom in those moments. She always hid her softer side–her vulnerabilities–around us. No more. This was different and we all knew it.

Nancy made it home for her 58th birthday on September 20th. Her body fought back, and we were all there to witness and celebrate together. There were teal roses, a cake from Aaron, and cards and gifts from the rest of us. Nancy sat in her favorite spot, the kitchen booth, nursing a can of ginger ale as we all sang "Happy Birthday." When she read the cards, she began to cry.

I think she knew that this could be her last birthday. If I comforted her, would that be like acknowledging that it might be? If I remained cheerful, would I be making light of her feelings? Giving her false hope? I felt pulled in different directions, the anxiety of yet another situation way beyond our control. Thankfully, Hank's antics had her laughing after a few minutes, which was good to see. I decided to hug her, and tell her I loved her. That was all I could think to do.

In October, Nancy was back at the Gibson Unit at MMC. It was my birthday month, and the nurses couldn't believe that, before she was re-admitted, Nancy bought and signed a card for me. She surprised me with it when I visited on October 25th. Nancy had prepared for Halloween too, changing from standard gray hospital socks to orange and black striped knee-highs for the day. She hung a sign by her bed that I'd given her years ago. It read, "The Witch Is In." The nurses loved it! That was our Nancy, still prepared for every holiday.

Most of us stayed at the hospital overnight, sometimes in the cots and recliners in Nancy's room, other times in the lounge across the hall. It had several couches, and the nurses on Gibson had thoughtfully reserved it for our family. We all rotated through the different sleeping arrangements, so we could stay nearby and each get some time with Nancy. Late one night when I was half asleep in Nancy's room in one of the sleeper chairs, Ken and Nancy had some quiet time together.

One of Nancy's favorite children's books was *Love You Forever* by Robert Munsch. The book was about a little boy going through the stages of childhood and becoming a man. It was also about the enduring nature of a parent's love and how it crosses generations. Through her oxygen mask in a soft voice, Nancy read the book to Ken as he quietly sat beside her. They held hands, while I pretended to be asleep so I wouldn't embarrass them or ruin their time together. They seemed to both be crying. So was I.

Nancy needed her abdomen drained of fluid buildup almost every other day. She lost more weight, was having difficulty breathing, and she was often in pain. Transfusions were frequent, and Nancy started having hallucinations. She mentioned seeing a donkey with big teeth,

Dad who passed away in 2005, and a school bus in her window. As she looked at the window, Nancy said, "Cheryl, I know there's not really a school bus there, right?" She knew they weren't real.

In addition to her other symptoms, Nancy had been constipated for days. Dr. Small gently explained this might be a sign her body was shutting down. None of us wanted to hear that, especially Nancy. But a few days later there was cause for celebration. "I pooped!" she yelled with joy. We had all been losing hope over the past few weeks, but now it was BACK! The light was back in Nancy's eyes. She had been to the brink so many times and always fought her way back. We were sure this was an early sign of yet another remission.

Sadly, it was short-lived. That morning, when Nancy's oncologist did rounds, she quietly told Nancy that, BM or no BM, her body was shutting down. Dr. Small asked me if I could get the family together for a meeting at 2:00 p.m. When I left the room, she spoke with Nancy privately. As I notified everyone, alarm bells were ringing in my head. In less than an hour, we'd gone from the high of anticipating a remission to a new low. We all dreaded hearing the prognosis at the family meeting.

At the meeting, Nancy was Dorothy at the end of her favorite movie, *The Wizard of Oz*. We were all there, seated around Nancy's hospital bed—she was in the middle with Aaron on one side and Dr. Small on the other. Mom was there with Joanne and Mark. Ken was there with his wife, Erin. Hank and I were there with Robert, who had flown in from New York. Andi and Dave were there. None of us, including Nancy, wanted her to go anywhere. We all loved her and she loved us. And unfortunately, we were all worried about what would come next.

Quietly, Dr. Small explained that Nancy's battle was over. Her body could not go on much longer, and Nancy had two choices. She could continue treatment for the cancer with no hope of remission, or allow the doctors to start morphine and allow her body to shut down naturally. Dr. Small predicted that if Nancy chose to stop treatment, she might live another three or four days. She promised us that the hospital staff could keep Nancy comfortable. These options must be what they had discussed earlier that morning as Nancy didn't seem as shocked as the rest of us.

When Dr. Small stopped speaking, it was quiet. Everyone's eyes were red, and everyone was holding hands, with Nancy and each other. Somehow Nancy found courage for what happened next, although I'm not sure how. She went around that circle, like the teacher she was, and asked each of the people who loved her what they thought she should do. It was awful, gut-wrenching, almost indescribable. Everyone started by telling Nancy how much we loved her. Then, each in our own way, we said it might be time to let go and let God make the decisions now, while the Gibson staff kept her comfortable. And that's what Nancy did.

Nancy was more comfortable over the next few days with the morphine onboard, although she still had difficulty breathing. She slept more, but was able to hear us better when she was awake. In addition to the family, some of the most special people in her life came to visit. Officials, now friends, from the Maine affiliate of the American Cancer Society came with an official document thanking Nancy for all of her volunteer work. Her best friend Betsy, her pastor and his wife, and the biggest surprise of all, David—the man who had broken her heart so many years ago, came to say their goodbyes.

David was a music teacher at the school in Wells where they both worked. In addition to teaching music, he was extremely talented and played piano at local restaurants and piano bars. They had been in a serious romantic relationship for over five years. David was her escort to every family function in the late 80s and early 90s. And then he got married—to someone else—without Nancy having any idea why. She was totally devastated.

It took Nancy a long time to get over David. No one ever found out what led to his unexpected marriage to someone he was not even known to have been dating. I guessed he may have still had feelings for

Nancy though. Here he was in the hallway at Maine Medical Center, all these years later, waiting for a private moment alone with her. When he came out of her room, I was in the hall. He had been crying and we hugged. David told me he had apologized to Nancy and given her a final kiss goodbye. He said she forgave him, and then he left, perhaps a little lighter than when he arrived.

These were not easy days for any of us, especially Nancy. She grew weaker and slept most of the time. Someone was with her at all times now, and we took turns napping and sitting at her bedside holding her hand. We softly played some of her favorite music as she slept. She and I both loved the soundtrack from the old Christopher Reeves movie *Somewhere in Time*, so I played that for her. I played her the ukulele version of "Somewhere Over the Rainbow" too, another of her favorites. Joanne made fun of my musical choices at times, and she put some rock music on so Nancy had a variety. I figured a little Huey Lewis couldn't hurt.

On Saturday evening, Hank, Aaron, and I went to Mass at Saint Peter's, the nearby Italian church in which Hank grew up. We didn't attend church regularly, but I found that I needed to call on my Catholic faith at times like this. Hank and I both needed to feel the warmth of St. Peter's enfolding us that night. When we left for Mass, I kissed Nancy goodbye, reminded her that I loved her, and told her I'd be back soon.

Before Mass, I asked the priest if he would say a special prayer for Nancy at this Mass, as we also did. The church was dark, smelled of incense, and there were few people. It was mostly elderly Italian ladies in black clothes and head scarves with rosary beads curled around their fingers. I cried throughout the service and took communion for Nancy.

After Mass, we planned to go back to the hospital, but I was exhausted. I had not gotten much sleep over the past few days, and I didn't argue when Hank suggested that he take me home for a good night's sleep.

He promised to bring me back to the hospital early Sunday morning. We said goodbye to Aaron, who returned to the hospital to spend the night with Nancy.

Sunday morning, Hank woke me with a gentle whisper. "Cheryl, she's gone." It was November 14th, 2010. My little sister, my very best friend in the world, was gone. Nancy was 58—our "Nancy with the laughing face" was finally at peace. For her, it truly was an endless summer.

Losing Nancy left me with a visceral emotional ache, a depressive emptiness in my soul, and a kind of angry anxiety that I worked hard to control. I didn't see how my life could ever be the same without her. I found some solace from seeing a counselor. The coping strategies I learned were helpful, but my sister was still gone.

*When I was small*
*And Christmas trees were tall*
*We used to laugh while others used to play*
*Don't ask me why*
*But time has passed us by*
*Someone else moved in from far away*

*Now we are tall*
*And Christmas trees are small*
*And you don't ask the time of day*
*But you and I*
*Our love will never die*
*To kiss and cry, "Come, first of May"*

Barry Gibb, 1969

*My last picture of Nancy.*

# *"Small Town"*

## John Mellencamp

Andover, Maine, 2011 - 2013

The next fall, Hank and I took a day trip through the Rangely Lakes area of Maine. It had been almost a year since we lost Nancy and I missed her every single day. Maybe a ride to New Hampshire on a crisp fall day would cheer me up.

We stumbled upon Andover, Maine, a lonely looking four-corners town that seemed as if it crept out of a Stephen King thriller. There was a general store with two muddy four wheelers parked at the town's only gas pumps, a row of abandoned houses and shops, a town green, and no people that we could see.

We stopped at the store, where Hank got out to stretch his legs and grab some snacks. He'd been inside for a while, so I got out of the car to photograph some of the deserted buildings. Ever since I was a kid in Connecticut exploring Tarkington's Barn, I'd been fascinated by old buildings and loved photographing them while wondering: *Who lived or worked here? What were their lives like? Why did they leave? Did they leave anything of themselves behind?*

Usually I stayed fairly undetectable in my photographic explorations, as I crept through the undergrowth or hid behind rafters for the perfect shot. But in small-town Maine, they don't let someone "from away" sneaking around with a camera go unnoticed for long. While I was outside, Hank later told me what had happened inside. A local in the store noticed me and commented to the cashier: "Big doins' in town. Some lady reporter from away is out there with a camera."

Hank, who thought I was waiting in the car, thought it couldn't be me until he looked outside just in time to see me slithering through the shrubbery. "Oh, that's my wife. She likes to take pictures of old buildings. She's harmless." He continued to make small talk with the store patrons, creating a perfect diversion for me—cub reporter, amateur photographer, and frequent creator of potentially embarrassing situations.

When I emerged from the thicket, I noticed an old guest house that appeared to be deserted. Its sign hung lopsided by one or two links of a rusty chain, which was a great photo op. I made my way along the weed-strewn driveway to take shots from the rear, but as I reached the end of the driveway, I discovered the mother lode: hidden at the back of the property was a 1964 vintage turquoise Scotty travel trailer begging to be photographed. I checked to be sure I was alone and snapped a photo—just as a screen door slammed to my left.

A man ran out, clad in only plaid boxer shorts, and headed right for me, yelling, "CAN I HELP YOU?" Time to turn on the charm... fast!

"Oh, hi," I said. "I didn't think anyone was around." The words nervously tumbled out. "I'm a vintage trailer lover, and I couldn't resist peeking at your Scotty. Mind if I take a picture of it?" I left out the part where I already had.

"Oh... okay", he answered. "Would you like to see the inside?"

"I'd love to," I blurted out without thinking.

He unlocked the Scotty's door and ushered me into its sweltering interior. As I proceeded inside ahead of my boxer-wearing friend, all of the Stephen King books I've read flooded my brain. Hank didn't know where I was, and I was all alone with a guy I didn't know—a practically naked guy who stood between me and the only door. What if he was a psycho who uses his cute little trailer to lure unsuspecting women from away into his camper?

I pretended to admire the vintage interior of the Scotty while my eyes frantically darted around in search of an emergency exit. There was only one way out, and it was the door he was blocking. I was trapped. Maybe if I asked him to show me how these yellow cots fold out, he would move so I could escape? Maybe if I asked him what was under the dinette, I could conk him over the head with my camera and make a run for it?

My thoughts of escape were interrupted when my scantily-clothed man friend stood up straight, looked me in the eye, and introduced himself with a firm handshake. "You may not recognize me. I'm Kevin Scott, independent candidate for Governor of Maine. I've put 44,000 miles on that Oldsmobile out there since the campaign started."

Oh, God, I did it again. I made a perfect fool of myself. Did stuff like this happen to other people?

Mr. Scott proved to be a pleasant guy who was restoring the old Scotty, as well as many of the deserted buildings in Andover. Once we both had pants on, Mr. Scott gave me a tour of the tiny town. He was so nice I couldn't bring myself to tell him I planned to vote for one of his opponents. Perhaps if I'd known he loved old Scotty's and old houses sooner, he may have had a chance.

Back home in Falmouth a few weeks later, we turned on WCSH Channel 6 to watch the gubernatorial debates. There was my guy, Mr. Scott, at the middle podium. Although he was wearing a suit, I couldn't help seeing him in his boxer shorts. It was a hard image to get out of my head. Just another day in my crazy life—saw some old houses, toured a vintage Scotty, and met the potential next governor of Maine in his underwear.

The following summer, we returned to Andover. This time, we made the trip with our new lightweight travel trailer, a 17-foot Casita we named "Cassie." We recently picked Cassie up from the one and only factory that makes Casitas in Rice, Texas. It had a small kitchenette, and an even smaller bathroom. I loved that I could take a shower and clean the bathroom at the same time! The queen bed was especially cozy in the rain, under a quilt I made. The dinette folded down to make a third bed, which was perfect when a grandchild, friend, or one of my sisters joined us at camp.

Earlier, we had stopped by the Portland camping show, and I noticed a pile of books in one of the booths. I wondered why it was prominently displayed at a camping show, so I walked over to investigate. The title was *We Took to the Woods* by Louise Dickenson Rich; it was written in 1943, and it was one of my favorites. Mrs. Rich and her husband raised five children in the woods around nearby Richardson Lake in the years between the two world wars. Life was difficult and supplies were hard to come by. What the family could not grow or make themselves, they acquired by taking a boat or sled, depending on the season, down the lake to "the Arm."

The Arm was what the locals called the small settlement at the south arm of the lake where supplies could be purchased. The book was in this particular booth because the booth was run by the owner of South Arm Campground, located right at the spot that Mrs. Rich wrote about in her memoir. We spoke to him briefly, asking about his campground, which he described as remote. Hank and I decided to reserve a campsite there for two weeks in July. We were warned to make sure we had good directions ahead of time because we were bound to lose cellphone service at about the halfway point. However, if we were desperate to make a call, we could always make our way to the top of one of the many mountains in the area.

A few months later, we called to verify directions before heading out so we wouldn't get lost. We were directed to take a right at the Andover country store and then the first left, before that turned into a dirt track for 12 miles, until we saw the South Arm sign. Our 4Runner and Casita were filled to the brim for our two-week stay, and we were anxious to get set up before dark. Spying the two rusty gas pumps we remembered from our previous trip, we turned right at the country store in the center of Andover and watched for the upcoming left turn.

It was a couple of miles before we spotted a store on the corner, which was farther than we expected. We turned left and settled in for the final 12-mile stretch to camp. However, the road seemed to end at a small lake bordered by summer cottages. But wait! It didn't end; it just turned to dirt. A couple on a four-wheeler roared by us with its occupants waving before they disappeared up the dirt track that climbed the mountain. We assumed this was the dirt path they were talking about and pushed on up the hill. We drove up and up and up, very slowly. The road became narrower, the incline steeper, but it couldn't go on forever, so we kept going.

Until we couldn't go anymore. The hill was so steep, the road so muddy, and the camper so heavy that our Toyota lost traction. It wasn't able to pull anymore, and we were stuck about halfway up the mountain. Worse than that, our camper was now very slowly starting to slide back down, pulling our Toyota—and its terrified occupants—with it. The camper was picking up momentum, and we were suddenly headed down the narrow mountain path with no shoulders—backwards! Since I hadn't paid enough attention to Galileo's experiments in Mrs. Colburn's Science class, I didn't think I would be much help to Hank. So, I grabbed a red blanket from the back seat, yelled, "We're going to die!" and covered my head. Problem solved.

Luckily, Hank the hero husband said, "Hold on!" He turned in his seat, doing his best to see where we were sliding while somehow managing to ignore every instinct one uses when driving forward to steer the camper. Finally, we came to a level area where our little motorcade stopped. It was quiet as I peered out from under my blanket. We weren't dead! But there was no place wide enough to turn the car and camper around, so we had only two choices: go the rest of the way up in forward, or try to go the rest of the way down in reverse.

In either case, we had to perform this feat without going over the steep drop on either side. We had started to wonder if the campground owner was downplaying the word remote. Since we had no cellphone service, as warned, with nowhere to get out, our best course was to keep going. Hank slid the Toyota back into four-wheel, hit the gas hard, and up we went—slipping backward every few yards before catching up to ourselves again. Finally, we could see the mountaintop! One last acceleration, and we catapulted over the edge with a deafening thud.

We tentatively opened the car doors to look around. Everything previously tied to the top of the 4Runner including our canoe, paddles, and camp chairs, was strewn around the vehicle. Except for our fallen load, there was absolutely nothing else at the very flat top of the mountain, besides many felled logs. There was definitely not a campground, no road, no sign, and no trees—unless you counted the felled logs. After all that stunt driving and blanket-grabbing fear, we arrived in the center of a clear-cut mesa in the Middle of Nowhere, Maine. We were finally ready to admit that we might have made a wrong turn.

Since we now had some time to think, it occurred to us that RVs much larger than us camp at South Arm, and they likely would not have been able to navigate this steep and narrow road which had almost claimed our lives. The more we thought about it, the more foolish we felt. How did we make it? Once we got over our fear and anger, we looked at each other and laughed out loud. We doubted anyone would believe we could have been this stupid. Remembering the four wheeler we saw earlier, it occurred to us that we had managed to drag two tons of metal up what we now realized was actually a four wheeler trail. The problem was now: how were we going to get back down?

The one good thing about being stuck at the top of a mountain was that the campground owner was right, we did have cell service! We called the campground, told them we were lost, described our surroundings, and asked for directions. They were very glad to hear from us. However, no one at the office had any clue as to where in the hell we were. They just suggested that we head back down, so we said goodbye so we could figure out exactly how we were going to do that. Considering there was no more up, our only option out of this forsaken place was to go back down on the same deadly dirt trail we rode up on.

The small mesa on the mountaintop was littered with our displaced items from the top of the 4Runner and logs from clear cutting. We had to move what seemed like a few hundred logs out of the way, in addition to reattaching our own gear, before we could turn the camper around. The moment I was belted back in, ever so helpful in a scary situation, I announced, "Okay. I trust you. Down we go," and put the blanket back over my head. Through some miracle, we bumped and rocked our way to the bottom, shaky, but alive. I whispered to Hank that he was my hero. Now, we just had to find the campground.

We retraced the route we had taken out of Andover and found our way back to the country store in the center of town—where we had started two hours earlier. Thankfully, there was cell reception at the store, so we called the campground office again. We explained that we had made it off the mountain and were back in the center of town. The office staff had been consulting some maps, and they believed we missed the first left and ended up on Flathead Mountain—that sounded about right to us. We got a new set of directions with landmarks. Then, they wished us luck and said we should arrive in about a half an hour.

Thankfully, we found South Arm Campground; we arrived at the office to a welcoming party of campers and staff. Word of our misadventures had spread, and they had all been worried. We had been pretty worried too! After introductions, thanks, and small talk, we bought ice and firewood before making our way along the lake to site number 17. The views were breathtakingly worth the trip. It was known as "the windy sight," but we didn't care. Our site was at the tip of the island, facing the sunset. Just as we backed our Casita into the site, a red sea plane came over and landed just down the lake. This place was perfect!

We set the brakes and unhitched the camper. Hank suggested I go open up the inside while he took care of hooking up our water and electricity. I unlocked our Casita's little door and opened it slowly. *OMG!* It looked like the inside of a moving van packed by a mad man. The bumpy road up the mountain was full of boulders, and not one thing was where it had been when we started out. Bed cushions blocked the doorway, and kitchen gear was spread across a floor covered in clothes and towels. All of the food that fell out of the refrigerator was sprinkled here and there among our belongings. If I were to make us BLTs, they'd be served on a bed of dishtowels with a side of toothpaste.

I fought back tears as I called Hank over to take a look. We were exhausted and losing daylight with a lot to do before we could even think of sleeping. Tired as we were, we encouraged each other, and in about an hour we had the campsite livable enough for the first night.

Hank lit a fire in our fire ring, and we sat together watching the last of the sun drop into Richardson Lake. As we gazed at the sun's rays and the fire's flames, we decided that being together here and now made it all worth it. Maybe someday in the distant future we were going to be able to laugh about our first trip "up the mountain" to South Arm!

*"Just sit right back*
*And you'll hear a tale*
*A tale of a fateful trip,*
*That started from this tropic port,*
*Aboard this tiny ship."*
Gilligan's Island, 1964

The "tropic port" was the south arm of Richardson Lake. It was now 2013, the third July we'd camped in Andover at South Arm. The "tiny ship" was a very safe looking aluminum pontoon boat. The day was beautiful and a perfect sunset was promised.

Among the passengers who set sail that evening were my husband Hank and I, our friend Rosalie, and eight or nine other unsuspecting campers. Our skipper Leon was brave and sure. I loved Leon. He'd been born in Andover and grew up on the lake. Every year when we arrived at camp, I would ask for him. He was such a kind man. In his 80s, he had a leathery face from working outdoors, a full head of white hair, an easy smile, and a mischievous twinkle in his eyes. I loved listening to his stories about life on the lake when he was a boy; it was so much like the stories Louise Rich told in *We Took to the Woods*. Like her children, he lived with a family in town each winter so that he could go to school. The roads to and from the Arm were impassable until Spring, and the only school was in Andover. Now partially retired, Leon helped out at the campground marina. That evening, he was our guide for an evening tour of the lake and its two dams. It had been a hot day for Rangeley, so most of us were dressed in shorts and sandals, some carrying margaritas to sip on the boat.

The sun was out and the sky was clear; a perfect night for the 17-mile cruise up the lake. After about half an hour of calm sailing, we disembarked to explore the Middle Dam. As we crossed the dam's cement top, Leon looked up at the sky and hollered for us to hurry back to the boat. We could tell he meant business. We ran. As soon as we got to the boat, he shoved off, heading us back to the safety of South Arm.

Then, everything happened at once. Our little boat was in the vortex of a violent thunder storm. I quickly realized that the term "golf ball-sized hail" wasn't an exaggeration; that's exactly what was pelting us. In a matter of seconds, the sky had gotten eerily dark. The winds were frantically whipping the boat. Our usually easy-going captain, looking very serious now, yelled over the wind, instructing us to get down and pointing out the location of the life jackets. He stood tall at the front of the boat, hands gripping the wheel, face to the wind, as he cranked the engines and steered for the Arm.

We didn't make it. What started out as a few hours of summer fun soon became a watery nightmare. Lightning was striking within feet of our metal boat as wind, rain, and hail pounded us relentlessly. The only safe place to dock was still miles down the lake. We took cover as best we could, under benches or huddled together on the floor of the boat. Hank pushed Rosalie and me down onto the aluminum bottom of the boat and lay on top of us, trying to cover us both with his jacket and his body. I closed my eyes and prayed. As we approached the South Arm marina, the storm was at its height. Rather than attempting to dock the boat, Captain Leon aimed it right up onto the beach and yelled, "JUMP!" Visions of my dad's stories about beach landings on D-Day swirled through my head.

So, I jumped... and landed right behind Hank and Rosalie, waist-deep in cold lake water. We half swam, half-waded to shore with lightning bursting all around us. Soaking wet, we sprinted to the nearby tiki hut for shelter, dripping on each other, hugging each other, and asking ourselves if this whole thing had just been a bad dream. I'd rarely been as scared as I was in the middle of that lake in the worst storm of the summer. Everyone was wet and cold but *safe*, thanks to our hero Leon.

Over the years, the story of Leon's heroism has taken on mythical proportions. To this day, whenever we go to South Arm, we run into people who recognize us and ask, "Weren't you among the people who were on that crazy boat ride a few years back when Leon had to run it aground?" Yup, that was us!

*Leon, our hero at South Arm.*

It seemed that every time Hank and I go to Andover, Maine, we found ourselves in unexpected situations. The first year. I ended up stuck in a Scotty trailer with one of Maine's gubernatorial candidates who just happened to be in his underwear. The next year, we got lost on the top of a mountain with our camper and had to *back* all the way down. And year three, the boat trip from hell.

Perhaps you thought no one could get into that much trouble in a small town of just 826 people. Unless of course you were Hank and I—or you were friends with Hank and I. We seemed to find a lot of it, or maybe it was finding us. Maybe Stephen King really was onto something. Andover? I was almost afraid to go back!

# CHAPTER 35

# *"Friends"*

## Elton John

### Falmouth, Maine, 2013 - Present

As much as we loved our time at Winn Farm, Hank said he always saw us as two in a long line of temporary caretakers of the historic property. If I looked at it that way, I felt happier about moving on. We were there 11 years, but at 4,000 square feet on three acres of land, it was too large for just the two of us. We knew it was time to downsize and pass Winn Farm along to someone else—hopefully to another family who wanted to make their own world of memories there and could give it the care it deserved.

It was hard to leave the magical wizards hidden in the trees, the little bridge, the tiny hobbit house, the pagoda, the grape arbor, the peach tree, and the fairytale hobbit house. It was difficult to say goodbye to the fishing hole, the hidden statue of Saint Francis, and the Jack-in-the-pulpits that pop up every spring. But when we left, we kept our memories of the Wizard's Forest and its secret paths in the mystical woods behind Winn Farm.

One gray Sunday winter afternoon, we went for a ride with no particular destination in mind. Hank and I drove along Route 88 with our grandson Brian who was visiting for the weekend. The road followed the shoreline in Falmouth Foreside, and we enjoyed the wintry views of Casco Bay. Brian noticed an open house sign and pointed at a neighborhood called Applegate we had never noticed before. As usual, we weren't looking for a house at that moment, but apparently one seemed to be looking for us. Since we had nothing better to do, we went in.

Immediately, we fell in love with 22 Applegate Lane. At 2,300 square feet, it was a lot smaller than Winn Farm, but big enough to accommodate visits from family and friends. It was walking distance to the Falmouth Town Landing, with its little general store, marina, and beach. How perfect: an apple-red Cape Cod house in a neighborhood called Applegate. The following spring, it became our retirement home.

I retired in June of 2013, freeing me up to begin a new project: renovating our new home at Applegate. I welcomed the change and the work. While we renovated, Hank and I got in the habit of starting our day at the nearby Dunkin' Donuts. We each drank one cup of coffee there, then got a second cup to drink as we scraped at stubborn wallpaper and painted each room at Applegate. Having breakfast at Dunkin' Donuts was like finding ourselves somewhere in time between the Mayberry Cafe from *The Andy Griffith Show* and the bar scene at the Mos Eisley Cantina in *Star Wars*.

Albert, the friendly bald manager, greeted us with a smile every morning. We headed for a table with our coffee and a *Portland Press Herald* to relax before the day's activities swept us up. Before we sat down, we would shim up one leg of the table with a napkin to keep it from wobbling. I was convinced there was not a single table with two legs the same length in the whole place. Shimming up a table leg was as much a part of the morning routine as adding cream to our coffee. Beyond our routine table-leveling, it was the regulars we saw most mornings who really defined the place. And, over time, we got to know them all.

There was "Mini Man," who loved his Mini Cooper and got a kick out of parking his blue one next to my red one. "Big John" was a heavy-set mild-mannered gentleman who stopped by most mornings. He was a limo driver, ever-cheerful and usually willing to share a story or two from his time behind the wheel. There was also a quiet man with military posture and a short gray buzzcut who always sat with his back to the wall. CIA? Special ops? Right here at the Falmouth Dunkin' Donuts?

There was also a group of runners. The spandex-clad older adults met a couple times a week for coffee after their two to three-mile jog. We sat near each other for weeks before we finally introduced ourselves. Hank used to run half marathons, so he admired that these men and women, who looked about our age, were still running.

Hank got a kick out of the fact that the Dunkin' Donuts staff learned to recognize our car whenever we entered the drive-thru loop instead of coming inside. They had our order, always the same, ready before we even got to the window. In addition to the manager, Albert, the other regular staffers were: Barbara, Phil, Mo, Charlie, Pauline, Casey, Kara, and Dabrya—who went by Angel.

When always-cheerful Barbara and her two children faced home-lessness last Christmas, we raised over 3,000 dollars from neighbors, family, and friends. Barbara was able to pay the first and last month's rent for a new apartment. Her family moved in over New Year's weekend and had a fresh start.

There was also a group of five or six elderly gentlemen, veterans of WWII and Korea according to their hats. They held court at the table in the far corner by the window, drinking coffee and arguing, sometimes loudly, about the news of the day. From the proposed height of the new buildings going up on Route 1 to why they thought Trump should win the upcoming presidential election, they could argue about anything. We found them friendly enough to us, nodding or smiling as we sat down. Maybe they hadn't yet figured out that we were staunch Democrats.

We were shocked one morning when one of their arguments got physical. Don—a thin, gray-haired vet who always wore a scowl—jumped up and started a fistfight by punching one of the other old guys. Thankfully, it was over almost as quickly as it started. The other vets held the combatants back until Don stormed out. Don always seemed to be scowling, and I felt sorry for him. I wondered what happened in his life that left him so unhappy.

A local veteran favorite was Arthur, who was a US Army WWII vet, Post Commander at the Falmouth American Legion, and Falmouth's Citizen of the Year. Because my Weight Watchers meeting was held in the basement at the Legion Hall, I first met Arthur there, of all places. He was always helping set out chairs or doing Legion paperwork in the basement, which I later learned was because he had a crush on our leader, Bernadette. He took a chance once and asked her out to dinner, but she declined, saying she preferred to continue as friends. After his death in 2013, she confessed to me that she always regretted that and wished she had said yes instead.

In addition to the table of vets, another regular at Dunkin' was a man named John—a tall scarecrow-looking man in his 50s who was pretty well known around Falmouth. He was a tinkerer, a renaissance man who picked up odd jobs like placing campaign signs at election time or distributing the free local newspaper, *The Forecaster*. Occasionally, John held art shows at local businesses of the paintings he did in oils and acrylics. He enjoyed carpentry and built colorful wooden benches, many of which could be seen around Falmouth. John also wrote and published two books of his photographs of Portland, both sold in area bookstores.

While John was seemingly successful at all of these endeavors, it did not explain why he never had any money. Some mornings he slinked to Dunkin' with a painting to sell. Other mornings, he'd just come right out and ask if we'd lend him a couple dollars for a cup of coffee, stating he was broke until the first of the month. My special education background led me to suspect that John was on the spectrum. He probably received disability and budgeting was clearly a challenge for him.

Most days, John managed to talk his way over to our table to visit or consult on the morning crossword puzzle. Other days he was completely silent and wouldn't even look up when we spoke to him, seemingly lost in a world of his own. We made two purchases to help keep John afloat. One was a painting he did, a take on a Van Gogh cafe scene, and the other was a bright green bench he built for the yard at Kristen's group home.

We also became friendly with two elderly sisters, Margaret and Jo. They lived together and shared the small yellow house where they grew up. Margaret—a stocky woman of average height with short white hair—was the first to introduce herself. Jo was heavy, with short gray hair and a prosthetic leg. Margaret was able to drive and Jo was able to walk with a cane, so together they managed to live independently with their little dog Gretel.

Although I had not met Margaret and Jo before Dunkin' Donuts, the saying that "Maine is just one big small town" proved uncannily true. They were retired cooks who spent years working in the cafeteria at Maine Medical Center when my ex-husband, Bob Underwood, was Food Services Director. Another peculiar coincidence was that they lived on Underwood Road. I was surprised when I learned that Jo was actually younger than me, while Margaret wasn't much older. I decided I'd be more careful in the future about who I described as "elderly," since I apparently am too!

Jo loved to share memories of her late husband named Bert. He was stationed at Pearl Harbor while serving in the Navy. I saw photos of Bert; he bore a slight resemblance to Barnie Fife from the *Andi Griffith Show*—skinny but handsome, with sandy hair and a nice smile. Other women must have been captivated by that smile too because Jo was proud to announce that she was his *10th* and last wife. Seemingly, after so many wives in so many ports, Bert finally dropped anchor when he met Jo. Bert amorously defied the adage that "cats only have nine lives." Before he went to his well-deserved eternal rest, Bert managed to squeak out 10!

Margaret reminded me of one of my very favorite people, my Grammy Smith. They had the same short gray hair, the same body shape, and the same can-do, take-no-prisoners personality. She used Grammy's Smith's familiar words like "t'aint" and "ayuh." She even cooked like Grammy, preferring traditional New England foods like hot dogs, beans, and brown bread on Saturday nights. Even though we were close in age, being with Margaret was a little like having my beloved Grammy Smith back.

Our friendship with Margaret and Jo extended beyond Dunkin' to their little yellow house on Underwood Road. It was tiny, with sagging floors and a moss-covered roof that was past due for replacement.

They were no longer able to do larger tasks around the house, so we helped them out when we could. Hank and I painted their little dining area a pretty aqua blue color they had chosen and added a shelf for their tea pots. One project turned out to be more than we bargained for: we almost killed ourselves attempting to apply a faux stone finish to their living room wall. The four of us laughed our way through that project. Eventually, we decided to ignore the useless stick-on installation instructions and just nail the damn "stones" right to the wall. I predicted they would last long after the little yellow house on Underwood Road was gone.

One tired-looking regular was named Sue. She stopped for oatmeal and coffee after pulling all-nighters at the local nursing home. As we became friends over coffee, I realized how much she relished that little bit of me time in her busy life. When she wasn't working, she cared for a husband with cancer and a grown son who didn't seem to do much of anything. Habitat for Humanity provided them a small but efficient house within walking distance of the Falmouth business district, which made life manageable for Sue.

She was also supporting her other son and his two children in Bath. One year, the regulars and some of our other friends anonymously gave Sue's grandchildren a Christmas to remember. The generosity of our little "donut" community was impressive. Not only did the kids get toys, but we didn't leave out their dad and mom. He got warm boots while she got a much-needed microwave oven. I realized that sometimes even a woman as tough as Sue needs help, even though she would never ask for it.

We became a little early-morning family, a curious band of very different people who slowly came to care about each other. If one of us went missing for a while, we wondered if something was the matter. "Have you seen Sue?" we'd ask. "Why do you think we haven't seen the 'CIA Guy' this week?" We took notice and, in a weird way, looked out for one another. Then COVID hit.

The dining room at Dunkin' Donuts closed, and coffee was only available at the drive thru. It was the end of an era. In a time of increasing social anonymity, Hank and I joked it was like our own small-town version of *Cheers*, with each regular playing their part. We looked forward to seeing our little Dunkin' family. But sadly, due to COVID, the regulars were not there anymore. No one was. When the pandemic was over, a few of them slowly returned. Albert, Phil, Barbara, and Angel made our coffee again, and we spotted some old familiar faces—including the "CIA man" with his back still to the wall.

One recent addition to the cast of characters at ye olde Falmouth Dunkin' was a man I called "Jack." He was a tall, thin man with long scraggly hair and a full beard who appeared to be homeless. Imagine Forest Gump after he'd been running for three years, two months, fourteen days, and sixteen hours. I didn't know where he slept at night, but he was often at the back table in the corner with a rolled-up red sleeping bag and two white trash bags—which I assumed contained his belongings.

The first day I saw him, I offered him a cup of coffee. His response was a loud, "Just leave me alone." So I did. Aside from raised eyebrows, so did everyone else. Being surrounded by the Dunkin' comings and goings didn't seem to bother Jack. He brushed his hair at the table he called home and constantly shuffled and reshuffled the belongings in his bags.

Albert the manager said Jack was harmless, which he seemed to be, but his presence and activities made people uncomfortable. Some patrons who noticed him there left soon after. A few times, Jack pushed nearby chairs out of the way, got down on the floor behind "his" high-top table and did an exercise routine. Jack worked out for 30 minutes, doing sit-ups, push-ups, and planks! I wondered if he might be a homeless veteran. Somehow, Jack seemed to fit right into our strange little crew. The only thing we were missing was a few bald-headed aliens with black eyes from the planet Tatoooine playing saxophones.

I had absolutely no idea why I kept going back!

# CHAPTER 36

# "I Love to Love (But My Baby Loves to Dance)"

## Tina Charles

Portland, Maine
Ireland
Portugal
Spain &
France
2016 - 2023

When Mom passed away in 2014, preceded by Dad in 2005, Joanne and Mark purchased their waterfront condo in Portland from the estate. The rest of us had already fulfilled our dreams of living in Maine someday, and we were glad Chandler's Wharf would stay in the family. They planned to use it as a vacation home until they could retire. Joanne and I spent hours cleaning, repainting, and scraping wallpaper. While she was working in Boston, I went over by myself and worked. I spent entire days removing the wallpaper in the master bathroom. Dad apparently didn't believe in using sizing before applying the paper, so it came off inch by stubborn inch.

Chandler's Wharf was built in the late 1980s, so it was a bit dated. Joanne and Mark gutted the place and created an open layout. This gave them a view of Casco Bay from almost every space. No expense was spared, and the condo was now replete with high-end finishes, Joanne's decorative touches, and yes, a built-in saltwater fish tank. Even without the renovations, what continued to make the condo special was the view of Portland Harbor with Casco Bay and Portland

Head Light beyond. It was magical. There were also the memories of Mom and Dad, and the good times we shared there with them.

While #310 belonged to them now, I still saw Dad sitting in the big flowered wing chair by the window, studying the boats with his binoculars and researching the flag, country of origin, and projected route of each ship. I missed the aroma of Mom's signature raisin bread pudding coming from the small condo kitchen, temporarily overtaking the smell of the salt air. Our parents were gone, but Joanne and Mark have honored their memory by breathing new life into the condo.

By 2016, Tim was out of prison and dying of cancer; Andi decided he could no longer hurt her. With Dave and her youngest daughter Kaylin, she moved back to Arizona. Her two oldest children were already there. Andi told us that she felt Arizona, not Maine, was her real home now. That felt like a betrayal to our childhood selves, especially after all we'd been through together. Yet, we accepted her choice.

What even was home, really? Was it a person or a place—someone or something fixed in time and space, or something more fluid than that? While I hated moving so much as a kid, I still seemed a bit rootless as an adult, with an adventurous spirit and wanderlust in my soul. These itchy feet had a hard time staying in one spot too long. For me, I've long thought Maine was and will always be home. However, once I finally made it to Maine, I still had a hard time staying in just one house. Not only do I have a bit of a house addiction, I also have a deep desire to run away at times—float down a river perhaps, go on a spontaneous road trip, or just hop on a plane.

Mark Twain was always one of my favorite authors. I read and re-read *The Adventures of Huckleberry Finn*, experiencing jolts of inspiration and bouts of belly laughter each time. I envied Huck and Jim for their ability to chuck it all and head down the Mississippi. When upended by difficult, tragic, or scary times in my life, I imagine myself lying on that raft with Jim and Huck watching the stars as we drift down the Mississippi, leaving my tangled relationships behind.

Yet, I also had this desire to be rooted–in Maine, but not necessarily in one house in Maine. While I longed to stay put, I was also addicted to houses, as if they were collectibles like stamps, or buttons, or sea glass; I would have one in every shape, size, and color. Maybe it was some kind of a compulsion springing from my nomadic childhood. Growing up, I went to three different high schools, which left me feeling as if I never really belonged at any of them. I'd envied my parents who lived in Haverhill, Massachusetts their whole lives. They always knew where home was. Every five years, Mom made a new dress for their 40th, 45th, 50th, and 60th class reunions. Mom and Dad were always eager to see old friends from their Haverhill High School classes of 1939 and 1941.

I made a vow that my children would never have to change schools. And I kept it–with the exception of Robert starting kindergarten in Vermont before our Kennebunk move. Since then, although we moved locally a few times, both Robert and Kristen went to school in Kennebunk/Kennebunkport through grade 12. I felt good when I heard Robert say his best friends are still the ones he made at Kennebunk High School, even though he made friends in his four years at Colby College as well. At his 50th birthday party in 2022, I was happy to see a few of his high school class of 1990 friends there. Some of them even flew with us to his wedding in Japan. That's what I wanted for my children. I'm proud that, even in hard times, I was able to accomplish it.

Still, these itchy feet longed to take me to far off places. Thankfully, Hank met my adventurous spirit so we could take on the world's splendors together, finding unforgettable adventures wherever we went. Whether it was an adventure by car or plane or boat, or simply buying a new house to start a new renovation adventure, Hank was by my side. We got lost in Rome, "crossed the ford" in Yorkshire, rode through Budapest in a tuk-tuk, explored windmills in the Netherlands, and dined on Nuremberg sausages in Germany. We sampled olive oils in Paris, savored hot chocolate with churros in Madrid, walked along Penny Lane, and sipped saki in Kyoto.

One place I wanted to explore was Ireland. It already felt familiar from Grampa Smith's stories and letters. Besides, I was still waiting for that pony Grampa Smith promised me. Maybe it was just lost in transit–60 years isn't too long to wait for a magical Irish pony, right?

In 2016, Hank and I boarded an Aer Lingus flight to Dublin, where we rented a car to drive along the coast of the Irish Republic. We followed the trail left by Grampa Smith in the many letters he wrote during his own trip to Ireland when he went to discover his roots. With his letters in my backpack and his stories in my long-term memory, I felt prepared for any castle, pony, or banshee we might encounter. Sometimes Grampa's trail went cold. I knew Grampa well enough to conclude that his letters might occasionally contain a wee bit of blarney, contributing to the difficulty of our search.

On our drive down a one-lane country road, I spotted an ancient-looking thatched cottage sitting all by itself in a pasture. The cottage looked abandoned, with no other houses or people anywhere within sight. A lover of history, I asked Hank to stop so that we could explore the old home. We parked, hiked across the grassy field, and looked around once more to make sure we were alone. Then, we stepped into the white-washed one-room house.

There was no furniture, there were no people, but there was a roaring fire in the home's little fireplace. Who built it? There were no trees anywhere near the lonely little house. Where did the wood come from? Was the fire fueled by peat? If so, where had the peat come from? The fire was blazing, not dormant. Who was keeping it going? From what I read in some folklore, if a banshee was seen sitting by a fire, it was an omen of death in the family. Death?

Needless to say, Hank and I looked at each other in apprehension and bolted out of there as if there were an Irish banshee close on our heels. It scared the hell out of us! We raced for our car. I wasn't sure if it was the wind I heard behind us... or a mournful wail. No matter. We locked the car doors and drove away as fast as we could. We never looked back.

Sadly, I wasn't able to locate the pony Grampa Smith promised me. I saw lots of castles though. I imagined Grampa standing in the tower of each one, forever protecting the homeland of his ancestors, the McCarthy Mors.

For my 70th birthday, in 2017, Hank surprised me with a romantic trip to Portugal! We stayed at the Villa Cascais Guesthouse, just a few miles south of Lisbon. The hotel looms above the ocean in the unforgettable seaside town of Cascais, pronounced Kash-Ki-sssh. The Villa Cascais was a study in understated sophistication. It featured exquisite patios, public spaces, and a quietly attentive staff. Our room was elegantly decorated in restful shades of deep blue with a king-sized bed that faced double doors opening onto a beach-front balcony.

Tired from driving, we decided to take a shower before we enjoyed the champagne and chocolate-covered strawberries that awaited. Feeling adventurously romantic on this eve of my 70th birthday, we decided to shower together. There we stood, ready for romance, unable to figure out how to turn on the shower. When we finally gave up, we grabbed the thick hotel robes and called the desk for help. I melted into one of the high-backed wing chairs by the window, hoping to stay unnoticed as Hank answered the door a few minutes later. The immaculately-attired desk clerk who had checked us in showed Hank the trick to turning on the shower and left as quietly as he arrived.

Crisis averted, we attempted our most acrobatic feat yet: both getting into the shower at the same time. As we jostled for position in the slippery, narrow space, we accidently knocked the sliding glass shower door off its track. Apparently, this shower was not designed to be shared by two porky 70-somethings. Embarrassed, we quickly finished our no-longer-romantic shower. Afterwards, Hank went to work in an attempt to reset the shower door. We'd been in our fairy-tale blue room for over an hour by then and still hadn't had a sip of champagne or a nibble of a strawberry. So much for sex at 70!

Once the shower door was fixed, we dressed and were finally ready to enjoy the elegant refreshments and view of the ocean below. Although it was October, Portugal's autumn was delightfully warm enough to open the doors of our small balcony. We were eager to enjoy the sea air while we relaxed. Except, when Hank pulled on the door knob, the door didn't just open, it came off its old hinges and fell into his arms. You likely guessed what happened next. Yup, we made another call to the front desk and had yet another visit from our dignified Portuguese desk clerk.

By the time he had the door back on its hinges, we were both embarrassed. Hank and I avoided eye contact as we shared our thanks by repeatedly saying "Obrigato" and showed him to the door once again. At that point, we had had enough excitement for one night. We headed to bed dreaming happy dreams of Portugal. Tomorrow was a new day, and we could start again.

You may recall that I actually have some history with the Alhambra. In sixth grade, my social studies teacher Mr. Howes assigned us a "major report," and the topic I drew was the Alhambra. I have no idea why Mr. Howes thought that a Moorish castle in Spain would have any relevance to the life of a 12-year-old girl growing up in Connecticut, but the Alhambra it was. I worked and worked on that report, consulting every encyclopedia in the Coleytown School library. I found some *Life* magazine pictures to include and spent hours copying over my first draft on white-lined paper in cursive.

After all that work on the first major "report" of my academic career, I couldn't wait to get to Spain to see the Alhambra for myself! In the summer of 2018, we boarded a little bus that would take us up the curvy mountain road to the palace I'd sweated over those many years ago. Begun in 1738, the Alhambra is one of the best preserved palaces of the historic Islamic world. The Moorish buildings and manicured grounds of the palace are immense and the view of the city of Granada below is breathtaking. I think Mr. Howes would have been proud of me for making the effort to complete this level of primary research 60 years later!

With two recent back surgeries, I was afraid that my ornery spine might be the end of our travels. I researched options that might minimize car renting and cobblestone-walking, which took a hefty toll on my back. That's when I remembered my old friends Huck and Jim's adventures on the Mississippi. Like my storybook friends, I decided that travel by river might be the perfect back-friendly way to go.

We've now been on three river cruises in Europe, but the most recent journey we took was a personal mission. I wanted to honor my dad by visiting the Normandy beaches in France. We flew to Paris and traveled to Normandy by boat; I'm sure Tim and Huck would have approved. The Paris to Normandy cruise down the Seine on the Viking Keri was perfect. In Paris, our ship was berthed almost directly beneath the twinkling lights of the Tour Eiffel.

While in Paris, we visited the Notre Dame Cathedral, which we hadn't seen since the disastrous fire in 2019. The church was covered in scaffolding; contractors and artisans were working overtime to get the cathedral ready for the upcoming 2024 Paris Olympics. It was sad to see beautiful Notre Dame in such a state. Oddly, what we noticed most was that years later, the smell of smoke still lingered in the air around it. After two days in Paris and a beautiful day at Monet's home and gardens in Giverny, we finally arrived in Normandy.

As suggested, Hank and I did some reading about D-Day and watched the movie *The Longest Day* before our trip. Because Dad was at Omaha Beach during the D-Day Invasion, I was fearful of the emotions the visit might stir up. Aboard the ship, the night before visiting Normandy, other passengers seemed to feel similar anxiety. I'm sure I wasn't the only one grateful for the considerate preparation our ship's program director provided. Mia was a lively young French woman who gave a slide presentation to prepare us for our visit. After the presentation, the passengers unanimously chose the veterans among the passengers who would act as our representatives. These were veterans on our ship who would lay a wreath at the grave of the unknown American soldier killed on D-Day.

The Normandy countryside was beautiful, dotted with ancient little French villages. Located in one of them, Colleville-sur-Mer, is the American Cemetery and Memorial. It contains the graves of 9,389 of our military dead, most of whom lost their lives in the D-Day landings. The graves, all in perfect lines, span acres and acres above Omaha Beach. The sheer number of graves was a sight that is difficult to describe because of the emotion it elicits.

*American Cemetery, Normandy, France 2023.*

The passengers and crew of our ship, including Hank and I, stood quietly in the semi-circle of the colonnade as a bugler stepped forward and played "The Star-Spangled Banner" and "Taps." It was a clear sunny day with bright blue skies highlighting the thousands of white marble crosses and Stars of David spread on the perfectly-manicured grass before us. The vets we chose the evening before stepped forward, saluted, and laid our wreath. There were few dry eyes among the passengers, crew, and dozens of French citizens who were also paying their respects in the colonnade that afternoon.

I stepped away from the other passengers because I knew I was about to cry more than a few tears, and I didn't want to bawl my eyes out in the middle of the group. I thought of my 20-year-old dad there at Omaha Beach in June of 1944. I thought of all of the men, boys really, just like him. I thought of all of those spread out below me in the thousands of graves, and I lost it. I was sobbing.

At that moment, a petite middle-aged French gentleman walked over to me. He stopped, put his hands together as if to pray, gave a slight bow of his head, and whispered "Merci." As quickly as he appeared, the gentleman turned and disappeared back into the crowd.

He must have guessed that I knew someone who fought at Normandy and understood my tearful outburst. His touching gesture caused me to cry even harder. That one unexpected moment summed up the gratitude the French people still feel for the British and American boys who liberated them from the Germans so long ago. Gratitude that is still symbolized 80 years later by the American flags flying in every little village throughout Normandy. As Hank appeared and hugged me and the crowd dispersed, I realized this was a moment I would hold in my heart for the rest of my life.

Once I pulled myself together, Hank and I took the stairs down to Omaha Beach. It was low tide, just as it was at the time of the landings on D-Day. There was a long expanse of sand between the water and the stone bulkheads the Germans had built along the shore. The Allied soldiers had to survive crossing the open beachfront with no protection from the German machine guns on the hills above. As I stood there looking out to sea one moment and then turning around to see the rows of crosses on the hilltop, I imagined what hell must have looked like on that day.

We spent time strolling the sands, watching families enjoy a day at the beach, all the while knowing that the ghosts of those whose life stories ended there would never be forgotten. Hank and I collected some sand in little commemorative jars, said a few prayers, and returned to our bus. Our hearts were so proud, so sad, and so thankful for the gift so many gave.

Back aboard the boat, we all seemed to need a little cheering up after a day in Colleville-sur-Mer. After dinner, Hank and I joined many of our fellow passengers in the lounge. As usual, there was a gentleman playing mostly old standbys on the piano near the bar. He played well, but our French program director Mia seemed to sense that we needed something more to lift our moods. Mia gave the pianist a break and cranked up some dance music on her Bluetooth. With songs like "Old Time Rock n' Roll" and "Dancing Queen" blaring from the bar, it didn't take long for the little dance floor to fill up.

Hank stayed for a while but admitted he was tired after the long day. He apologized as he headed to bed, but he encouraged me to stay and relax. I loved the music and bad back or no bad back, it made me want to dance. As I looked around, I noticed many other couples were in the same predicament. The women wanted to dance while the men wanted to sleep. Thankfully, we had one passenger who was always up for a dance.

His name was Bill, and he was ready to come to the rescue any night there was music and a willing dance partner. Bill was a short middle-aged guy with a crew cut, jeans, a plaid shirt, and a mischievous smile. He was on the cruise with his wife, who sat quietly smiling up at him. Thankfully, he stepped in and saved our little group of female wanna-be dancers whose husbands had either gone to bed or retreated to the bar. All was well on the Viking Kari that night, because we had Bill!

As if on cue, up sauntered Bill, beckoning to all of us to join him. Program Director Mia egged him on (whispering in French to the pianist to take another break: "Arrete! Arrete!"), and cranking up her Bluetooth as she headed for the dance floor. For the next few hours, we rocked, twisted, strolled, and YMCA'ed the evening away. All of us sang along and Bill loved it. He managed to dance with all of us at once; the only guy out there. He was our Dancing King. By the end of the night there were no language barriers; it was as if we'd all known each other for years—or at least since the day disco died.

*Mia and Disco Bill, Viking Kari, France.*

Although Huck and Jim didn't have balconied staterooms and chef-prepared meals, I think they would have enjoyed spending time with some of the interesting humans we've met on our recent river adventures. I won't ever give up my sense of adventure, my love for exploring new places, or the joy I find in meeting people from around the world. After losing Nancy, I reminded myself of a favorite quote from Robert Frost: "In three words I can sum up everything I've learned about life: it goes on."

CHAPTER 37

# *"Take it Easy"*

## The Eagles

### New Mexico & Arizona, 2021 - 2022

On Memorial Day of 2021, while relaxing in our camper at Searsport Shores, Hank and I got a phone call. Andi's oldest child Kieran was found dead of a drug overdose. In 2001, Kieran called me for help to save his mom. Tragically, 20 years later, he couldn't save himself.

My eldest-sister protective brain went into overdrive. We packed the camper, rushed back to Portland, and the next morning I was on a Southwest flight to Phoenix. Over the next few days, I went to the funeral home with Andi and Kieran's sisters to make the arrangements. At Andi's request, I drafted Kieran's obituary.

I knew Kieran had demons, many likely invited by Tim. Years before, Kieran unintentionally drank too much absinthe, developed alcohol poisoning, and almost died. As a chef, Kieran loved to cook for people. As the occasional Mainer, Kieran loved to fish. He even enjoyed dropping a line off of his grandparents' deck at Chandler's Wharf when he visited.

Kieran was a sweet guy who wanted to please. He loved his family and was always happy to cook for a crowd. He had so much potential. I hated the drugs that killed him and the culture that supported it. Kieran didn't deserve this. He would be missed.

After a week, we hugged goodbye at Sky Harbor Airport as I boarded my flight back to Maine. I couldn't imagine Andi's grief. It was heart-breaking and another blow to our fractured family. Yet, it was then I realized—*Mom, I tried my best.* I knew I loved my sister dearly, but I just couldn't protect Andrea anymore—not without losing myself.

Later that year, Joanne and Mark finally fulfilled their dream of becoming snowbirds. They were going to spend summers in Maine and winters in Arizona, not far from Andi and Dave. Mark sold his landscaping business and semi-retired; Joanne planned to continue working as a physical therapist on a per diem basis. They purchased a new home in Gold Canyon, east of Mesa, where Andi and Dave lived. It had the layout they liked, and most importantly it had perfect views of the Superstition Mountains. They began their move during COVID. Their cat Tabby flew back and forth with them, comfortably stowed under their seats on Southwest.

In the spring of 2022, Hank and I were looking forward to a trip out west: a week in New Mexico and two weeks with my sisters in Arizona. Andi had been begging us to visit her in Mesa and Joanne was anxious to show us her new Gold Canton home. After a snowy Maine winter and two years of COVID isolation, a getaway in the sunny Southwest sounded perfect.

Hank and I loved exploring unique places, especially those with interesting histories. We always wanted to take a road trip along what's left of old Route 66, the primary route for those who migrated west during the Dust Bowl of the 1930s. We planned to visit the quickly disappearing cultural icon, and take the old road as far as we could.

We flew to Albuquerque, New Mexico, where we rented a car before spending the day in Old Town Albuquerque. Then, we followed Route 66 (the "Mother Road") east to Tucumcari, once a popular stop for cross-country travelers.

Some of the vintage motels and restaurants built in Tucumcari in the 1940s and 50s were still in business, while others were in ruins. Those still in operation were sporting bright art deco neon signs and shiny vintage cars out front. We stayed at the Blue Swallow Motel, which looked like a place that time forgot.

Each motel room had its own narrow one-car garage. In the evening, guests danced to oldies in the parking lot or sat in webbed lawn chairs watching the New Mexico sunset. The interior continued the 50s theme, with each room decorated in mid-century style, right down to the bathroom fixtures and bedside clock.

After two days at the Blue Swallow, we headed to Taos via the High Road, Routes 74 and 518. Our travels taught us that it's often unplanned side trips which lead to the most memorable adventures, so we decided to turn off the main route and stop in the little town of Chimayo.

Chimayo was named for one of the four nearby hills the Tewa people hold sacred. In 1816, the area was settled by Christians who had similar beliefs about the hot springs in the area and the soil itself once the springs dried up. They constructed a little chapel on the site called Santuario de Chimayo, the most visited Catholic pilgrimage site in North America. Many visited the chapel for healing, as evidenced by the crutches and other castoffs left behind in the holy shrine. People claimed that by rubbing the dirt on their injured and ailing bodies, they had been miraculously healed.

At 74, I wasn't about to pass that up! I got a plastic spoon and empty food container from the car, entered the little adobe room at the back of the sanctuario which contained the holy dirt, waited my turn, and began to dig. I made a point of getting some of the healing dirt on myself while I was at it. I wondered if it worked on back pain and anxiety, but I figured it couldn't hurt. I dug enough dirt to give some to my sisters and a couple of my Catholic friends at home. We said a few prayers, left a donation for the dirt, and eventually got back on our way to Taos.

We had stopped to browse the crafts that Navajo artisans were selling at the Rio Grande Gorge when a local woman suggested we try the "nearby" Chili Line Depot for lunch. It sounded so delightful that we decided to check it out. Although "nearby" in rural New Mexico ended up being about 20 miles through the desert, I'm glad we made the effort.

*New Mexico.*

The Chili Line Depot is located in the small town of Tres Piedras—*three rocks* in Spanish—for the massive pink boulders nearby. It was only a crossroads in the vast desert with nothing more than the cafe, a cemetery, and an abandoned kudzu-covered building. Chili Line Depot was formerly a train depot and sat beside the dusty track, which was all that remained of the historic Chili Line Railroad. It ran from Denver to Mexico City, carrying travelers, livestock, lumber, mail, and supplies.

The rustic restaurant was about the only building still habitable in the little town. There was a little wooden stage on one side of the restaurant where a young Glen Campbell used to perform with his uncle. The whole scene reminded me of the imaginary Whistle Stop Cafe in one of my favorite movies, *Fried Green Tomatoes.*

Not long after we arrived, we met the vivacious owner Deb, who was about my age. Deb sat with us while we ate the best chili burgers we ever had. She had come to the area as a young dreamer in the late 60s to "ski and save the Indians." Deb did make it to the Olympic trials but has not yet managed to save the Indians. We spent most of the afternoon with Deb and her Chili Line Depot crew. She was larger than life: loud, friendly, and quite the storyteller. Nancy would have loved her!

A day later, we boarded an early flight from Albuquerque to Phoenix, where Andi and Dave met us at the airport. Our two-week Arizona itinerary was planned by Andi, our family's best tour director. The plan was for us to stay with her and Dave in Mesa during the week, and with Joanne and Mark on the weekends. It sounded perfect.

The only foreseeable downside for our trip was my back. I had a bad case of spinal stenosis and was scheduled for back surgery shortly after we returned home. I was limited as to how far I could walk without a break, but I was determined to do and see as much as I could. Unfortunately, my back started to act up on the first day when Andi took us to the Phoenix Arboretum.

The arboretum was huge, with every variety of flowering cactus, succulent, and other desert species. Hundreds of massive saguaro cacti were in bloom. It was beautiful. There was a lot of walking and it was hot, at least for someone who had just arrived from Maine. As much as I was enjoying the desert beauty, I had to let the group walk on ahead while I frequently took breaks. I could tell that Andi was frustrated with me.

During the next few days, we visited a lot of local attractions. Andi had planned our itinerary well! We went to an interactive Butterfly Wonderland, a rainforest greenhouse where butterflies flitted past, and sometimes even sat on your head or outstretched hand. Organ Stop Pizza was an almost Radio City-sized auditorium where an organ rose up out of the floor. An organist entertained us while cats danced alongside and pizza was served.

My favorite event was the immersive Van Gogh exhibit in Scottsdale. The exhibit brought us on a digital trip *inside* the paintings. I couldn't stop the tears from the beginning of the show to the very end. We also enjoyed Mexican food, a cookout at Andi and Dave's in Mesa, hors d'oeuvres at Joanne's in Gold Canyon, dinner at a restaurant specializing in fine wines, and a big Italian lunch at Rigatoni's. We went horseback riding through the hills, walked the dogs, swam in the pool, and streamed *1887*. Every day was memorable.

Then we got sick. Andi got sick first. It came on suddenly and she was violently ill. Just as she started to feel better, Hank and I came down with whatever she had. Hank got over it in a day, but for me it lasted two days. Being sick wasn't on the itinerary for any of us. We still had almost another week in Arizona, so I hoped to get well quickly and enjoy whatever adventure Andi had planned for us next.

# CHAPTER 38

# *"I Will Remember You"*

## Sarah McLachlan

### Arizona, 2022

When I felt better, my sisters took me shopping. Since all three of us loved everything Mexican, our first stop was a huge Mexican Supermarket. I loved the Mexican grocery store and its variety of foods—tres leches, hot sauce, chiles, papayas, tortillas, carne, frijoles, and even cabeza de cerdo, pig's head! Attempting to read the colorful signs and labels provided a valuable opportunity to practice the college Spanish I took as "Carolina" at Sage with Senora Perez-Lopez.

Our next stop, the jewelry shop, sold expensive pieces made with stones native to the Southwest. That stop was not fun at all. Joanne was apparently a regular, so the owner was all over her, while ignoring Andi and me. As we waited, I imagined how Julia Roberts' character in *Pretty Woman* must have felt when she went into the Rodeo Drive boutique in her working-girl clothes. The two of us sat awkwardly in straight-backed chairs while Joanne paraded around the store modeling expensive jewelry, followed closely by the Mexican owner who kept repeating that she looked, "Hermosa!" and "Divina!" and "Preciosa!" Joanne had to know that Andi couldn't afford that jewelry. It was painful to watch, and I couldn't wait to get out of there.

Our final stop was a huge indoor/outdoor Mexican pottery store, which I loved. I purchased some Mexican tiles, black with humorous Muertos on them. Unfortunately, as much as I enjoyed the store, there was something awkward about this stop as well. No matter which part of the huge indoor-outdoor store I was in, Joanne and Andi left and went to another. They were talking to each other but not to me. When we got home later, I tried to explain it to Hank, but he couldn't understand. I taught both junior and senior high school for 25 years and I recognized this game. "Mean girls" play it to let someone know she isn't in the "in" group.

Even as a feminist, I considered that maybe only females would recognize this middle-school behavior. Mean girls talked about a person while keeping them at a distance. They demonstrated the fine art of appearing disinterested. It was a subtle way of letting someone know they don't fit in. Here was a typical me to mean-girl sisters conversation:

Me: "Look at these great tiles I found!"

Mean Girls: (Pretend they don't hear, and move to the next showroom together)

Me: (Catching up to them) "Did you know that if you pay in cash, everything is 10 percent off?"

Mean Girls: (Pretend they don't hear, and move to the next showroom together)

On that day, I was "out." I wasn't sure why, but it really hurt.

On the following day, Friday, we took a sightseeing cruise of Saguaro Lake on the Desert Belle. Before we left, Andi said she and Joanne planned for lunch after the cruise. Sounded perfect! As we headed out, Andi pulled me aside with a warning that Hank and I should ride the twisty roads to the lake with her and Dave rather than Joanne and Mark. She said Joanne would want to "hit all the bars." If we rode with them, we'd be taking our lives in our hands because Joanne would drive home drunk.

While Andi did enjoy a gin and tonic or glass of white wine if I poured it for her, she wasn't much of a drinker. Joanne drank more; it was one of her hobbies, like collecting guitar picks. She mixed fancy drinks at home and, when not at home, she and Mark were at one of their favorite bars. They seemed to personally know every bartender in Portland and Gold Canyon. Bar-hopping was something they did for fun. I was somewhere in the middle. I had a glass of wine or, if it was summer, a gin and tonic before dinner most evenings. Hank rarely drinks, so as much as I might like to, we never hung out at bars. To each her own.

We rode to the marina with Andi and Dave. The boat ride on the deep canyon lake allowed us to enjoy views of steep mountains and colorful rock formations on all sides. Although Joanne and Andi were still acting distant, Hank and I really enjoyed ourselves. After the Desert Belle docked, we headed to Tortilla Flat in the Superstition Mountains.

As promised, the road was a dizzying series of twists and turns, crossing two single lane bridges before reaching the restaurant and the small strip of western shops next to it. If you ignored the parking lot full of recent model cars and motor cycles, you could almost imagine stumbling onto a long-forgotten cowboy town hidden in the mountains. My sisters and I headed for the shops, losing track of the guys.

Yet again, I was trying to keep up while Andi and Joanne kept leaving me behind. As we browsed the shops at Superstition Mountain, their behavior was weirdly similar to the previous day at the Mexican store. When I entered one shop, they moved as a unit to the next. I was uncomfortable and not sure what I'd done to anger them.

We eventually found our husbands seated at a table in the dining room of Tortilla Flat Saloon. They'd requested a large table and ordered drinks. Joanne seemed upset and blurted out, "This wasn't the plan!" Apparently, she and Andi hadn't planned on eating there. I had no idea what the plan was, and it appeared that the guys hadn't been read in on it either.

With the Arizona heat and saloon's commotion, plus the discomfort of my sisters' unknown distance, I lost it. Two days of my sisters' passive-aggressive behavior had finally gotten to me. I stood and loudly asked something to the effect of, "What plan?" before I walked out of the restaurant like a crazy woman, tears burning my eyes. I was embarrassed by my own behavior.

When I got outside, I sat on a bench where I cried and cried. Hank came outside to check on me. I tried to explain my totally inappropriate actions, but I couldn't. He hadn't seen the subtle meanness I'd been subjected to for the past two days. Even if he had seen it, I'm not sure he would have recognized the shunning behavior it was.

Why was it that when there were three sisters together, one of us had to be the uncool one—ostensibly part of the group, but emotionally walled out by the other two? And then, if one dared to mention the behavior, it was minimized. Responses historically included: "Gee, I never heard that" or "I never saw that" or "You're overreacting." And the gaslighting began.

A few minutes later, the rest of our group came outside. Without any conversation, we headed to our cars. Joanne led us to another restaurant, where we finally had lunch. There was live music and country line dancing here, so luckily, we didn't need to face any uncomfortable silences at the table. It seemed that the singing of "Lonny Cash" relaxed us all. I held onto the hope that the day was saved.

By Saturday, we had already had a very busy week. Andi's plan was a quick trip to Costco and a quiet day by the pool. As we drove home from Costco, Andi stage-whispered to Dave, "You'd better put the window down; Cheryl will be complaining about the heat." The comment was clearly meant for me to overhear. Had I been complaining about the heat too much? I didn't realize I had. In fact, I was beginning to doubt everything I did or said. Andi seemed so annoyed. I was having a good time, but it was as if Andi couldn't see that.

After the trip to Costco, Hank and I got ready to walk to the nearby community pool. Andi was texting and said she'd join us later. When Andi finally arrived, Hank and I had already gotten out of the pool and were reading at one of the poolside tables. Andi had purchased a floating pool chair at Costco and she was anxious to try it out. She left her phone and towel on the table and jumped in.

Andi's phone was face up on the table right next to my book. I heard the beep when a text came in. While I knew it went against all the rules of cellphone etiquette and I should not look, I suspected the text had something to do with me. I hoped it might explain my sisters' behaviors in the past few days. Even though I knew reading it was wrong, my curiosity got the better of me. I'm ashamed to admit that I did it anyway. I should have respected Andi's privacy. This was definitely something I'd need to go to confession for.

The text was from Joanne and as I scrolled, I saw that it was only a tiny part of a lengthy digital conversation that had been going on for days. I was right, the incoming text was about me, as were the rest in the lengthy diary of our time together. Andi and Joanne had critiqued my every move since I arrived in Arizona via daily texts. Even the slightest misstep or unexpected behavior—including my sickness—was unkindly documented, dissected, discussed, and assigned unintended meaning. I couldn't hold the tears back. I was shaking. The more I read, the more I cried.

I never made it to the end. It seemed to go on forever, and I'd already read enough. I felt like such an idiot. My face was burning. The tears wouldn't stop. I was unable to form words, so I silently pushed Andi's cellphone over to Hank. While he started to read, I waited, still crying. When he finished, he looked up. I said, "We have to leave. You know that, right?" He nodded. We quietly slipped out of the pool area and walked back to Andi's condo, leaving her cellphone on the table.

As we walked, their messages flashed through my head. They certainly didn't hold back or cut me any slack. They texted that I was mentally ill and diagnosed me with bipolar disorder. I didn't know where that came from.

When we first arrived as houseguests, Andi and Dave had very little in the house to eat but protein shakes. I purchased enough gin and wine to share for the two weeks we'd be there, plus some staples for quick meals. While Andi didn't cook, Dave did enjoy making breakfast for us. One day, Dave and I shopped and prepared a big cookout for the whole Arizona family, including Andi's daughters, their husbands, and grandchild. Except for that evening, we went out to eat for every meal. Hank and I had been paying, and it was getting expensive. Because I offered to shop and cook at Andi's a few of the nights we stayed there, my sisters texted that I was cheap for not wanting to go out to eat instead. I couldn't win.

Andi sent a message to Joanne that she couldn't wait to get rid of us. That broke my heart. Joanne replied she didn't want Andi to send us back to her house; we weren't welcome there either. Andi commented the last time I stayed at her house, for Kieran's funeral the year before, I left early because I found out she voted for Donald Trump. Yet again, there was meaning assigned that entirely left out my reality, which of course they couldn't have known if they didn't ask me about it.

While I knew how Andi voted, it had nothing to do with why I left early after Kieran's funeral. We finished all of the arrangements for Kieran within a week of my arrival, including my writing Kieran's obituary as Andi requested. Kieran's girlfriend Becky was grieving and praying with Andi at the house much of the time. After a week, I began to feel as if I was in the way. I didn't want to be a bother, and I'd done what I came to do, helping with the arrangements and offering support. I wanted to give them time alone to mourn. Apparently, Andi saw that as the wrong decision.

In the final portion of the texts I read, Joanne wondered if Hank knew "what she's really like" and that really hurt. Wow! I assumed that after 35 years of marriage, Hank had a pretty good idea of what I was "really like," warts and all. Joanne also texted she was angry that I had called her an alcoholic. WHAT? I didn't say that at all. That was Andi's mantra about Joanne, the day of the Desert Belle boat ride and many times before. I was broken and couldn't read anymore.

Maybe I shouldn't have been surprised by the intensity of the hatred in my sisters' texts. Since about 2016, our sisterhood was strained by our differing political and religious views. Like many families, we dealt with it by not talking about politics. Hank and I were the odd ones out in the family: still Catholic, Obama/Biden supporters, MSNBC watchers, East Coast "libs." However, most of our Arizona family were conservative megachurch-goers, former Catholics who had found Jesus, watched Fox News, and supported Donald Trump. It seemed that the division sown in our country by self-serving politicians had come home to roost.

Phoenix was a poppy field of red hats, and I'll admit to being thin-skinned about politics, so I'm sure some of the blame is mine. We did our best to maintain our familial bonds outside of the political arena—or so I thought. It seemed there was more damage done by being on opposing aisles than I realized. Yet, was that really the ammunition behind the amount of hatred in those texts? Or was it something else, some long-seated resentments resurfacing? Sadly, I burned bridges reading those texts, so I may never know.

When Hank and I got back to Andi's condo, it was quiet. He went upstairs to change and start packing. I went out to the deck and called Southwest Airlines to see if we could change our return flights. Andi came home from the pool, and I was sure my face was still red from crying.

When she stepped out onto the deck, I looked her in the eye and said softly, "I read your texts. We're leaving." She turned and headed back into the house, adding the fatal blow in a loud voice that trailed behind her, "Well, now you know what we really think about you." There were no more words after that. I was totally broken. Nancy was dead and I had just been disowned by my two remaining sisters, who clearly had become closer since Joanne and Mark joined Andi in Arizona.

Since the guest room had an ensuite bath, Hank and I stayed in our room all that evening. Andi and Dave met Joanne and Mark for dinner that Saturday night, and I'm surprised my ears weren't burning! I doubted Mark or Dave, both really nice guys, had any idea of the cattiness that had been going on. I believed they would not have liked it. They probably hadn't heard a fair accounting of why we were leaving. If they knew about or had seen the text messages, which wasn't likely, I wondered what their response would have been.

*I Will Remember You – Joanne & Cheryl, AZ.*

We left early the next morning; the house was quiet. Andi and Dave were at church. On the hall table I left a thank-you note and the Muerto I purchased for Andi in Albuquerque. Both Andi and Joanne collected Muertos—a Day of the Dead symbol that resembles a skeleton dressed in colorful traditional Mexican clothing.

Because we couldn't get a flight out until Tuesday, Hank and I took an Uber to the airport Holiday Inn Express, where we spent the next few days. It had a big pool, a decent bar, a restaurant, and a couple of streaming services on the TV. While unexpected, the few days rest was very welcome since we were both emotionally exhausted.

We had a very early flight Tuesday morning, boarding the hotel shuttle before dawn. As I was squeezing into my window seat on the plane to Boston, my phone pinged. I received a text. Surprisingly, it was from Joanne. It said simply, "You have no right to call me an alcoholic." I didn't respond. There was no point in even trying to defend myself.

It seemed like my lived experience was unimportant to Joanne and Andi. They apparently believed the stories they told themselves about me with no input from me. The last two days of calm at the hotel had put our departure in perspective, and I found myself in tears again as the plane began to taxi. I felt hollowed out and couldn't wait to get out of there.

Sadly, that's how the story of the Stunning Smith Sisters ends. I'm done and I'm pretty sure my sisters are too. Too much was said that can't be taken back. I knew I should forgive my sisters and ask for their forgiveness. But I couldn't do it—at least not yet. There was a strong possibility that going through this drama with them again could quite literally kill me, so I have withdrawn from them in order to save myself.

When we were little and hurt by playground name-calling, Mom always said, "Sticks and stones may break your bones, but names can never hurt you." That was reassuring when I was six, but now I know she was wrong. Words hurt too. And they hurt much more, and sometimes last longer, than the wounds left by sticks or stones.

*Sisters' Last Ride.*

# CHAPTER 39

# "*Imagine*"

## John Lennon

Falmouth, Maine, 2025

When Hank and I saw the premier of a play called *Almost Maine* at Portland Stage Company back in 2004, it resonated with me. The playwright John Cariani was born in Massachusetts and moved to Presque Isle in faraway Aroostook County, Maine as a child. Because John was raised but not born in-state, his friends conceded that he was almost a Mainer—thus, the play's name. Although born in Connecticut, my sisters and I traveled a long, often bumpy, road to get here. So now, like the playwright, I think of myself as being "Almost Maine." It's a perfect description of someone from away who chooses to make Maine their forever home.

I've lived in Maine for over 47 years—not counting those long-ago college summers at the Arundel—but I'm still not considered a "Mainer." Hank is lucky; he can honestly claim that title. The fact that he grew up on Munjoy Hill, which is Portland's Little Italy, gives him even more Maine creds. Maine is still my favorite place in the world. I love its craggy coast, four seasons, bucolic small towns, iconic Italian sandwiches, chocolatey whoopie pies, and especially its hardy, unpretentious people.

Applegate was our last move. I moved 24 times in my life. Sometimes, I forgot where home was, simply because I'd had so many. I was tired of being new, getting visits from Welcome Wagons, and bringing innumerable pot luck dishes to meetings of Newcomers' Clubs. I wanted no more joining and then leaving, or starting but never finishing.

I was sick of painting, and I lost the energy for any more wallpaper removal. Planting rhododendrons, packing and unpacking had gotten old. I had gotten old. I was done with any and all redecorating or doing-it-myself that went beyond the confines of my craft room—goodbye, HGTV!

I'm almost a Mainer—as close as I can get according to the old-timers. As I make my way down the stairs of our little red Cape, I think once again about how much I love it. It is so close to the ocean that we can smell the salt air through the pine trees that line the shore. We were so in love with our home when we moved in that it didn't matter that we worked all day scraping wallpaper, ate takeout, and slept in sleeping bags until the job was done. Memories were made here whether we were exhausted or excited, sad or happy. We filled the space with stories, friends, family, love, and—most of all—laughter.

Our house is located in a small community called Applegate, situated on what was once orchard land. I liked the symmetry of that: red apples; red house. I liked symmetry in general I guess: predictability, closure, happy endings. Most mornings I found Hank in our pleasantly dated Applegate kitchen - Corian counters and white appliances, oh dear! - where the coffee was hot and last night's dishes were put away.

On Sunday mornings, we sometimes walk from our house to the iconic Town Landing Market for coffee and croissants followed by the nearby Catholic Church for Mass. The town beach and marina—the Landing—are just down the hill. There is an orchard at the back of our aptly-named community, where we picked apples in the fall. It borders the community garden that connects Applegate to the Falmouth trail system. Everything we need, including the daily inspiration of the sun rising over the bay, is right here.

The living room holds many of our favorite mementos. The matching tortoiseshell sunglasses my parents bought on their Wells Beach honeymoon in 1946 are framed on the wall. My favorite painting—faceless dancers by my friend, the late Susan Tobey White—hangs over the couch. The caricatures of Nancy and I, done so long ago by the artist at Perkin's Cove, hang in the living room as well. Nearby, the old steeple clock my parents left us rests on the mantle, quietly marking the passage of time. Next to the old clock sits one of the last photos of my sister Nancy, for whom time no longer matters.

There are keepsakes from trips we've taken, including the huge conch shell Hank found on a St. Augustine beach. Our friend, Survivor winner Bob Crowley, contributed a wall-sized tobacco basket he dragged home from Charleston for us. On the shelves across the room are our little collection of Mexican pottery and my vintage McCoy vases, nestled between scores of my favorite books. A vintage stereo cabinet from Hank's aunt is surrounded by comfy mismatched furniture and lots of books.

I spend most of my time in the craft room, an updated version of the one I had at Winn Farm. It has a big skylight, providing natural light for sewing, painting, or writing. There is also a large bank of windows facing east, which capture the morning sun. We use one end as an office, home to my desktop and printer, while the other end is for sewing and craft projects. I love inviting friends to sit around my big craft table, formerly a door I found at the ReStore. We drink wine and make things together. Our projects have included stenciling, needle-felting, origami, and quilting, with a big side of talking, crying, and wine-drinking. I go to the craft room when I need alone time to write, read, sew, think, or do my favorite *New York Times* Sunday crossword puzzle.

While I love my indoor pursuits, Hank loves to get outdoors. In November, Hank gets his hunting gear ready for the big day: the opening of deer season in Maine. As a gentle giant, Hank never shot a deer in all the years I'd known him, but he loves to go out into the woods with his brothers and hunt. Hunting to Hank means sitting in his spot—each brother has a "spot"—and embracing the sights and sounds of the deep woods. A modern-day Robert Frost, Hank still sits in the woods on snowy mornings before dawn and listens to the world wake up.

He likes to study the layers of color as dawn creeps into the deepest part of the woods, waking up the animals who sleep there. He watches and waits, quietly listening as each newly-awakened forest creature adds its unique sound to the morning symphony. Hank loves to tell me about it over coffee when he gets home. Beyond the woods, sounds, and deer, he tells me it is the time spent in nature with his brothers that he loves the most about this time of year.

Throughout all the moves, one thing that hasn't changed is my annual level of anxiety as Christmas approaches. I wonder if others feel this way too—those who bear the weight of holiday prep and planning. It's as if I need to duplicate the perfection of Christmases past. Often, the stress overtakes the joy of the holiday. In recent years, our Christmas has consisted of leftover Thai food, Netflix, a tiny table-top tree, and no presents. Parents, grandparents, siblings and friends have passed away, leaving deep holes in my heart.

The empty seat at the table, the unwrapped present under the tree, old stories no longer told and old songs no longer sung—all remind me of people I miss at the holidays. Every Christmas Eve, Grammy Boocock sang her favorite carol, *Silent Night*, in her Yorkshire accent. Grampa Smith danced the jig and tapped his tambourine on his knee. Grammy Smith, tough as a bird, made me feel safe and loved just by being in the room. Nancy baked dozens and dozens of cookies, sparkling with red and green sugar in her flour-stained Mary Engelbreit apron.

After so many big family celebrations at Winn Farm, it's quiet here at Applegate on holidays. This year I sent out 38 Christmas cards, mailed countless boxes of gifts, made treats for the crew at our local Dunkin' Donuts, donated to the Salvation Army, helped a homeless family obtain an apartment, tipped the paperboy, and tried my best to be kind to all. Even so, our mailbox, tree, and living room were almost empty of hugs, stories, music, and cards.

Big events for the holidays are no longer hosted by us. Instead, we go to Kristen's group home to celebrate with her and her housemates on

Christmas Eve and Christmas morning. At 50 years old, Kristen's belief in Santa Claus is still going strong. As I watch her innocent excitement as she hangs her stocking or unwraps a simple gift of Tic-Tacs, it brings meaning back to Christmas for me. Yet, when we return to Applegate where it's quiet and we're alone, I can't help asking myself, "Is this all there is?" I miss family. I miss my sisters. Then I sit and cry.

Although we seem to have fewer family relationships as we age, Hank and I have always made friends easily. Hank and I are both *"people people"* and take pleasure in getting to know all kinds of folks—whether we have a lot in common, are close in age, or have entirely different backgrounds, languages, and cultures.

Our dear Applegate friend Bernadette just celebrated her 83rd birthday. She still sports her trademark bouffant white hair, hot pink accessories, and cheeky sense of humor. I love hearing stories of Bernadette's youthful adventures working at the telephone company in the 1960s and 70s.

One of my favorites was the night she came home from work tired and cranky. Unexpectedly, she found her musician husband jamming in the kitchen with... Wayne Newton. That woke her up! She slinked across the room saying, "Well, Hi-i-i-i, Wayne!" Bernadette remains young at heart and does her best to stay active, even while battling lymphoma. I know I can always count on Bernadette, a devout Catholic, to get her beads out and put in a good word with the Big Guy whenever I need a rosary said.

Many of our friends came to us through our travels: Corlia from South Africa, Hernan from Spain, Mia from France. Sometimes we made friends closer to home, like Linda and Rich from New Jersey, with whom we spent a long day stranded in the Munich airport.

No matter the time of year, we've found no shortage of activities when friends visited. One year, we had more snow than I had seen since I was a kid. It was fortunate that the big storm hit when our friend Corlia visited from South Africa. She had planned her trip in the hope of experiencing snow, something she had never seen in her home country.

Hank wanted to help Corlia enjoy the snow to the fullest, and what started out as the construction of a small igloo in the front yard turned into a neighborhood winter carnival. A juvenile court judge in her 60s, Corlia was like a kid, rushing out each morning to make first tracks in the drifts that had fallen overnight. She and Hank dug and dug to expand the little igloo until it would hold three or four adults. They even added a center firepit and a snow chimney. When they noticed the snow plow pile at the end of our driveway, they made it into a smaller igloo and scooped out a frosty tunnel to connect them.

The two igloos wouldn't hold enough friends for Hank and Corlia, so they kept building in the hope of including even more. They built a huge fire pit in the center of the front yard, and it was surrounded by a circle of snow benches long enough to seat fifteen people. Soon, some of our neighbors decided to join in their fun. Susie dug her own snow igloo at the base of her driveway, right across from ours. Marilyn added food coloring to the icicles forming under our mailboxes. Lane Two in Applegate was quickly becoming a winter destination.

Excited by our wintry creations, we invited friends and neighbors to our unplanned celebration of snow. Hank got out the Bailey's, marshmallows, and red hot dogs. Thermoses were filled with hot chocolate while wine chilled in the snow banks. Susie dubbed her snow igloo the Shrimp Shed, inviting one and all to stop by for appetizers. It mattered little that both the shrimp and the cocktail sauce were frozen solid. Kristen, with her friends and helpers, bundled up and joined us on the snow benches for hot dogs and s'mores. We met many of our neighbors for the first time, sitting around Hank and Corlia's bonfire. Snacks and drinks continued to arrive, sleighing songs were sung, igloos were explored, and Corlia had the snow day of her life!

*Our snow igloo.*

Besides our overseas travels, Hank and I met many special people camping, especially during our frequent visits to Searsport Shores, just above Belfast on the Central Maine coast. This magical place is an artsy vision created by friends Astrig and Steve—an inspiration to me with their kindness, creativity, hard work and caring spirits. Since my first visit to Searsport Shores with Nancy all those years ago, I've returned every year with Hank, who has also felt the magic of this special place. On our subsequent visits, Astrig and Steve continued to enrich our lives by encouraging our imaginations and renewing our sense of wonder.

Between them, Steve and Astrig have maintained fairytale organic gardens, raised chickens and goats, kept bees, woven and dyed fabric, played instruments and cooked pizza in a handmade beehive oven. They've driven tractors, taught classes, grilled kabobs, seeded the clam flats, and run a busy seasonal campground on the shores of Penobscot Bay. They each have a knack for making each person they meet feel special.

Astrig and Steve organize many events at the campground. One of my favorites is "Fiber College" held every September as a celebration of food, music, friendship, and fiber arts. Fiber is defined loosely at Searsport Shores: fabric, yarn, paper, leather, straw, wood, and even metal are all embraced as potential materials for creations. Classes by Maine artists are offered in everything from knitting to painting, bookbinding to dyeing fabrics with plants, paper crafts to Japanese rock wrapping, stenciling to wood carving.

We've met amazing people at Fiber College, many who have now become old friends. "Santa Steve" offers classes in making chainmail, small metal rings linked together in a pattern to form a medieval-inspired mesh, which is then used to create jewelry and even clothing. Steve is a certified graduate of Santa School and, even when not in his red suit, he looks just like the real thing. In real life, Steve is a physicist from Virginia whose work for the federal government was so secret that he spent much of his career in a SCIF, Sensitive Compartmented Information Facility.

*Astrig & Steve, Searsport Shores.*

One year, I arrived at Fiber College dragging a huge plastic tote full of fabric scraps for quilting class. When I stopped to ask Astrig where I should put my tote, she introduced me to Kendra, a local woman of about my age who was helping out with the event. An outgoing, energetic woman, she was Searsport, Maine's unofficial Volunteer of the Year.

She was a gourmet cook, a quilter and sewer, a leader and organizer, and a generous giver of her time and talents. As soon as I met Kendra, I knew I'd met a friend. Even though we had both been involved with this merry little band of Searsport makers for years, it seemed impossible that we hadn't met each other until the year I joined the quilting class.

The highlight of Fiber College for me was meeting the Gee's Bend Quilters, who Astrig and Steve invited to Maine to teach us how they make their extraordinary quilts. Ms. China Pettway and Ms. Stella Pettway were our instructors. Descendants of enslaved people who lived on the Pettway Plantation in Gees's Bend, Alabama, most of their ancestors (who were freed after the Civil War) took the last name of the plantation owner Mark Pettway. The plantation was isolated with no bridge and the make-shift ferry only ran when wind and weather allowed. Ironically, it used to shut down on election days. Determined to vote, the residents of Gee's Bend found ways to get to the polls anyway.

When the Great Depression hit, winter was especially hard on the former enslaved people who had remained at Gee's Bend since Emancipation. The women made quilts to keep their families warm. Since they had no cloth, they used feed sacks and old clothes as their material, the more colorful the better. Without rulers, they judged the size of quilt pieces by eyeballing them. Without scissors, they ripped the fabric into desired shapes. The women sang spirituals as they worked together making their quilts.

Each generation of quilters at Gee's Bend taught the next; grandmother to mother, mother to child. In 2002, their quilts became recognized by the world outside of Gee's Bend, as significant works of African American folk art. Their quilts were exhibited in America's most prestigious art museums, people near and far wanted to purchase Gee's Bend quilts, and the Gee's Bend Quilters were enlisted to teach workshops and speak about their history around the country. The previously poverty-stricken African American families of Gee's

Bend finally had a degree of financial security and recognition for their time-honored tradition.

As the ladies from Gee's Bend sang their traditional spirituals, they encouraged us to sing along with them while we sewed:

*Come on sister an' don't be a-shame,*
*Want to go to Heaven when I die;*
*Angels waiting for to write your name,*
*Want to go to Heaven when I die.*

Ms. Stella showed me how to choose colors, rip the fabric, and lay the pieces out on the sweet summer grass of Searsport Shores—rearranging them until I was happy with the design. I made my quilt from the fabric of old pajamas, faded blue jeans, and the t-shirts I made for my first road trip to Searsport with Nancy in 2007. When it was finished, Ms. Stella and Ms. China each signed a block with a Sharpie. Making a quilt with Ms. Stella and Ms. China Pettway was one of the highlights of my life.

*Miss. Stella, Kendra and Mary Elizabeth*
*at Fiber College.*

The last day of Fiber College fell on a Sunday. Ms. China was an ordained minister of the African Methodist Episcopal Church. She conducted a worship service on the beach, shared lessons from the Bible, and gave a sermon about fellowship and love. Spirituals were sung by Ms. Stella as we felt the wind off Penobscot Bay soft on our faces. Her voice intermingled with the waves of the incoming tide, and I had tears running down my cheeks as the service concluded. I knew I'd have the memory of those precious days with the quilters of Gee's Bend until I wrote my own name in heaven.

In my time at Fiber College that September, I got to spend more time with Kendra. We enjoyed getting to know each other. Kendra was a force of nature, and she is one of the women I most admire. She ran a backpack program for children with food insecurity, took in homeless teenagers from the high school, and hosted a monthly sewing group. They made clothes for children in Guatemala and scarves for chemo patients in Augusta. As a gourmet cook and baker, Kendra volunteered her culinary skills at the many multi-cultural events sponsored by Astrig and Steve at Searsport Shores.

Kendra shared my sense of adventure and wanderlust, so it was no surprise when she moved across the world. After recovering from a serious stroke, Kendra decided to live with her daughter, Thai son-in-law, and their children—in Thailand! For two years, Kendra and I remained close in spite of the distance with the help of technology. As I write this, Kendra is on her way from Bangkok to stay with us for the summer and just maybe, to return to Maine forever.

Chosen family, our friends have always held a special place in our lives and our hearts. As I've ached for my biological sisters—Andi, Joanne, and Nancy—I turn to our friends for solace and hugs. I like to talk to Nancy when I sit among the flowers in the shadow of her grave and before I fall asleep at night. Always my best friend, it's ironic that I can still talk with Nancy but not my two living sisters.

Hank and I have been married for over 37 years, and we are more in love than ever. We've lived over a decade at Applegate—the longest I've lived in one home my entire nomadic life. This house suits us, with plenty of room for friends or grandchildren to visit. We've added a deck and planted the slowest-growing, most stubborn rhododendrons known to man around the edge. Hank built a cedar privacy fence from which he hung the birdhouse Mike from Searsport Shores made for him. Above the little hole where the birds enter, the words "Hank Hom" were burned into the wood by Mike, who is a much better friend and woodworker than speller. That birdhouse means a lot to both of us.

I started out painting the names of special people who have passed away on rocks. I placed them in the shade of a large flowering shrub behind the garage. Nancy's rock is there and Diana's, Kieran's, and Susan Tobey-White's too, alongside Mom and Dad's. Sadly, in the past few years, there has been no keeping up. The older we got, the more loved ones we lost. At this point, I have tried to just hold them all in my heart.

I am no longer a rolling stone. I plan to stay here with Hank in our little red Cape. It reminds me so much of the one Dad and Grampa Smith built for us in Connecticut after the war. The circle of life seems to be completing itself for us at Applegate. Although there isn't a Checkerberry soda or a chestnut tree nearby, I'm happy to have ended up right where I am.

Are we there yet?

Almost.

*Forever home.*

# *"Dream On"*

## Steven Tyler

Falmouth, Maine, 2025 - 2026

My faded blue Russell Sage Blazer doesn't fit quite like it used to in 1966. I've often replayed my years at Russell Sage College in my mind, as if I dreamt them. They've softened and become more nostalgic with age—although they still remain vivid. Those were some of the happiest days of my life. Although there was still the stress of exams and social interactions, times were simpler then, perhaps because we didn't know what we didn't have. There were no computers, cell phones, or social media sites then, but now, almost 60 years later, they keep us connected even when our memories falter.

The Blue Angels of 1969 have formed an active Facebook group, which I recently joined. It's been a joy, though sometimes bittersweet, to reconnect with old classmates. We've all begun to show our age, and some of the Angels have passed away, but the class spirit is still alive. On the rare occasions when I meet another Sage alumna, we find ourselves trying to stuff our no-longer-young selves into our blazers and giving in to the urge to sing the long-remembered Rally Day songs. The mythology of the Blue Angels still exists, and we'll always be sisters, if only in memory.

On a recent visit to the Russell Sage campus, it looked as if everything, and yet not much, had changed. The old brownstones are still there, as is the bronze statue of Emma Willard in front of Sage Hall. There are men on campus now and more commuters than resident students. Rally Day is gone, and blazers have been replaced by cardigan sweaters. There is nary a skirt to be seen, and the faculty teas are no more. Still, I choose to remember Russell Sage as it was, a remnant of the age of small women's liberal arts colleges founded by early generations of suffragettes. Sage gave women like me confidence in a time of great social turmoil. We carried on, in part, due to one another's support. We will always be sisters.

My generation, born just after WWII, has lived through a number of historical events that have affected the way many of us see the world. I'll never forget the silent train ride on the day that President Kennedy was shot in 1963. I remember coming home from school and grabbing the latest edition of *Life* magazine—my parents were subscribers—and seeing nothing but the faces and bios of young men not much older than me who had lost their lives in Vietnam, pages and pages and pages of them in just one week. I recall sitting in our little third floor room at the Port House in 1968 in disbelief at news of the death of Bobby Kennedy so shortly after the murder of Martin Luther King. My grief was shared with millions of other Americans. I recall arriving at our apartment in Worcester late one afternoon in 1970, my first year teaching at Worcester North, turning on the news, and hearing that four college students had been shot and killed at Kent State by National Guardsmen during a campus protest against the war. It seemed so tragically unreal. The pictures of students my age running for their lives are still vivid, all these years later. Those events changed us. They made even polite school teachers from oh-so-proper women's colleges mad as hell. Those memories inform my politics still.

In February of 1964, my sisters and I joined 73 million others who turned into the *Ed Sullivan Show* to watch the Beatles perform. I doubt many of our peers strained to hear the Beatles over their mom smashing their dad on the head with a harvest gold telephone receiver. Still, the Stunning Smith Sisters can say that we did tune in; we just had more of a show than most. That was how our lives were—up one moment, down the next. Fight or flight. We lived on high alert, always waiting for the other shoe to drop. That continues to be a difficult response to overcome.

The understanding of epilepsy has come a long way in the almost 50 years since Kristen was born. Researchers have identified many rare epilepsy syndromes since her initial diagnosis, including Lennox-Gastaut syndrome, named after the two French neurologists who first identified it. Lennox-Gastaut, which Kristen has, is a severe condition characterized by repeated seizures that begin early in the first years of life.

Most individuals with LGS have some level of permanent cognitive impairment. Many also develop behavioral problems ranging from hyperactivity and irritability to autistic-like symptoms. (We certainly have dealt with our share of those!) Seizures typically continue throughout childhood and into adulthood.

While Kristen has had all of these symptoms, she is now leading a fulfilling life thanks to all of the supports that have been put in place for her. Her mood and seizure frequency have stabilized thanks to the development of newer medications. Physical therapy has kept her mobile. She has a cozy home nearby that she shares with three friends and 24-hour support by loving caregivers, some of whom have been with her for over 20 years. She is a beautiful, happy young woman. She is one of the lucky ones, as am I.

My son Rob continues to make me proud with his commitment to his work and his children. He and his wife, whom he met while teaching in Japan through the JET program, will celebrate their 25th wedding anniversary in April of 2026, cherry blossom (sakura) season. They have three amazing children, two in college and one in high school. After years of shared camping trips and time spent in both Brooklyn, their home, and ours in Maine, we're close to each of them. They are all kind, bilingual, and excellent students. We can't wait to see what these amazing young people will end up contributing to the world.

When I leave my dentist's office, which happens to be in Wells, I always take a detour down memory lane. I drive past the Indian Moccasin Shop and through the marsh to the center. I park between the old Casino and the beach, open the windows, and just sit. When I close my eyes and breathe in the salt air, Nancy is still there, as are the pie man, the trash man, Frankie Avalon... and maybe even Uncle Donald's teeth. The nostalgia is so strong I sometimes catch a whiff of popcorn from the deserted little window in front of the casino. Even 70 years later, I still feel the ghosts who live there in my memories as they mix with the soft sounds of the breaking waves below.

When I've had my fill, I drive to the end of Webhannet Drive and back, stopping before each of our cottages to reabsorb the memories made at each. At Howgate, I see my toddler self carefully putting my dolls to sleep on the porch. I stop beside Laura Lee and conjure Grammy Boocock clamming in her polka dot dress and straw hat—the only time we saw this proper English woman from Yorkshire without her stockings and shoes.

Sometimes I cry for those magical days so long ago when I was young and still had my parents, grandparents, and sisters. Although bittersweet, those childhood Coppertone-scented memories of Wells Beach summers will live in my heart forever. It was the one place we could count on, our collective touchstone. For me, it still is.

Walled off behind all the happy Wells Beach memories are a few darker ones. I don't like to be reminded of those moments, because they interrupt my fantasy of Wells Beach as a safe harbor for my sisters and I. It was a place where we didn't need to hide in my big closet, where we could be happy forever, and where the pounding of the surf blocked out raised voices. Wells Beach was a place where parents didn't get drunk and yell at cocktail hour, and moms didn't try to run dads down with their kids in the car and then pretend it never happened.

"Whatever goes on in this house is not to leave this house" was our family mantra. Today we might call it being gaslit, but as kids, we accepted it. I often wondered, where were our fears supposed to go if they couldn't ever leave the house or the cottage? Since no answer was ever forthcoming, I stuffed mine. They still live inside me. Many times over the years, I thought I had overcome them. No one warned me that sometimes the past and its long-buried traumas can continue to haunt you later in life.

Not far from Wells is Kennebunkport, where the Arundel holds its own memories. I remember how, on my walk to the dining room each day, I looked up and daydreamed about the huge oak tree that lent its cool shade to the cocktail lounge and living room on humid summer days. I wondered who planted it and when and why they chose that exact spot. Because Kennebunk didn't have many chestnut trees, that old oak became my summer talisman. Hank and I had our picture taken under that same tree a few years ago, its arms spread wider now. Every time I look at it, I'm glad some things remain just where they were.

After Grampa Smith passed away in 1977, we came upon a letter he wrote to his niece Ethel. Grampa wrote of his "production at the Arundel House" and how much it meant to him. He called it his "last show." He shared every detail in the letter and ended with his belief that it was the best gift his granddaughters had ever given him. I cried. While he used a different one during that show, I still have Grampa's vaudeville tambourine.

Over 70 years ago on a hot summer day in 1953, I found a four-leaf clover in the yard of our little red Cape in Newington. I've kept it close as best I could. I framed the little resin encased clover for additional protection. It has always hung in my various bedrooms throughout our moves, except for about two decades when I misplaced it. My luck wasn't the best during those years. I've concluded that a four-leaf clover may only work when you know exactly where it is.

We lost our dad in 2005. Among the things he left behind was the book he used to build our Newington home, *Your Dream Home: How to Build It for Less Than $3,500*. His signature was inside the front cover. As I look at Dad's signature and hold his book, beloved memories are rekindled. I display it on my living room bookshelf, next to one of his well-worn tools.

Looking back, I've always liked to think of Mom and Dad the way they were back when they made root beer in the kitchen of our little red Cape Cod while I kept busy imagining the comings and goings of the wallpaper people next to my chair. With the war behind them, they were both young and optimistic. Like so many others of the Greatest Generation, they looked ahead to growing their family and achieving the American Dream.

As I've sat in my own craft room staring out the window, I've often wondered if my mother ever looked out the window of her sewing room and pondered her life. Maybe she thought about being the oldest sister, like me, with all of the attendant expectations and responsibilities. Part of her learning to sew was an effort to look stylish in high school on a tight budget, set herself apart from her circumstances, and fit in with her peers. But while Mom had a knack for turning one thing into another on her old Singer Featherweight, she couldn't mend her dreams. No matter how fine her stitches were.

After she passed away in 2014, I found a little bag wrapped in tissue paper at the bottom of her bedroom drawer. One Mother's Day when I was about eight years old, I used my toy loom to weave Mom a little toiletry bag for Mother's Day. I embroidered "MAKE-UP" on the front with yarn, and I rode my bike to the old drugstore in Newington Center to buy a 25 cent Cutex pink pearl lipstick to put in it as a finishing touch. I was so proud of that gift! I didn't know that she'd saved it all those years. It now sits proudly on a little white shelf where I can see it when I put on my own lipstick.

I treasure the few happy memories Mom and I had together and still wear the silver bracelet I saved up to give her as a gift for Mother's'

Day in 1966. Whenever I think back to all of the costumes she made me, I smile, especially when I look at the tiny black tap-dance shoes that I keep on display in my craft room. I know she tried to be a good mother in spite of her demons. Finding that little makeup bag, knowing that she kept it all those years, suggested that Mom really did love me. I never remember mom saying the words, "I love you" to any of us. What she wasn't able to put in words, she communicated through her actions, like her sewing, cooking, and decorating. I watched her demonstrate her love and strength as she sat in the hospital and held the hand of her dying daughter. I will always wish that she and I could have had a better relationship as adults.

Nancy is sorely missed, not just because she was my sister, but because she was my best friend. There is so much of life that she was present for, so much Andi and Joanne were there for too, but some that they weren't. It's as if a piece of my past, almost of myself, is missing without her. Those memories of madcap adventures that only she and I created have to be held on my own now. Therapy helped soften the rough edges off the unspeakable hurt from the loss of Nancy. The tools I have learned do provide some comfort—but that grief still finds me in unexpected moments.

Only Nancy seemed to share the understanding of not being good enough for our mother. First it was Andi who kept Mom and Dad busy with the whirlwind that always stirred around her. Then Joanne came along—their favorite, replacing Andi before her— so Nancy and I became a bit of an afterthought in many ways. Of course, I still needed to do my duty as the oldest, maintain the role of the "responsible one," even when I didn't want to. I always remembered Mom's words from those early days in Newington when we headed out to the school path: "Watch out for Andi." And I tried to... Dutifully. Until 2022.

I've done a lot of reading to try to understand the dynamic between us, the older and younger sisters, Nancy's "queens" and "drones." It's no surprise that studies claim that children raised in families where favoritism exists can be more prone to anxiety, depression, and low self-esteem. That certainly seemed to be the case in our family; favoritism and the jealousy it created impacted our relationships as sisters.

From my diary:

*January 9, 1959*

*Dear Diary,*

*After I arrived home from church this morning, I went right out ice skating. For New Year's Day we didn't do anything special but I had a lot of fun skating. In between skating I watched the Tournament of Roses Parade on television. The theme was Adventure in Flowers and the floats were beautiful. I was thinking about how wonderful it would be to be the Rose Queen (my dream!).*

*Love, Cheryl*

How innocent I was at 12! Although I never became the Rose Queen, the first five years we lived in Westport were mostly happy ones. I arrived on Patrick Road as a young girl and left as a teen. Sometimes when I drive to Brooklyn to visit my son and his family, I get off the Merritt Parkway in Westport and relive those days, letting memories be my GPS. There are so many familiar things that take me back to that time, so many familiar sights. Right at the exit from the Merritt Parkway nearest our old house, the Red Barn still sits. It is closed now, but if I pull into the vacant parking lot and listen hard, I can just hear the laughter of young girls enjoying a fancy birthday party inside, complete with stylish waiters and finger bowls.

Nearby is the old Three Bears Inn, where Sandy Yoder and I met for our day-long bike adventures. After over 200 years as a post office stop, inn, and restaurant, it is closed now, but its exterior holds a storehouse of memories. Just down Wilton Road from the Three Bears is Sandy's old house—a tiny Cape Cod set back from the road—in which mattresses flew through dining rooms, English muffins were buttered before they were toasted, and Spin-the Bottle was played by nervous sixth-graders at our first "Boy-Girl Party."

The smell of fresh balsam takes me back to our living room in Westport, transfixed by the magic of the Christmas tree. Strung with big colored lights, it glowed, while the silver tinsel Dad put on strand by strand added the final sparkle. Now, whenever I smell balsam, I see my sisters and I lying under that glittering tree: young, innocent, and unaware of what the future would hold for us.

At 65 Partrick Road, I pull over for a few moments by the stone wall in front of our old "40,000-dollar house" and relive some of the childhood memories it holds. Maybe those leaves blowing across my windshield were once the walls of little girls' leaf houses, or even the remains of imaginary bowls of "leaf soup." When it all becomes too much, I fight back the tears and head back to the Merritt Parkway.

*Our Family, Westport, 1959.*

I still collect chestnuts when I can find them. There are few chestnut trees left in New England, but when we were at El Retiro Park in Madrid in 2018, they were everywhere. I ran from tree to tree, filling my pockets like the child I once was all those years ago in Newington. Perhaps one of the reasons I like collecting chestnuts so much is that they remind me of our family—sometimes we looked much better on the outside than we felt on the inside.

In my imaginings, we are still together, all four of us: the Stunning Smith Sisters. This book is my love letter to them... and to the other "sisters" I've adopted along the way, all of whom have left their marks on my soul. You know who you are.

*Lobster: Cheryl, Joanne & Andi.*

# *Life's Dream*

By Blue Whimsy Dulac

When I open my eyes I'm smiling, not just my usual 75-year-old smile, but the youthful smile I remember from yesteryear. A tandem Huffy bicycle arrives on a whirlwind, and Andi waves as it skids to a stop, telling me that Kieran says hi. Joanne is on the back wearing her rocker guitar pick necklace, and after they dismount, she pulls margaritas and homemade ceviche out from the basket on the front. We walk down the Summer Place driveway and into the house. Nancy hands us each a Tab so we now have a drink for each hand. The Four Stunning Smith Sisters sit around Nancy's kitchen booth and catch up—our weekly ritual. Sisterhood knows no bounds—not space, not time, not life or death. It remains, always.

After many hours, and many more Tabs, we get ready to leave. I notice how invigorated I feel, my steps lighter than when I arrived. We each hug Nancy on our way out, and I go last to hold her for just a few extra moments. I hug Andi and Joanne before they climb back onto their tandem Huffy and pedal off into the sky, while I climb onto my English bike that appeared at my beck and call. I'm off to visit with Mom and Dad at #310 Chandler's Wharf, where there is never any yelling. My heart feels full as we laugh together and recount many stories from my childhood—only the good ones, as if the bad ones never happened.

It's dark when I leave, and there's a car waiting out front. It's a shining black and white '57 Chevy, and I know it's there for me. I climb into the passenger seat next to Bob Underwood, who invites me to spend time with him and our children, Kristen and Robert. It's not how we were for very long before the Christmas card, and we will never be again. I hug Robert and Kristen before Bob and I climb back into his '57

Chevy for a long ride to Chicago to meet his wife and son. During the trip, we talk and joke like the friends we once were. When we arrive, I like his wife Carol right away. She's kind and welcoming, and their son, who looks a lot like his father, is a delight. It's clear that Carol and Bob are in love and I'm happy for them. I'm devastated for Carol when Bob passes away from Parkinson's disease a few years later; he was too young and they deserved more time together.

Still dreaming, I find myself back in Maine at the Arundel, visiting with Deidre Reid, John Goddard, and my sister Andi in the dining room. Shortly after we arrive, Grampa Smith puts on an encore performance of his famous sand dance while Grammy sits in the audience cheering him on. I wave goodbye to everyone and give Grampa and Grammy a hug before my dream transports me—as only dreams can do—to the Wells Beach Casino. As I pass a mirror, I notice my hair has a more lustrous sheen and my wrinkles have faded. I look down to see the beautiful aqua gown Mom made me, and I twirl around the dance floor a few times before I make my way to my favorite tree. My arms wrap around it, and I squeeze—a hug for all of the joy and comfort it brought me in those years.

When I open my eyes, I'm no longer under the oak at the Arundel but looking up at the maple tree Mom and Dad planted outside our kitchen window in Westport. I run around to the front of the house, where we all pile into a big old car. Somehow the four of us fit in the backseat instead of three—Joanne came early, I suppose—that's just like her to arrive unexpectedly. As we pull out of the Westport driveway, Mom and Dad are singing along to the radio while wearing the matching tortoiseshell sunglasses they bought on their honeymoon. In the back seat, we—the Four Stunning Smith Sisters—are making a pinky promise to all live in Maine someday.

As we drive through the clam flats on the road to Wells Beach, we roll down the windows so our four bouncing, mostly blonde, heads can hang out to yell, of the marsh, "I smelled it first!" We grin at each other and the beautiful sights around us. "Home," I smile as I lovingly look at my sisters. Grampa Boocock's old 1937 Chevy pulls up in front of Life's Dream, and I clamor out with my sisters while Dad and Mom unpack the car. The four of us girls hold hands and run for the waves, giggling. I wonder if we'll find Uncle Donald's missing teeth. Stranger things have happened.

Mom and Dad join us for a while on the sand, and we watch the sunset together. A perfect day spent in a perfect way—all of us together, no yelling or fighting, no divorces, no epilepsy, no cancer, no memories to block out later in life. Just a family spending time together, sisters spending time together. If only it were that simple... I blink and wipe a tear as I return the framed clover to my bedroom wall. I head off to find Hank for a hug. Perhaps somehow, somewhere, the four Stunning Smith Sisters will all end up in Maine together again.

*Cottages and Bathing Beach, looking East*
*from Casino, Wells Beach, Maine.*

# Book Group
# Discussion Questions

1) For the author, Wells Beach was a magical place, a place of reflection, a touchstone. Do you have a special place to which you retreat, step away from the madness of everyday life and reconnect with your memories?

2) If you have siblings, have you ever faced challenges or jealousies in your relationships with them? How did those relationships change as you aged?

3) Have you had to face a chronic illness or significant disability in your family? How did you deal with it? How did it change you? How did it change the family dynamic?

4) Have you ever been betrayed by a close friend or significant other? How did you cope with the betrayal? What did you learn from the experience?

5) One theme of this memoir is resilience. What does resilience mean to you? How have you demonstrated resilience in your own life?

6) The author has friends who have become like family to her. Do you have friends who have become part of your chosen family?

7) The author shared some of the crazy adventures she experienced with her sisters; in fact, the healing power of laughter is one theme of this memoir. How has laughter helped you cope with difficult times? Do you have a silly story of your own to share?

# Acknowledgements

My sincerest thanks to the people who had faith in me and supported my work along the way. Without them, this memoir would not have been possible.

Thanks to my dear "Epiladies" friend, Jeanne Cahill. It was Jeanne who encouraged me to begin this memoir and who helped me edit it, chapter by chapter. We spent weeks on her big front porch in Atlanta sipping sweet tea with one hand and holding our red pens in the other. As I wrote, I carried Jeanne on one shoulder and Stephen King (*On Writing*, Scribner, 2000) on the other. Both whispered in my amateur ear as I struggled to drop the perfect words onto the page. Jeanne recently published her memoir, *Call Me Jeanne* (Colorful Crow Publishing, 2025). If she retells even half of the stories she has shared with us on her front porch in Atlanta over the years, the book will be a testament to *Steel Magnolias* throughout the South.

A special note of gratitude goes to my book coach, Bailey Morse. She has walked me through the steps of the publishing process; I never could have done this without her. At a time this fall when I was about to give up—an editor had turned down my manuscript on the same day my husband was diagnosed with renal cancer—Bailey wrote, "I am sticking with you all the way." Those words meant the world to me and got me back on track. If there were no Bailey, there would be no memoir. Sincerest thanks!

Very special thanks go to my editor, Blue Whimsy Dulac. Blue describes herself as a "trailblazing unicorn, non-binary human, mom to one and sometimes camper van adventurer who offers resources, insights, and skills to encourage the forward momentum of humans seeking clarity and direction." Wow! When we were introduced by Bailey, insights, clarity, and forward momentum were just what I needed—and Blue delivered. Blue really "got" me and my story, so much so that she asked to write the afterword! Her editing was invaluable to the quality of the final draft. Blue—you are amazing; it was a pleasure to work with you. Thank you.

This memoir would not be as carefully crafted if it were not for the vigilant eye of proofreader Chloë Siennah. I appreciate your hard work on my manuscript, Chloë.

I also would like to thank Nelly Murariu at PixBee Design for her creative cover design, layout and use of photos throughout my memoir. Her graphics made my memoir come to life. Nelly is a pleasure to work with—flexible and attentive—and a talented graphic artist. I am so glad that Bailey introduced us. Thank you, Nelly!

Thank you to the friends, near and far, who have supported and encouraged me over the years. Friends from the "Gourmet Group," the "Train Group," and Searsport Shores have always been there for me. Special thanks to the friends who have read and commented on specific chapters, making suggestions that have improved my writing.

Thanks too to my son and grandsons for their IT help when I occasionally got stuck.

And thank you to the Stunning Smith Sisters. For better or worse, without you there would be no funny stories, no shared memories. There would be no memoir.

I'm saving the best for last: thank you to my husband, Hank, who has encouraged me every step of the way for the past three years of this project. When I was discouraged, he was there to pick me up and point out how far I had come. He read and re-read chapter after chapter, making corrections and suggestions. He let me bounce ideas off of him ad nauseum and always provided thoughtful and honest responses. Since he was there for many of the latter events in the memoir, his comments on content were invaluable. He never let me down. Thank you, Hank!

*The Arundel, Under the Oak Tree 60 Years Later.*